Wisdom from a Rainforest

Wisdom from a Rainforest

The Spiritual Journey of an Anthropologist

STUART A. SCHLEGEL

To Dan and Elaine —
Welcome to Santa Cruz.
John Schlegel

THE UNIVERSITY OF GEORGIA PRESS   ATHENS AND LONDON

Published by the University of Georgia Press
Athens, Georgia 30602
© 1998 by Stuart A. Schlegel
All rights reserved
Designed by Erin Kirk New
Set in 12 on 15 Centaur by G&S Typesetters
Printed and bound by Maple-Vail
The paper in this book meets the guidelines for
permanence and durability of the Committee on
Production Guidelines for Book Longevity of the
Council on Library Resources.

Printed in the United States of America

02   01   00   99   98   C   5   4   3   2   1

Library of Congress Cataloging in Publication Data

Schlegel, Stuart A.
    Wisdom from a rainforest : the spiritual journey
of an anthropologist / Stuart A. Schlegel.
        p.   cm.
    Includes bibliographical references and index.
    ISBN 0-8203-2057-9 (alk. paper)
    1. Tiruray (Philippine people)—Social
conditions.   2. Tiruray (Philippine people)—
Psychology.   3. Tiruray (Philippine people—
Ethnic identity.   4. Deforestation—Philippines—
Mindanao Island.   5. Rain forest ecology—
Philippines—Mindanao Island.   6. Rain forest
conservation—Philippines—Mindanao Island.
7. Mindanao Island (Philippines)—Politics and
government.   I. Title.
DS666.T6S36   1998
959.9′7—dc21   98-7608

This book is dedicated to

Len,

who lived so well and died so young.

And to

Will,

who taught us all to be strong.

Things fall apart; the center cannot hold:

Mere anarchy is loosed upon the world . . .

Surely some revelation is at hand . . .

William Butler Yeats, "The Second Coming"

Contents

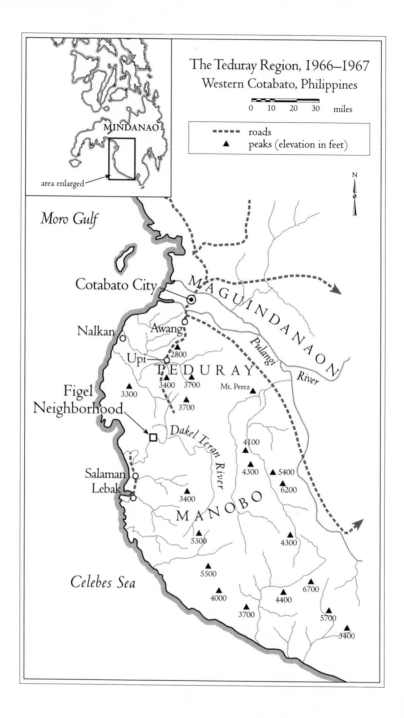

The Teduray Region, 1966–1967
Western Cotabato, Philippines

0   10   20   30   miles

----- roads
▲ peaks (elevation in feet)

MINDANAO

area enlarged

N

Moro Gulf

Cotabato City

MAGUINDANAON

Nalkan

Awang

Upi

2800

TEDURAY

3400   3700

Mt. Perez

3300

3700

Figel
Neighborhood

Dakel Teran River

Pulangi River

4100

4300   5400

6200

Salaman
Lebak

3400

MANOBO

5300

4300

Celebes Sea

5500

4000

6700

4400

3700

5700

3400

Prologue

This book is a love story.

In the middle of a dark night in July 1967, deep in a Philippine rainforest, I realized that my son Len, sleeping beside me on the bamboo slat floor of my tiny house, was sick. The heat of his feverish body had awakened me. Rain, which had begun the day before, pounded loudly against the grass roof, but I could still hear him moaning. Len was only six years old, and his mother—who knew much more than I did about sick children—was far away. But I knew that he was too hot. I woke him up and gave him an aspirin with a little water I kept by the sleeping mat. As the night went on he became hotter and hotter. I lit a kerosene lamp, climbed out of the mosquito net we were sharing, and poured more cool water. I sponged off his arms and legs, hoping that by cooling them I might bring down the fever. Perhaps it helped; I couldn't tell. Len kept moaning and I waited impatiently for morning, my mind filled with dark apprehension.

We were in a place called Figel, a small Teduray settlement alongside the Dakel Teran River on the island of Mindanao. Len and I had walked in the day before, wading across the wide river numerous times. It was a long, hard, full day's trek into the heart of the forest.

Morning finally came and—at last—I heard the playing of gongs which greeted each sunrise in Figel. I saw several Teduray friends up and stretching in the morning mist, their sleeping sarongs cowled over their heads against the damp coolness of the new day, and I called for them to come over and look at my son. By then he seemed to be much worse. He had lost control of his bowels and bladder, and he was obviously seriously ill.

Several women and men discussed the situation among themselves. They saw my fear and concern, and some of the men said that they would leave immediately and carry Len out to the coastal town of Lebak, where there was a large plywood factory that had "my kind of doctor." Normally the trail to Lebak involved fording the winding river about a dozen times as it snaked its way to the sea. But I knew that would be impossible now: the night's hard rain had swollen the river, removing any hope of crossing it. It was strong and swift and twice its usual armpit depth. People never tried to go to town under such conditions. But my Teduray companions saw that I desperately wanted my son to see the coastal doctor, and knowing this touched a deep chord in them, in their understanding of how life should be lived. The Teduray I knew in Figel never ever took someone's wants or needs lightly. They were willing to risk their lives to take him there.

They would attempt this unimaginably dangerous trip even though they were certain that Len's illness was due to his having unintentionally angered a spirit. The Figel people had no concept whatsoever of germs, or even any awareness of what my kind of doctor did, and although no one said anything, I knew they had informed one of the Figel shamans, who would litigate with the offended spirit as soon as possible to effect a cure.

One of the men quickly cut down two six-foot lengths of bamboo from a nearby grove and hung a sarong between them.

We then put Len, who seemed to me barely conscious, in this makeshift stretcher. The trek would be agonizingly slow with the river so treacherous; no one would ever attempt it unless forced to by an emergency. But within twenty minutes of the gongs' announcement of the dawn, we were off. Our little group—six Teduray men, Len, and me—made its way, deliberately and torturously, along the full length of the flooded, furious river, clinging to its banks. Fear for myself and my friends' safety now joined my anxiety about Len's condition. In many places the men carrying Len had no firm footing and, their muscles taut and glistening with sweat, were forced to grasp exposed tree roots or shrubs as the river crashed by just below them. The going was slow. Although we stopped for very few breaks, the day passed all too quickly and we were still far from the coast.

After sundown darkness filled the forest, but our little band struggled on. There was a half-moon for part of the night, but not much of its light penetrated the canopy of high trees to reach us on the forest floor. When the night became too dim and the darkness too dangerous we paused and made torches of tree resin applied to the end of short sticks. As we continued along the river banks, we held the torches high with our free hands so that we could see where to put our feet and grasp for firm handholds.

I stumbled alongside my sick and frightened son trying to comfort him, awkwardly keeping up as best I could with these men who had spent their whole lives on this river and in this forest. I put cool cloths on his forehead and spoke to him whenever we stopped for a break or to switch litter bearers.

The trip was a twenty-hour nightmare of physical exertion and danger. We crawled along the river through most of the night, resting only occasionally for a few short moments—which seemed to refresh the Teduray but which did little for my fear and heartache. I knew the breaks in the pace were necessary—it was incredible that these men didn't need more of them—but Len seemed to be getting hotter and weaker, and the horrible possibility that he might not make it weighed on me.

Just as morning was about to dawn we finally dragged ourselves out of the forest and reached the road that led to Lebak. I found someone who had a jeep, and he agreed to take Len and me into town, while my Teduray friends rested a few hours before starting back to Figel. At the plywood factory, the doctor checked Len carefully and told me that my son was not really all that critical, that he had a kind of viral flu that produced nasty symptoms but was not actually life-threatening. My feeling of relief at that welcome news soaked into every cell of my weary mind and body. I remember the moment clearly still today.

But what especially sticks in my mind, and continues now, many years later, to cause me wonder and even awe, is the gift that those Teduray men gave me and my boy by rallying around us and risking themselves so willingly to do what I felt Len needed. It was a true gift, given simply; a gift of life, and of themselves. It was a gift of love.

In February 1972, five years after my Figel friends carried Len along the banks of the Dakel Teran, I was standing in one of the main lecture halls at the University of California, Santa Cruz. The day was lovely, sunny yet crisply cool. From behind the lectern in that familiar room where I had so often taught I looked at my students with tears in my eyes. In a few pained words I told them that the Teduray people of Figel, the community of people I had lived with in the rainforest for two years, had been massacred by a ragged band of outlaws.

My cracked voice and the horror of my message brought gasps from throughout the room. These were upper-division anthropology majors, and they had heard me speak at length about Teduray life and culture. From slide shows and many informal discussions as well as in classes, they had grown familiar with the ways and even the faces of the far-off Figel people. I believe most of my students admired the forest Teduray greatly, and they all knew that I had been personally touched by them in a way that went far beyond professional respect. They knew that I loved these people of Figel.

I could not teach that morning and merely dismissed the class. But first I asked them to stand with me for a few moments of silence in honor of those good and peaceful people, who never wanted any part of the violence that raged outside of the forest but who nonetheless had fallen before its terrible fury.

This book began to be written in my mind on that day. I believe that in their death the Figel Teduray left their story to me, that they commissioned me to be their voice to a wider world. Ever since, in formal teaching and research volumes, in conversations, in lectures and homilies to the communities where I have lived, I have told the story of the Teduray of Figel and their gracious way of life. In this book I pass on their wisdom to you. I waited a long time to write it, until I could retire from scholarly writing, until I was freed from the demands of two careers, and until a heartbreak in my family had run its course.

This is an intensely personal book, because it is not only about the Teduray; it is about me as well. I lived in Figel as an anthropologist for two years. But the story is much more personal than just an ethnographer's report from the field. In the pages that follow, I will take you into the Teduray's rainforest and deep into their understanding of reality. I will also take you into some extraordinarily sensitive times in my own life. I want to introduce you to the thinking of these people in all its beauty and elegance. But beyond that, I want to tell you about the tremendous impact their thinking had on me as a human being and the wisdom that it offers us all.

Their gracious, life-affirming, compassionate ways transformed the foundations of my life: my thinking, my feelings, my relationships, and my career. I hope a wider world will hear the voices I heard in that remote forest and realize, as I came to, that the Teduray speak eloquently to us all of tolerance, cooperation, grace, and gentleness, that their understanding of the world contains lessons that all of us pursuing "the good life" need to hear.

I hope that the Teduray move you in a deep and fundamental way, as they did me. Knowing and living with them was one of the greatest gifts of my life. This book is my gift of them to you.

Wisdom from a Rainforest

1 🌿 Beginnings

The Philippines is a nation made up entirely of islands, the exposed tops of a long range of undersea volcanoes lying south and east of China. There are two quite large Philippine islands and a whole array of medium-sized and little ones. Luzon is the big island in the north, where Manila is located, and Mindanao is the large southern island. The mists of prehistory hide the origins of the Teduray and of their neighbors, the Maguindanaon, but the ancestral home of both societies is the southwestern quarter of Mindanao. The Teduray live in the rainforest-covered mountains south of the Pulangi, a major river that empties into the Moro Gulf at Cotabato City and from there into the South China Sea. The Maguindanaon, who are Muslim, occupy the lowlands to the north and west of the mountains. The old myths of both people say they have been there since the beginning of time.

The Teduray people number some thirty thousand and are subdivided roughly into three main groups. Until the twentieth century, the majority were "forest people" who were relatively isolated from and unknown to the outside world and who lived by gardening and foraging for wild foods in the mountains of the Cotabato Cordillera. Egalitarian and peaceful, their primary contact with the world outside the rainforest was through trade pacts established with the Maguindanaon. A second type of Teduray was the "coastal people," a relatively small scattering of families along the beaches of the Moro Gulf who lived and thought much like the forest people but who, in addition, extensively fished in the sea. The third division comprised the Teduray of the Awang area, the northern foothills close to Cotabato City. The Awang people, some of whom lived as far into the hills as the Upi Valley, twenty-five miles south of Awang Village, were the closest neighbors to the Maguindanaon and, as we shall see, interacted with them in many important ways that other Teduray did not.

The Maguindanaon are a larger tribal group than the Teduray, numbering half a million, and their territory spreads widely through the lowlands surrounding the Cotabato Cordillera. Unlike the Teduray, who remained animists, the Maguindanaon adopted the faith of Islam some five hundred years ago. For centuries they have lived by wet-rice paddy farming. Maguindanaon society is hierarchical, with an aristocracy composed of datus, who fight fierce, bitter, and protracted dynastic wars with each other. Until recent times, the forest Teduray allowed a few Maguindanaon traders, representing powerful datus, into the mountains under the terms of strict trade pacts, but on the whole they feared and disliked their Muslim neighbors' propensity to look down upon them as primitive and ignorant. Indeed, the Maguindanaon treated most Teduray with contempt and occasionally took them as slaves.

The Awang/Upi Teduray, in contrast, came to terms with the Maguindanaon many centuries ago. Living as close to Cotabato City as they do, their long history of greater contact and interaction with the Muslim lowlanders gave their way of life a distinctive flavor. Even before the Maguindanaon converted to Islam, the Awang people were military allies of the "lower-valley" datus in their ancient and seemingly endless dynastic warfare with the more inland "upper-valley" datus. Many bits and pieces of both Awang Teduray and Maguindanaon oral tradition (and even some old Maguindanaon genealogical documents) make reference to Awang people fighting alongside the lowlanders.

Quite early on, Awang Teduray adopted many of the Maguindanaon social and cultural ways. Presumably dazzled by the larger group's comparative wealth and splendor, their political power, and their demonstrations of military valor, the Awang people must have decided the Maguindanaon made better friends than enemies. The Awang Teduray emulated them, creating chiefs with political titles and power who proceeded to coerce obedience from their followers. They developed concepts of personal ownership of property, including dry rice fields on land that they cleared and plowed in the Maguindanaon manner with draft animals. They learned to prize violence, and to be good at it. Like the datus, Awang Teduray men considered multiple wives to be a sign of high status. Some of the most wealthy and powerful even imitated the Maguindanaon custom of owning slaves.

Awang Teduray never converted to Islam, however; they preserved their animistic belief in a world of spirits. Nonetheless, like their Muslim Maguindanaon allies, they considered their more isolated forest sisters and brothers to be, if not infidels, at least rustic and unsophisticated.

The place of these Teduray and Maguindanaon peoples, the southwestern quarter of Mindanao, is to this day part of one of the world's great cultural fault lines, running between the Crescent of Islam and the Cross of Christianity.

In the middle of the sixteenth century, when Islam was just beginning to penetrate into the southern islands of the Philippine archipelago, Spanish conquistadors began pushing their way into the central and northern islands. So right from the beginning, the Catholic Spanish battled the Muslims of Mindanao. They named them *Moros* (Moors), as they had called North African Muslims, and the word persists to this day.

In spite of Spanish imperial claims, southern Mindanao did not become a recognized part of the Philippine nation for three centuries. Two Jesuit padres established a small mission in Cotabato in 1748, but were forced to evacuate just six months later by implacable Muslim hostility. The Spanish began to turn the tide in their three-hundred-year-long campaign against the Muslim peoples of the south only in the early 1860s, when, with the help of newly developed steam-powered gunboats, they were able to establish limited political control in Cotabato.

One of the first moves of Spanish rule in southern Mindanao was to invite the Jesuits to resume missionary work. In 1862 a group of Jesuits opened a mission and school in Tamantaka, between Cotabato City and Awang, and set about trying to convert both the Muslim Maguindanaon of the lowlands and the animist Teduray of the mountains. Awang people were therefore the first Teduray to encounter Christianity. The main Awang Teduray leader, who bore the Maguindanaon title of Datu Bandara, became a protégé of the Jesuits, and the Spanish government soon named him *presidente* of Awang municipality.

One of the Jesuit priests, Padre Guerrico Bennasar, took responsibility for the Teduray work. The first Teduray people to accept baptism were Bandara's family, supplied by the Spanish with the last name Tenorio. The baptismal ceremony took place at the Tamantaka Mission in 1863 and included a young man named Sigayan. Given the Christian name of José Tenorio, he became Padre Bennasar's prize pupil, and at the Jesuit's request dictated a little volume, which was published in Madrid with the missionary's rendering of Sigayan's Teduray on one page and his own Spanish translation on the facing page. The book, titled *Costumbres de los indios Tirurayes* (Customs of the Teduray People), was surely one of the first times the name of the Teduray people appeared in print, spelled as it must have sounded to a Spaniard, to whom a *d* sounded like an *r* and the closest sound to the Teduray *e* was the Spanish *i*. It is a fascinating document and, to my knowledge, the earliest "ethnography" to be written by a native Filipino of his own indigenous customs. The Teduray have since been known in Spanish and English as the Tiruray, a practice that at their recent request I no longer follow.

Sigayan's account of Teduray customs reveals some characteristics common to all Teduray: the same language, the same house styles, similar marriage patterns, many of the same names for spirits. But in matters that pertain to social ranking, political power, and a commitment to violence, Sigayan's description reflects the heavily Maguindanaon-influenced thinking about heirarchy and domination that was characteristic of the Awang people. Teduray men were portrayed by Sigayan in several places as dominant over women and as warlike raiders led by political headmen or chiefs.*

In spite of Datu Bandara's influential family, Christianity did not take hold among the Awang Teduray, any more than the Islamic religion had centuries earlier, and when the American

---

*The depiction of the Teduray by Grace Wood Moore, their only other modern-day anthropological observer, like Tenorio's describes people who are hierarchical and violent and seems to be clearly about the Awang variant and not the forest Teduray such as the people of Figel. See Grace Wood, "The Tiruray," *Philippine Sociological Review* 5 (1957): 12–39.

period began some two generations later few Teduray Catholics were to be found.

Maguindanaon political factions have made war on each other since well before the late fifteenth century. The United States entered this scene militarily when it wrestled titular control of the Philippines from Spain in 1898 (part of the settlement of the Spanish-American War) and joined the ranks of nations with overseas territorial holdings. The Americans immediately found themselves engaged in a bloody and repressive war in the new colony. From the Filipino point of view, the desperate, losing struggle against the United States Army was merely the second phase of a revolution they had launched against colonial rule in 1896. American journalists and historians of the day, who viewed our military conquest as part of our "manifest destiny" to gain an overseas colony rich in natural resources, as well as an economic foothold in Asia, named the resistance against the United States "the Philippine Insurrection." The fighting was especially fierce in the Islamic areas of the southern Philippines, where the Spanish had been able to establish only tenuous control over the local Muslims, and even that for only about thirty-five years.

In 1903, just five years after their arrival, the Americans forced the Muslim regions, which they renamed the Moro Province, to become part of the Philippine nation. This threatened the ancient isolation of the forest Teduray as nothing ever had before, and that isolation soon began to break down around the edges. The Americans thus began a historical process that ultimately resulted in destruction of the rainforest and, as a consequence, the radical acculturation of Teduray society.

One of the American officers in the Moro campaigns around Cotabato City was Captain Irving Edwards. Staying on after pacification as a colonial administrator, Edwards became intensely interested in the Teduray people. In 1921 he married a young Teduray woman from the Tenorio family of Awang, a relative of Datu Bandara, the old friend of the Spanish. Edwards lived among the Teduray until his death in the late 1950s, serving in a number of official and unofficial capacities including head of the military constabulary, provincial chief justice, governor, and superintendent of schools. Captain Edwards—as everyone called him throughout his life—devoted himself tirelessly to the furthering of what he considered "progress" among the Teduray: education, proper government, law and order, economic modernization, and religious conversion. In 1916 he established a public school at Awang, and in 1919 opened an agricultural school in the Upi Valley, linked by a winding road with the lowlands. By the 1920s he had established primary and elementary schools in dozens of Awang and Upi Teduray communities.

Encouraged by Captain Edwards, Christian homesteaders from other parts of the Philippines, particularly Cebuanos from the central Philippines and Ilocanos from the large northern island of Luzon, began to settle in the Upi Valley. Maguindanaon Muslim farmers as well, now protected by American rule, for the first time began to occupy and own land in the Teduray area. The number of Maguindanaon settlers in Upi increased greatly after World War II, and they took permanent political control of the area in the mid-1940s, holding it to this day.

Teduray in the rainforest beyond Upi employed a form of forest gardening that had served them well for untold centuries. The Upi agricultural school teachers and the lowlander homesteaders, however, all agreed that the forest Teduray way of cultivation was hopelessly primitive. "Why, they know nothing of plows," one earnest teacher told me in 1961, "and they don't even clear the forest. They just poke holes in the ground with pathetic little sharpened sticks!" So everywhere around Upi, and all along the road down through Awang to Cotabato City, the forest was zealously cleared, the fields plowed, and corn and sugar cane planted in neat Iowan rows. Teduray people in deforested places were issued titles to their land, but their unsophisticated grasp of the unfamiliar concept eventually resulted in the loss of almost every Teduray-owned farm to homesteaders.

Captain Edwards organized the villages outside the forest, Teduray and homesteader alike, into units of the Philippine government, with Upi as the main municipal center. There courts administered and police enforced Philippine national law. He wanted to "pacify" all the Teduray, but at that time he had little reach into the remaining rainforest. Although deforestation was proceeding steadily, it did not become intensive until the post–World War II years, when the independent Philippine government began giving franchises to lowlander timber companies to cut and haul away the trees.

In addition to all these drastic changes in local life, Captain Edwards was determined that his Teduray charges would be brought out of "pagan darkness" and made Christians. He asked several church groups, including the Roman Catholics and the Methodists, to establish missions among the Awang/Upi Teduray, but was told by each that there were no funds to support such a venture. In the mid-1920s the Episcopal Church responded to his invitation by sending an American missionary priest to open the Mission of St. Francis of Assisi. By 1960, when I arrived to be a priest at the mission, it had chapels in some fifty-four Teduray communities and a large parish church and medical clinic in Upi. After World War II Roman Catholics and several Protestant churches also began vigorous work among the Awang and Upi Teduray and the homesteader families.

Awang people—who made up most of the Teduray population not only of Awang but also of the Upi Valley—took to the new regime and way of life quite congenially. The changes, however, utterly transformed and bewildered the forest Teduray, who, as the rainforest was progressively cleared, were unwittingly caught up in them. Some responded by moving farther into the forest, in hopes of escaping all the change and confusion. But others— often after several such retreats proved insufficient to keep them ahead of the relentless loggers and homesteaders—simply surrendered and joined the peasant world. Typically, in one great convulsion of change, Teduray families would begin to dress like the homesteaders, learn their languages, send their children to school, ask for Christian baptism, and join a mission congregation. Most essential of all, they sought a landlord who would provide them with a work animal and a field to plow. They still thought of themselves as Teduray, of course, but most of them knew that the peaceful, egalitarian life they had cherished so dearly in the forest was over.

The economic consequences of deforestation and the process of becoming peasants were devastating. In contrast to the rich variety of foods the forest people were accustomed to, the cleared and plowed fields of the Upi Valley specialized in just four crops: rice, corn, tomatoes, and onions. Hunting, fishing, and gathering, of course, played almost no role at all in the cleared regions; the forests were gone and the rivers and creeks all seriously depleted. Besides, the streams were now private property and fishing them was considered trespassing.

In place of the foraging that had always abundantly supplied forest Teduray, assuring them a good life even if their garden crops failed, now the market dominated their lives, with its unfamiliar cash and credit system and its very different values. This meant a far less assured, less varied, and less interesting natural diet. Moreover, it meant that the Teduray outside the forest were now full participants in the rural Philippine peasant market system, as much so as any immigrant or Maguindanaon homesteader in the Upi Valley. And that meant that they lost the significant independence the forest had allowed them. With it gone, they were only a tiny part of the world economy, and sharecroppers to boot, occupying the lowest possible status other than beggars or homeless.

There was, however, one way to rise above this status. Fostered by the school system, a whole new set of elite Teduray emerged, persons of high social standing and influence whose roles reflected not Teduray traditional life but the Filipino mainstream. By 1967 some forty-eight Teduray women and men had become schoolteachers, three men had been ordained Episcopal priests, two more were lawyers working with the national government, two Teduray women were nurses, and one young man had become a provincial agriculturist. But the old specialized roles of the forest folk—as legal sages and shamans, skilled hunters and basket weavers—had disappeared. Captain Edwards felt very proud of all that the Teduray people achieved, but traditional Teduray were far less enthusiastic.

In short, as a consequence of American rule a whole new distinction between Teduray came into being. There were now the "forest people," the traditional communities still living the old way in the ever-shrinking rainforest, and there were the profoundly acculturated "peasant Teduray" outside the forest. By the 1960s half the Teduray population, some fifteen thousand, had become this new ethnic version of Filipino peasantry and were largely out of touch with their forest counterparts.

My wife, Audrey, and I first arrived in Upi in June 1960, sent by the Episcopal Church in America to be missionaries on the staff of the Mission of St. Francis of Assisi. Our initial task was to found St. Francis High School, the first academic high school in the Teduray mountains. Not long after our arrival, even before the school was built, I was named priest-in-charge of the mission.

At that time, Upi was a frontier town. We often thought that life there must be similar to life in Dodge City in the 1880s. Many people carried guns. The buses plying the slow, rough road between Upi and Cotabato would occasionally be stopped and the passengers robbed. Maguindanaon bandits were common in the mountains, where they took refuge from the law in the lowlands, unofficially protected by the datus who were in control, and every so often gangs of these bandits would come into town, get drunk, and shoot the place up.

Despite this, our life at the mission was virtually idyllic and we always felt safe. Most of the inhabitants of the Upi Valley were either peasant Teduray farmers or Christian homesteaders from other parts of the Philippines. The political power was firmly in the hands of two strong Muslim Maguindanaon datus of the upper-valley faction; one was mayor and the other, his cousin, was police chief. The mission had excellent relations with them both, partly because they had residual respect for Americans and partly because I welcomed their children as students at St. Francis High School and, to their surprise, excused them from Christian worship and religious instruction. I offered to let the Muslim students receive Islamic instruction, if their families would send an instructor. So the Muslim authorities were friends and watched out for our safety. They discouraged the bandits (who were often their relatives) from hassling us and always sent a messenger to warn us if they heard about plans to rob the mission office safe. The police chief once told Audrey that, if anyone came to bother us, we should lock our house up tight and bang a washtub with a wooden mallet; they would hear and come right away. In a place without telephones or even electricity, this was an effective alarm system.

Looking back at those missionary days, I realize that I never felt much fire in my belly to convert anyone. I wanted to care for and serve our parishioners and our community—and the mission did a lot of each—but I was little concerned with people's beliefs. This was not because I perceived that Teduray traditional spirituality was arguably a finer expression of what Jesus proclaimed as the Kingdom of God than what we were up to at the mission; I had not discovered that yet. It was because, like many other Episcopal missionaries in the Philippines, I was mainly concerned to keep the institution growing and to provide regular services, attractive liturgies, and interesting sermons. Transforming Teduray people's cosmology or moral sensibilities—which I didn't know anything about anyway—was not part of my sense of the job. What got me excited were the ministries of care and service, such as the high school, the clinic, the farm project, and the complex of cooperatives I helped put together to enable Teduray newly out of the forest to ease more gently into a cash-and-credit economy.

I remember that time now with nostalgia. It was a heady period in my life. I was just in my late twenties, but thanks to residual patterns that can only be termed neocolonial, I was in charge of a vast complex of people and institutions, and my creative juices were able to go wild. I had been trusted to found the first academic high school in the region. And since I spent half of each week hiking up and down hilly trails visiting the chapels in the outlying peasant Teduray communities, I had never been in better health (and never have been again). My family was growing; both of my sons, Len and Will, were born in those mission years. I had good friends in the missionary and local communities, and I was blissfully ignorant of how unintelligible much of what we were doing must have seemed to the people we tended.

Happy as my life was during my three years at the Mission of St. Francis, however, I grew increasingly restless and dissatisfied. In planning St. Francis High School, which I knew should not be simply a replica of the schools I was acquainted with in America, I sought the assistance of several anthropologists in Manila, who helped me make it fit the special needs of the remote rural area and people it would serve. They put me on to some marvelous studies of Filipino life and culture, and the more anthropology I read, the more the field attracted me. By my last year at the mission I was convinced that I was in the right part of the world but, at least for me, had the wrong relationship to it. Audrey felt the same way. We wanted to be learners from these people, not teachers.

In the summer of 1963 my family and I moved back to the United States, to the University of Chicago, where I affiliated with the Philippine Studies Program and began working on a doctorate in anthropology.

After two years of rigorous course work at Chicago and six months of special studies at the University of Michigan in Ann Arbor, I returned with Audrey and our two sons (then age four and three) to the Upi Valley to launch my dissertation research.

Hamilton Edwards, a good friend from mission days, invited us to his farm in Mirab, just four miles north of Upi along the road to Cotabato City. "Hammy" was in his mid-thirties, as was I. He had been a close friend and invaluable source of information when I was at the mission in Upi. He was also the son of the formidable Captain Irving Edwards, who had played such an important role during colonization and was famous beyond words among the Teduray people. With his dad, Hammy spent most of the World War II years in a Japanese prison, where he learned his high school lessons under interned Catholic and Protestant missionary school teachers, receiving probably the finest education available in Mindanao in the early 1940s. After liberation from the Japanese occupation he went to the United States for college, but soon after graduating came home and took over the family farm in Mirab. Half American and half Teduray, Hammy lived a thoroughly Filipino-style life. People respected him greatly as a patron and a leader. His knowledge of the Teduray—at least those outside the rainforest—was immense.

Hammy helped clarify my research plans as soon as we arrived in Mirab. I had never actually been into the forest, and I arrived on the scene with no inkling that the community of Figel existed or that I would do my fieldwork there. I only knew that I wanted to live for two years among the people in the forest, among those Teduray who still followed "the old life."

I was even less sure just what aspect of Teduray life I would primarily study. I had proposed to investigate the traditional forest Teduray legal system for my dissertation research, but, truth be told, I didn't know for certain that they even had a legal system! A few comments I had heard at the mission suggested that they settled disputes in an unusual way, so I figured there would be *something* for me to study. Hammy confirmed my guess the first night we were in Mirab. Over a bottle of scotch, he told me that the forest people indeed had an elaborate system for mending disputes.

I needed to find housing for my family, and Hammy helped with that too. When I told him the first night we were in Mirab that I wanted to stay somewhere deep in the forest for a couple of years, coming out only every six or eight weeks to visit my family, he suggested that we build a house there on his farm for Audrey and the boys.

We put up a little house near Hammy's house. There, Audrey, Len, and Will would be within reach of medical services, and the Edwards family would be close by to help out if needed. It was nothing fancy; we just sketched a rough design on the back of an envelope and hired Ramón, a local carpenter, to build it with lumber we brought up from Cotabato City in Hammy's truck. There were three small bedrooms, one for Len and Will, one for Audrey and me, and one for a live-in helper, as well as an office, a living room, a large kitchen, and a small porch. Mirab, like Upi itself, had no electricity or running water, but Ramón built a little privy in the back, a dip-from-a-bucket bathing room beside the house, and a small tank to catch rainwater from our plaited-leaf roof. There was no glass in the windows, and we could see outside through knotholes in the walls, but our new house took just two weeks to build and the total cost for all materials, labor, and furnishings was a little under five hundred dollars.

The boys soon met other youngsters on the farm and began acquiring dogs, chickens, and various other small pets. Audrey and I split our time between settling into the new house and preparing me to go into the interior. For Len and Will, Mirab was the Philippine equivalent of Tom Sawyer's Mississippi. They swam naked with the other kids in the rice paddies and water buffalo wallows, they ran around chasing their chickens, they learned a whole raft of rural skills, and they turned brown in the tropical sun.

Not all aspects of our arrangements were completely positive. Audrey said nothing at the time, but years later she told me that she felt abandoned by her fledgling anthropologist husband who planned to camp out so far from her and the little boys for such a long period of time. Still, staying near the Edwards was some consolation. Audrey had grown up in a small rural town in Wisconsin so looked forward to farm life, and she had long felt close to the Edwards family. Although Captain Edwards had died in the 1950s, his extended family still lived on the property. I felt confident about leaving her and my boys there; I knew that Hammy would be like a brother to Audrey and an uncle and surrogate father for Len and Will during the long stretches of time I would be in the forest.

Where exactly I would do my work remained an unresolved question. I asked many people in the Mirab/Upi area where I might find the old way of life in full swing, and most of them didn't have any idea. These Teduray were all from families who had left forest life more than a generation ago and they had remarkably little real idea what it had been like. They were, in fact, fascinated that I actually wanted to live there and expressed eagerness to hear about the old-style Teduray from me.

There was one man who knew quite a bit: Fr. Simeon Beling, one of the mission priests. Simeon was then about forty years old. Although he had gone to the Episcopal seminary near Manila a number of years before, unlike most of his fellow Filipino priests he had a compelling interest in his roots and maintained contact with people in the interior. He even went into the rainforest from time to time. Simeon came up to Upi every few weeks from his post at Nalkan along the coast, so I passed the word that I wanted to see him, and before long he showed up at Hammy's farm. I had always been fond of Simeon, and it was good to see him again. He had a great sense of humor and a hardy frontiersman-like quality.

Simeon assured me that Hammy was right in thinking that a lively practice of traditional law went on among the forest people and that certain women and men were renowned for their ability to restore justice. He suggested several possible fieldwork sites, but thought the best might be the community of Figel, where Balaud, one of the most skillful legal specialists, lived.

"It is far into the interior. Is that okay for you?" he asked, during an early conversation.

"That's exactly what I want."

"It's along the Tran Grande River—the Dakel Teran, we call it in Teduray—a day's walk into the forest. So there aren't many changes from the old ways."

"Do you think they would let me and a couple of assistants live and study there?" I asked. I was excited, but feared they might not be open to the idea of strangers observing them.

"Of course," he said. "They will want to help you out in any way they can."

Little did I know how true this was! But Simeon said it with such confidence that we made a plan, right then and there, that in a couple of weeks we would go to Figel, with Simeon acting as guide and entrée to this forest community.

There was much to prepare. I bought numerous boxes of batteries for my tape recorder, assembled a medicine kit, purchased film, and had a tinsmith make me a watertight metal box for my valuables. The list went on and on, but provisioning was the least of my challenges. I needed to find a couple of Teduray men to work with me in the forest. The forest Teduray were virtually unknown in the anthropological world, so, if possible, I planned to learn the outlines of their general cultural and social ways, in addition to their legal system. I also hoped that I could do some systematic analysis of their virtually unstudied language, which I would need to learn to speak. Attempting so much within a two-year stay meant I needed help in gathering information.

I decided to ask Fr. George Harris, my successor at the mission, whether I could co-opt the services of Mamerto, one of his several full-time lay assistants. I knew Mer (as everyone called him) well. The two of us were roughly the same age and we had spent many hours and days together on trails up and down the hills around Upi, hiking to outstation chapels for Mass. I knew Mer was good company, cheerful and bright. George, Mer, and I agreed that for 1966 and 1967 I would pay Mer's regular salary, that the mission would continue his benefits, and that he would work as my field assistant.

I asked Mer if he had any suggestions for another fieldwork helper. He thought about it for several days and then showed up at the Mirab house with Aliman Francisco, a man I had not met before. Like Mer, he had a great interest in learning about the old ways. Though only a few years older than Mer and me, Aliman looked much older. His face and body showed the strain of chronic malaria and of recurring pain from a serious accident he had been involved in on the Upi road. But Aliman had been farming in the last couple of years, which was harder physical work than I would be asking of him. He was a gregarious fellow, and I soon decided he would be a good companion to Mer and me.

My little team began at once to discuss our stay in the forest. That night after dinner we all sat in front of the house listening to the sounds of the night, watching bats feed from the fruit of a nearby tree. My older son, Len, grew tired of adult conversation and asked, "Why do bats only come at night?" In my best dutiful-parent manner I explained that bats are "nocturnal creatures" (graduate students talk that way), but Aliman quickly launched into the first of many stories from his rich memory of Teduray fables.

"Once the birds and the animals had a terrible war because a bird severely offended a wild pig, and the animals were unable to contain their anger," he said. "Bats, of course, are birds because they fly through the air." He made a slight flapping motion with his hands. "But they were afraid that the birds, mostly small, would have no real chance against the animals, who were much larger." At this point Aliman seemed first to shrink, then to grow, which got the boys and then the rest of us laughing.

"So the bats, who are tricky, went to the animals and said, 'Let us fight on your side. After all, we have hair, not feathers.' After some discussion, the animals agreed to have the bats on their side, thinking that they might be of some help.

"The birds, when they saw what those sneaky bats had done, tried a little sneakiness of their own. Bees are also creatures who fly, even though they are not really birds, so the birds went to them and said, 'We are just small and the boars and the monkeys are much bigger than we are. Please help us that we don't perish and we can set things straight.'

"The bees thought for a while and, not wanting to hurt the birds' feelings, decided that they would help them. So in the first battle they zoomed in and stung all the animals so badly that they ran away. When the bats saw that, they went right to the birds and said, 'Actually, we were mistaken. We are really *birds!* As you well know, we fly through the air.'

"The birds said to the bats, 'What you really are is cowards! You should forever hide yourself with shame from both birds and animals.' The bats were horribly shamed, and from then on they have always come out only at night."

Aliman was less educated than Mer, but I soon developed an admiration for his love of detail, and I felt I could trust the information he would record.

Finally I knew I had done all the preparing I could and was ready to go. I felt considerable anxiety about the unknown world that lay ahead of me—I would, after all, be entering a strange community deep within a totally unfamiliar rainforest—but I was satisfied that I had gathered a workable research team and I was excited to start the great adventure.

2 🌿 Trekking to Figel

Even though we had stayed up late making final preparations, I got up before the sun for my first trip to Figel. It was early March; just ten weeks earlier, Audrey, Len, Will, and I had stepped off the plane in Manila and, a few days after that, flown on to the Teduray region of southwestern Mindanao. Careful planning, hard work, good friends, a lot of support, and some old-fashioned good luck had filled those weeks. We were reasonably settled in Mirab, and I was about to embark for the rainforest. Hammy would take Mer, Aliman, and me down to Cotabato City in his truck.

I knew the trip would not be easy, not even this first leg. The road to Cotabato City was a road in name only, made of crushed coral and certainly not suited to automobiles. Since it was just slightly over a single lane wide, all the vehicles making their way around the sharp curves needed to honk loudly to warn anything coming the other way to stop. By local custom, a truck or bus proceeding uphill had the right to keep going, while whatever was coming down stopped and pulled over. Most of the traffic on the Upi road consisted of huge flat-bed logging trucks, which bumped down from the hills loaded with large logs, a bevy of hitchhikers clinging to their back bed, and returned up the road empty of cargo but still packed with travelers. Otherwise only a few small trucks, like Hammy's World War II weapons carrier, and a daily bus ran between Upi and the coastal town.

We passed several of the big loggers, each time pulling over as far as possible to let them by. Every time one passed us I cringed, thinking of Aliman. Several years earlier he had been riding on the back of a logging truck when it hit a deep rut and overturned. Aliman was struck in the lower abdomen by one of the logs. It was amazing that he was not killed instantly, but his bladder was crushed, and although a Cotabato City surgeon more or less successfully repaired it, Aliman said it was never the same and from time to time he experienced intense pain in his lower belly.

In the rainy season the road was often impassable, with countless ruts and pools of muddy slush. This was the dry season, and the trip up or down its crushed coral surface was possible. But it brought to mind what riding on early American "corduroy roads" must have been like. We bounced and jostled and thumped along this road for a couple of hours, even though Mirab is actually not far from Cotabato City, only about twenty miles. We were in high spirits and tried to chat about our venture, but the noise of the vehicle pounding the rough surface made talk almost impossible.

When our truck pulled into Cotabato City restorative therapy—a plate of fried rice and a cold San Miguel beer at Mariano's little Chinese café—was our first priority, just as it had always been when I trucked down to the coast for provisions during my first stay in the area. Mariano was an artist with a wok and a good friend. There was a national bank in the city, where one could cash large checks or keep a balance, but, like Hammy and numerous friends of Mariano, I had learned years before to use his café as a sort of private rural bank. If we were short of cash, he always put a hearty meal on the cuff and, on several occasions, loaned us enough pesos to get through the day.

Cotabato City, predominantly Muslim, stands at the inlet end of the muddy delta where the Pulangi River flows into the Moro Gulf and the South China Sea. It always seemed too small a place to be called a "city"—just a few streets criss-crossing each other, several shops, a couple of modest restaurants and rooming houses, two frontier-style hospitals, and a sprinkling of government buildings. But it was the capital of the province, and that must be what made it a city.

We were at Mariano's for only half an hour, and then Hammy, Mer, Aliman, and I set off to the wharf to find out when the next morning's launch would leave for Lebak. It was scheduled for six in the morning, and the three of us who made up my little fieldwork team booked on. Then we returned to Mariano's for a substantial lunch. We said our thanks and good-byes to Hammy, did a little last-minute shopping, and went to see a movie in the newly air-conditioned cinema. The wooden theater had been rebuilt and "modernized" while I was away at graduate school and was now the pride of the little coastal town. Rats ran across the floor, and the seats were loaded with bedbugs and fleas, just as before, but taking in a show was well worth the inconveniences because of the respite the deliciously cool air offered from Cotabato's midday heat and humidity.

That night we settled down to sleep on the deck of the launch. We wanted to be sure to have seats, since by morning many other passengers would be crowding the deck. Stevedores loaded cargo much of the night, and the mosquitoes whining and buzzing in my ears were fierce. Normally I would never even have *thought* of braving a night in the open air without rigging my mosquito net, but there was no way to do that on the deck. So

I knew I would get precious little rest and that by sunrise the next morning I would have sacrificed some blood to the muse of anthropology.

We took off bright and early, if not quite on time. The boat chugged slowly through the Pulangi River delta toward the Moro Gulf. A light mist felt cool on our faces, but didn't obscure our vision. We could easily see a few scattered homes of poor Maguindanaon fishing families built on stilts in the mangrove groves covering the banks of the delta, and every so often we heard the splash of a startled crocodile sliding into the water. Beyond the mangroves, the sight of tall, thin coconut palms on plantations reminded us that there were people along the river who were far wealthier, by local standards, than those who scratched out a living through fishing.

Upon reaching the open sea in under thirty minutes, our launch revved up its engine and labored hard for the seven or so hours to Lebak. I had never been on one of these coastal vessels before. A diesel-powered cargo boat about sixty feet long with a crew of two or three, ours was full that day with two dozen other people on benches in the passenger area just aft of the wheelhouse. Most of them spoke English, as did all Filipinos who went beyond third grade, at which point English became the language of instruction throughout the country. The other passengers all spoke Pilipino, the Philippine national language based on Tagalog, which most people used with Filipinos of other language groups than their own. I had learned enough Pilipino myself when I was a missionary to carry on a simple conversation. Two Teduray women were among our launch companions, and I tried out my beginning skills in that language with them. Since I regularly spoke English with Mer and Aliman, and could manage some simple greetings and inquiries in Maguindanaon with the Muslim family sitting beside me, the launch trip was an exhilarating quadrilingual experience.

Every so often as we progressed down the coast the launch would stop just offshore from a small village to unload or take on a passenger or to pick up an outrigger canoe's load of coconuts consigned to someone in Lebak. When we stopped at Nalkan at about 10 A.M. Simeon climbed aboard, his backpack slung on his shoulders, and squeezed himself in beside Mer, Aliman, and me on our bench.

I enjoyed the launch trip immensely. I had quiet, relaxed time to catch up with Simeon and to chat about old times, and the hours went by quickly. I could smell the seaweed and the salt air. The southwest portion of Mindanao was surely every Westerner's tropical island fantasy come true: vivid blue water under the near-equatorial sun; white sandy beaches that gave way to grazed grass and a narrow strip of coconut palms. And then, just a few hundred yards back from the water in most places, the blue-gray hills of the Cotabato Cordillera rose. Although everyone calls them "mountains," the highest peak is less than four thousand feet. They were blanketed with tropical rainforest wherever lowland farmers, coconut palm growers, and timber companies had not cleared it away.

Perhaps I should have been filled with calm scientific rigor of purpose and spent the trip outlining my notes and queries—something I knew my professors at the University of Chicago would have approved. I felt some of that, to be sure; I was excited about my enterprise. But it was the adventure of it all, not the science, that had hooked me, and I surrendered to a feeling of well-being as the canvas canopy of the launch flapped in the wind and the stench of diesel oil filled my nose.

Lebak appeared on our bow at about four that afternoon, and a small outrigger canoe, called locally a *vinta,* ferried us to the rock jetty that doubled as a wharf. The town itself was a fifteen-minute drive away. Visitors all arrived, as we did, by launch because otherwise Lebak was isolated, unconnected to the rest of the island by road, let alone airport. In the 1960s it was a sleepy place, where local fishermen sold their catch, coconut growers loaded their produce onto seagoing vessels, and everyone within walking distance came to the weekly market on Saturday. Simeon told me that Lebak was where the Teduray of Figel came to do what little marketing they did.

After a bite to eat from a jettyside vendor and a warm San Miguel beer—no ice here—we loaded ourselves and our gear into a jeep bound for town. There we reloaded everything onto pedicabs and went to the home of Carlos and Priscilla Concha. Priscilla was an Edwards, Hammy's older sister. She had married Carlos and moved to Lebak many years before. They were warm people and, like almost everyone else I met, interested in what I hoped to learn about the old ways of the forest Teduray. Mamerto, Aliman, and I were invited to stay with them whenever we came through Lebak, on the way to or from Figel. Their house was small but pleasant; we slept in their *sala* (living room), rolling out our sleeping mats on the floor and stringing our mosquito nets to handy nails or doorknobs.

The following morning Simeon and our little three-man anthropology team got up at five o'clock and ate a hearty breakfast of rice and dried fish prepared by Priscilla. A jeep took us from Krusing—the most inland part of the town of Lebak, so called because of a large road crossing—to the point where the road ended a mile or so outside the forest. A small store stood there, a last outpost where hikers could buy a soda or some coffee before heading into the forest. I drank a cup of strong home-grown coffee, and with a final check of our packs we took off for our day's trek to Figel.

The path took us first through a stretch of wet-rice paddies with scattered houses. Here and there as we walked past a home a voice would call out and invite us in to chat or eat. Simeon knew these people. (I sometimes think he knew everyone in Mindanao!) He told us they were homesteaders from the Visayas—the middle group of islands in the Philippines, north of Mindanao—and were accustomed to people passing by on their way into the interior. Even their watchdogs would eventually know us, he said, and stop their barking. He told us a bit of their story and how they had come to farm near Lebak, with more hope than real promise. He said that they had found little but grinding hardship in their lives and that they were frequently raided by bandits.

Before long we began to hear a faint rush of water. Soon we stood at the edge of the forest, gazing some fifty feet across the Dakel Teran at a dense wall of green. It was an imposing sight. We knew that later in the year, at the height of the rainy season, this river would often be impossible to cross; within a few hours after the start of a heavy rain, swollen from runoff from the mountains, it could double in width and become dramatically deeper and faster. But at the moment it could be waded across.

I knew that people accustomed to the river thought nothing of striding in when it was relatively calm, as it was then, and, their belongings held overhead, hopping barefoot from rock to rock until they were on the other side. But when I tried that, my tender feet slipped and stung from the sharp rocks. I soon returned to shore and, greatly chastened, put my shoes on. From then on I determined to wear my canvas shoes whenever I was in the river, even when bathing and otherwise nude. But even with tennis shoes on to help my feet gain some small purchase it was hard work to negotiate the current, and I arrived on the other side exhausted by the struggle. Still, the water's coolness was a refreshing break from the hot, damp air of the forest.

Once across the river we plunged into the lush, green mass and were immediately swallowed up by sweltering heat and humidity. From here we would hike steadily for the entire day, fording the river a dozen times before arriving at Figel.

My mind drifted pleasantly as we trudged along, hour after hour. I thought the natural beauty was breathtaking—the huge trees, the hanging vines (many with brightly colored flowers), the occasional glimpse through a break in the canopy of the deep blue sky. We were striding into the mountains as well as the forest, and soon wooded slopes rose on every side of us. Carrying my heavy pack was tiring, especially when we encountered mud or had to climb abruptly, but for the most part we ascended gently along the winding valley of the Dakel Teran. We could see the steep, striking beauty of mountains all around, but we never were higher than five hundred or so feet above sea level.

About four hours into the forest we paused, and I stretched and looked around. I remembered a time when I had flown over these mountains and could see clearly that the forest was a place of water as well as trees. Rainfall being somewhat seasonal but generally heavy, the streams that lace the mountains flow into a few larger rivers like the Dakel Teran, which in turn curve and twist toward the coast. From the air they gave the appearance of a delicate web. I recalled seeing from the plane tiny clearings scattered here and there throughout the forest, each with several small houses. In my imagination I pictured Figel as just such a clearing, a speck in the sea of green. It was on no map, but Simeon had told me that it was some twelve miles up the winding Dakel Teran. In geographic terms, it was located between 6 and 7 degrees North latitude, and sat at an elevation of 400 feet.

Walking into a rainforest is like walking back in time; the first thing I sensed was its age and how alien it felt. To Simeon it was familiar, but to me—and to a certain extent to Mer and Aliman as well, who were encountering it for the first time—the forest was awesome. Rainforests are so old, so rich, and so complex. I had seen them on TV and in films, of course, but I was utterly unprepared for what I was experiencing in person.

Once we were well into the forest I saw that it was not really the green tangle it had appeared to be from outside. The tropical sun beat down on the forest's edge, but inside little sunlight made its way through the dense canopies far above us, and I was surprised to see that in the old-growth areas there was little underbrush. I noticed many buttressed trunks of huge trees and a fair number of low plants, seedlings, and saplings. Vines climbed among the trees, as did sharply spiked rattans, and I saw an array of clinging mosses and lichens.

In the parts of the forest that were no longer pristine, where Simeon said the Teduray had at one time or another cut clearings and raised crops, thorny and bushy scrub grew in thick tangles, especially along the banks of the river and larger streams. We came across a few swamps where the ground was soaked and treacherous.

There was one especially happy surprise for me on the trail as well: no leeches! I had expected leeches to be one of the givens of forest life, and as I walked in they were my greatest apprehension. I hated the way the little bloodsuckers would climb or fall onto their unsuspecting hosts, then would numb the skin at the point of the bite, swell to grotesque size with blood, and leave a sore that was slow to clot and itched fiercely for weeks. But we never saw a single leech between Lebak and Figel! I eventually discovered that there were plenty of them in other parts of the forest, and so they remained a part of this lush, wild scene that I had to struggle to accept.

We followed foot trails that were clear and well worn by many passing feet; probably they had been there for many generations. Getting around on them was not difficult and certainly didn't require the furious right-and-left slashing with a machete that is the jungle cliché in so many Hollywood movies. Even the occasional grassy fields we came upon—seas of tall, harsh elephant grass crowding out all other plants, often bounded by impressive stands of bamboo—were traversed by clearly delineated trails. Simeon reminded us always to stay on the trails, because the deadly cobras of the forest were not aggressive unless you threatened their nests, and they never made nests on established walkways. In any case, off the trails the forest floor was difficult to travel through, strewn as it was with fallen trees, some dead of natural causes, others felled as part of shifting cultivation practices.

As we moved along the trails, from river crossing to river crossing, the silence of the forest impressed me profoundly. The gurgle of the river against the rocks could almost always be heard softly in the background, and once in a while a bird would trill or caw. As night fell, the forest insects began their soft, high whine. But the atmosphere was more like the solitude and grandeur of a medieval cathedral than like a zoo with its loudly chirping birds and monkeys.

I also did not find the profusion of colorful flowers that I had expected; instead there was a sort of dim gray-greenness everywhere. Although a scattering of orchids and other flowers grew high in the canopy, where the sunlight was strong and white, down in the damp dimness of the forest floor were only the shade-loving fungi and plants whose flowers were small and inconspicuous.

Animal life, too, was less evident than I had supposed it would be, and it was also distributed among the various layers. I later learned from friends in Figel that most of the animals in the uppermost canopy were plant eaters, though there were a few exceptions, such as the Philippine eagle, locally known as the "monkey-eating eagle." We saw many small, acrobatic monkeys, some furry flying mammals called colugos, and on the ground, a few small deer and a wild pig that snorted loudly as it scurried away. Our little group delighted in the many-colored tropical birds, and we ran into countless snakes, frogs, and insects. Most memorably, there were moments of pure magic when brightly colored and startlingly beautiful butterflies would flutter by the trail. Not many of any one plant or animal seemed to be in a single area. The various layers of the forest offered a multitude of niches, of course, many of them high up and out of sight. The extreme diversity of both flora and fauna struck me that first day in the forest, and I eventually learned that the diversity went far beyond my initial impression.

Rainforests are old and majestic. Their trees were among the first ever to grace the earth, and it was these trees that cleansed the acid-saturated atmosphere of our young planet so that animal life could begin. Ever since those first hours on the trail to Figel, the forest has seemed to me a palpably sacred place.

As we made our way into the interior, we not only waded across the river again and again, but we also passed through several small Teduray settlements. The people in them would wave in a friendly manner, then look startled when they saw a tall white person in the group. We waved in return, occasionally exchanging a few words before pushing on. Finally, as the forest light was dimming with evening, we climbed a short but steep cliff and came to a wider clearing than I had yet seen. Several small houses and one large one, all on stilts, stood in the midst of considerable activity—chickens squawking, pigs rooting in the ground, and children running around. We could smell coffee roasting and soup simmering, and the aroma made me realize that I was ravenous.

We had arrived at Figel.

Simeon had previously sent word to the people there about me and my crew and given them an idea of when we would be arriving. A small boy standing on the brow of the low cliff we had just climbed was the first to see us. As we drew near to the settlement he turned and ran, excitedly calling, "They're here!" When we actually walked into the settlement itself, six or seven men and women gathered to meet us. Simeon made a brief speech to the group, and each of the Figel people said something in return. There were solemn traditional "handshakes" all around. These were the first I had seen—the Teduray outside the forest no longer follow the practice—and I watched with fascination. Simeon held his hands together as in prayer, and the woman standing across from him took them between hers; both then slid their fingers slowly back toward themselves. When their hands parted, the two touched their hands to their chests, then spread them wide, palms facing forward. The communication of welcome and openness could not have been more clear.

The sun set soon after our arrival and darkness replaced the tropical brightness of day in the Figel clearing. In the fading light I saw that the settlement stood about fifty yards in from the Dakel Teran, at a place where the river narrows a bit to a width of about seventy-five feet. Simeon told me that in the Teduray language the name Figel means a narrow place in something that is usually wider—"like a Coca-Cola bottle." Although he said that the community was home to seven families, I counted fourteen small houses plus the large one, forming a rectangle around a large central work and play area.

That night the four of us slept in the large house, which had a wide open floor space for our mats and nets. Despite my general state of intense awareness, I felt very tired almost immediately after eating the plate of rice, vegetables, and boiled chicken we were given for supper. But the evening was clearly not over. Some fifteen or twenty people gathered and sat on woven sleeping mats that were scattered around the large split-bamboo floor. I listened and watched with fascination as, during speech after speech, both men and women periodically leaned over to let their spit—dark red from betel leaf mixed with areca nut and a little lime—drop through the nearest crack in the floor. Munching the betel quid is not intoxicating, but it gives a slight tingle to the mouth, and almost all adults chewed throughout most of their waking day. The nuts had to be smashed before being mixed with the other ingredients, and as visitors we were each offered a well-prepared chew. I accepted mine and chewed it briefly, but decided that its bitterness must be an acquired taste. As soon as it was gracefully possible to do so, I discreetly spit the masticated quid out through the floor.

My Teduray language abilities at that time were such that I didn't understand much of the talk, but it all seemed friendly, and Mer, sitting next to me, gave me the gist of each address. Simeon was explaining that I was Mo-Lini, "Father of Lennie"—he used the Teduray way of naming me by my first-born child—and that I was well known to him and to many Teduray in the Upi area as a good and kind person with no malign intent. It impressed me that they named fathers and mothers after their oldest child, male or female, rather than giving children their father's last name as in my society. (By this practice, Audrey would be known as Ideng-Lini—"Mother of Lennie.")

"Mo-Lini is a writer of books," Simeon said, "and he wants to write about your customs and ways." None of the Figel people were literate, but they knew about books from their trips to the Lebak market and from their awareness that their lowland Muslim neighbors had a sacred book. In fact, the word used by forest Teduray for book was *kuran*, from the Muslim scriptures. What they had trouble understanding from Simeon was why someone would want to come to their forest and write a book about them.

Some of the Teduray expressed concern that I had come as a conversion-minded missionary. Two of the people present had once run into a Wycliff Translator working with some Cotabato Manobo people near Lebak. The Wycliff Translators are a group whose primary interest is putting the Bible into local languages around the world, but this particular linguist had also been aggressive about evangelizing. They recalled that the experience had been quite unpleasant and that he, too, claimed to be working on a book.

One other person said that he recognized me. "I have seen this man before," he said cautiously. "He is Father Schlegel from the Upi mission."

Simeon, himself a priest and clearly trusted by these people, reassured them. "He is no longer with the mission. Mo-Lini is here for a different purpose; his book will be a story about your customs and lifestyle. Don't worry, he doesn't want to change you. He only hopes to learn about your way of settling disputes."

I finally surrendered to fatigue, lay down, and burrowed into my sarong. Mer whispered to me of other concerns voiced in the evening's speeches, such as whether Simeon was certain I was not a point-man for a logging company. But Simeon apparently assuaged all such fears, and Mer said, "There doesn't seem to be any opposition to our settling in Figel."

Tired as I felt, I was too stimulated to go quickly to sleep. Too much was new; too much was exciting. A sense of wonder and excitement filled my heart and mind. I had just walked into a throbbingly unfamiliar place, where I expected to live for two long years and which I knew would have a huge impact on the rest of my career, indeed my life. Living in the forest was no longer just a dream; I was actually in a community of "the other."

I was up with the first light, awakened by loud gong music. It was a beautiful day. I set forth, as I would most every day for the next couple of years, in a pair of blue jeans, a T-shirt, canvas shoes, and a big straw farmer's hat. The local folks dressed more like Upi Filipinos than I had expected them to, with many wearing store-bought clothes—basketball shorts, T-shirts, occasional straw hats for the men, and simple dresses (of the sort my mother and grandmother always called "housedresses") for the women. Several of the adults, however, were in traditional Teduray dress—pajamalike trousers and shirts for the men, sarongs and fitted blouses with three-quarter sleeves for the women— and unlike in Upi, almost everybody had long hair. No one seemed to have sweaters or jackets: except in the early mornings, when people wrapped themselves in their sleeping sarongs, it was consistently hot.

After breakfast Simeon left immediately for Lebak and Nalkan, and we sent him off with plentiful thanks. I then started to look around, with Aliman by my side to translate. We spoke to several people, who proved surprisingly friendly and helpful.

Although I had feared that the women might be too shy to talk to me, I was mistaken; the Figel women I met were self-confident and articulate. One told me the Dakel Teran was a good friend to the Figel people and they held the river in affection. From it they were able to extract a large assortment of good things to eat, not only many different kinds of fish but also crabs, prawns, eels, and frogs. And they bathed in it daily. The spirits held it in equal regard, for all the same reasons.

I saw an older man, up early making coffee under his house. We approached him and, with gestures and halting Teduray, I asked him about the gongs that had awakened me. His reply in a burst of rapid Teduray had me looking immediately to Aliman for help. The old man, Aliman explained, was telling us about spirits, saying that they were people just like human beings, except that you could not see or talk to them. "They are all around, Mo-Lini, but you don't need to worry. Most spirits are friendly and helpful. We humans have an agreement with them about the river. We use it during the day," he said, "and the spirits use it at night. That's why we play gongs every morning and at dusk: the spirits can hear the music. It honors them, and it signals the transfer of rights to the river. Once the gongs are played at sunset, don't go to the river again until sunrise, when the gongs say that the spirits' river rights are over."

Were there any exceptions?

"Oh yes, Mo-Lini," Aliman translated. "It is not a problem. Sometimes we have to fish at night; we just make a speech to the spirits and ask them to understand our need to be at the river."

On the side of Figel opposite the river was a clearing approximately one hundred yards square which people called "the grassy place." It was covered in the sharp, tall grass known in the

Philippines as cogan, impossible to cultivate without a tractor, but prized for many domestic purposes, especially roofing for houses. Beyond the grassy place I saw the dense forest hemming Figel in in every direction. I would soon learn that, like the Dakel Teran, the forest was a close friend and provider of many goods to the community, the valued backdrop for almost all life.

The houses in Figel intrigued me. The large house that seemed to dominate the settlement, Simeon told me, was the home of Balaud, the legal sage who was highly esteemed among the Teduray. It measured some thirty by one hundred feet, and Balaud and his two wives shared it with another family. I assumed at first that he rated this extraordinarily big dwelling because he was the leader of this community, but after the assembly that first night I wasn't so sure. For one thing, people gathered in this house in large numbers and without noticeable deference to the old man. Indeed, it appeared to be more an open public area than merely Balaud's personal residence; he didn't so much hold community meetings in his house as reside in the community meeting hall. I noticed that he and his wives occupied one small corner, partitioned off to make a sort of apartment within the larger space, and that they lived in exactly the same simple way all the other families of Figel did in their smaller houses. I saw no indications of rank or high status other than Balaud's having more than one wife, and that proved, I later learned, not to be a sign of rank either and to carry no special honor.

Only five of the smaller houses were occupied. When I asked why the others were vacant, one of the men (I had yet to learn my new neighbors' names) answered that a house took little time or effort to build, and they had been put up by families in nearby settlements as places to stay when the larger community came together for special events. They could, of course, stay in the big house, and often did, but sometimes singing and talking would go on there all night; having their own place gave them more privacy and the option of getting to sleep a bit earlier.

The houses were all single rooms, made of wood and bamboo and roofed with grass like native buildings in many other parts of Southeast Asia. Most doors were hinged at the bottom and came down like a medieval European drawbridge, and several of the houses had no other windows or openings. They measured about nine by fifteen feet and with one exception were on stilts. Running from the ground up into the houses were notched log ladders, which gave access during the day and which could be pulled up during the night.

I quickly noticed that most living and eating took place underneath the houses. Pots simmered on hooks hanging from the floor overhead, and chickens and other small animals were all about; I assumed that they found refuge from the frequent rains in these open-air "basements." I also observed that families did not have regular meals together. Through Mer, who had just joined me and Aliman in our survey of Figel, I mentioned this to a short, wiry man eating some cold rice under one of the small houses. His name was Mo-Tong; he was a complete stranger to me then, of course, but would become my good friend and next-door neighbor. While he and Mer chatted about my question for a few moments, I stood by, increasingly frustrated and impatient to learn the language. Mer told me that, according to Mo-Tong, food was always available—rice or minced corn, fruit, a pot of vegetables—and that adults and children just ate whenever they felt hungry. Mer and Aliman were as surprised as I was at this practice; it was certainly not characteristic of the plow-farming Teduray outside the forest.

Inside the houses, most family life seemed to take place on the floor. The houses all had small earth-filled fireboxes built into one corner, where food could be cooked in wet or cold weather.

During the day sleeping mats and mosquito nets were rolled and set against the wall.

While the three of us were having some rice, fruit, and a cup of coffee with Mo-Tong, a woman and a man came to show me a small dwelling just across the central yard from the community house. My pack and other gear had been placed inside. The house was smaller than the others and not on stilts, and it had a tiny porch with a sitting bench, but in all other respects it was like the rest. It may have been too small for a whole family, but it was perfect for me—as though made to order—with just enough room for a small desk beneath a window on the north side and for me to stretch out my sleeping mat. The house had clearly not been put up in expectation of my coming; it was weathered and looked lived in. I tried to imagine why it had originally been built; perhaps it had belonged to a childless couple. I wondered whether they were offering it to me not only because it was small but also because, with its porch and easy access, it would be a bit more comfortable. Mer and Aliman were set up in the house next to mine.

On that first morning in Figel, Ideng-Emét and Mo-Emét, a young couple who lived in an adjacent corner of the big house with Balaud, offered to cook for us as a regular arrangement; we would join them for meals under the big house. We were grateful not to have to perform this task ourselves, since we could then put in longer days on our projects. We wanted to offer some gift in return, but all we could think of was to carry in special treats from the coast whenever we hiked back from trips to Mirab. We provided rice in the off-season when they were down to only their next year's seed, and occasionally brought candy or sweet rolls. The arrangement worked out well. The couple and their preadolescent son Emét were good companions and excellent sources of information. They said that preparing food for us posed no hardship for them, and it was certainly true that not having to cook and chop firewood allowed my team to do much more anthropological work than would have otherwise been possible.

While I was arranging my belongings in my house I saw men in the grassy area nearby digging a hole in the ground and erecting a partition between the hole and the residential area. They knew about outhouses from contacts outside the forest and were making me one, another unrequested kindness. The Figel people seemed unusually sensitive to what they thought would make me maximally comfortable, something I knew to be a general Filipino trait. The work on the privy reminded me of the time almost a decade earlier when, before going to seminary, I lived for the better part of a year as an unordained missionary in a remote community in the mountains of northern Luzon, and on my first day there folks had carted a brass four-poster bed up the main street to my place, assuming that I wouldn't want to—or couldn't—sleep on the floor. This time I didn't feel the embarrassment or resistance I had then. In fact, I was delighted to be provided with a place where I could attend to my private physical needs in a more or less familiar way. It was a thoughtful gesture, and I was pleased. That day I didn't truly recognize what was happening, or understand the full extent of the Teduray desire to do such kindnesses, but eventually I would look upon my outhouse and the offer to cook for us as early encounters with the most central of Teduray moral precepts.

Another brush with Teduray attitudes came the next morning. I was bothered on my first night in my little house to see the large number of house spiders that emerged at dark from the woven bamboo walls. They seemed to be everywhere I looked—large spiders with bodies as big as pecans and leg spans the size of the palm of my hand. And although they didn't seem interested in me, I found them creepy and I shuddered more than once as I looked around. I commented on the spiders the next morning to one of the Figel women, and she smiled and said brightly, as though commenting on an old friend, "Oh yes, the spiders. They live there too." I adopted that same friendly stance as my own and soon found that, when left alone, the spiders left me alone as well, and we all got along just fine sharing our mutual residence.

During that first week, Figel began to feel like home. I learned to bathe, brush my teeth, and shave naked in the cold, clear water of the Dakel Teran. For a few uncomfortable nights I grappled with an unforeseen sleeping problem. It wasn't my spider companions, nor was it the hard floorboards: I had carried in a fluffy American-style pillow and in any case was accustomed to sleeping on Philippine floors. The problem was tiny chicken mites, which were terribly itchy. (I would learn that their name was used by Teduray to refer to people who were always horny!) I soon realized, however, that putting the mat out in the hot midday sun and turning it repeatedly did more to discourage the mites than any chemical insecticide, so that problem didn't last long. And although I had none of the bookshelves I love to surround myself with in my own home, I did have my large watertight metal box for my film, my tape recorders, the many cases of batteries needed to run them, and, of course, the few books I had carried in.

Yet even as I was settling into this new home, I knew it was in many ways very different from any I had ever experienced. I wished I could share with Mer and Aliman my attraction to Figel ways and the uncommon graciousness of these people, but I had no inkling yet of their importance and of the personal journey that lay ahead of me. I had come to this exotic corner of the world as a "participant-observer," to engage in a classic anthropological rite of passage and gain professional status. I certainly never dreamt that, as I learned more and more about the forest Teduray, I would be powerfully pulled to explore as well some of the unknown regions of my own soul.

3 ✿ Animals That Fly Are Birds

One morning, about six weeks after I had arrived in Figel, I heard a conversation taking place beneath a nearby house. My neighbor, Mo-Udow, was talking to his two-year-old daughter, Miliyana, about a small furry animal with big eyes he had shot with his blowgun that morning just as dawn was breaking. He gestured toward the little animal and said several times "*kobol*," the name for a colugo (*Cynocephalus volans*, a squirrel-like mammal with membranes between its body and its legs which leaps gracefully, and even soars, from branch to branch in the lower canopy of the forest). "It is a kind of bird [*manuk*]," Mo-Udow told her.

Miliyana said after him, pointing with great glee, "Kobol. Manuk."

After every few repetitions of the word, Mo-Udow told his daughter a little bit about the colugo. "The kobol goes around at night, and it eats at night too. The kobol jumps from one tree to another."

"Kobol," she repeated.

"It is a bird," he taught, "because it flies through the air."

"Kobol. Manuk," she crowed.

The two of them, often joined by Ideng-Udow, her mother, played this game frequently. And little Miliyana continued it by herself during the day. She gestured in typical Teduray fashion, nodding her head and pointing with her lips at all sorts of things. And as she gestured she said their names, as though she was some sort of primeval Adam naming the world—which, of course, is exactly what she was. She reminded me of my children, who at her age played the same game in California with different things and different names. Miliyana was in the "one-word stage" of learning her language and her world. Sometimes she got a word wrong, perhaps calling a certain insect by the name of another one, and a passing adult would correct her. "No, child, that is a taro beetle, not a coconut beetle," or "That is a spiny bamboo, not a zigzag bamboo." And she would laugh and gesture and say the word herself, sometimes over and over, utterly delighted with herself. The world was becoming familiar to her—the Teduray would say "tame." It was becoming home.

I recognized our kinship as learners. Day by day I, too, was gaining familiarity with Miliyana's language and her world in much the same way. Humans—wherever we live and whatever social and cultural reality we are raised within—need to learn the words for our world, and we all seem to find pleasure in do-ing it. As with Miliyana, so with us all, another entity loses its strangeness when we learn its name.

The most memorable of my early encounters with a Teduray's notions of what the world was like occurred in 1961, a number of years before I arrived in Figel. A brand-new priest at the mission in Upi, I was not long off the plane and much more full of my-self than I realized.

On the mission compound in Upi—in addition to the large church, the homes of clergy and lay workers, the nuns' convent, and the new high school that was being built—we had a free clinic with a resident nurse, where we dispensed Western-style medical care. One day an older Teduray man, a sharecropper on a homesteader's farm near the mission, met me outside the clinic. He had just been treated for, as he called it, "having cold." At that time, I knew only a very few words of his language, but he spoke a bit of English, and so we stood in the shade of a tree and chatted for a while.

"Ah, Father," he said, "your clinic does the most surprising magic."

"Magic!" I said. "That's not magic. It's modern medicine."

"Oh, no, Father. It is truly magic. I am sick, and I know why I am sick. I have offended a spirit. The nurse is not a shaman but still makes me better. She gives me two little white stones to swallow, and if they don't work, she sticks a pin in my arm." He shook his head in wonder. "These things have nothing at all to do with what made me sick, but soon I am better. I don't give the offended spirit any chicken or anything. It is true magic."

I said very earnestly, hoping to deliver him from his naive beliefs, "No, no, no! Spirits do not cause sickness; germs cause sickness." I still cringe when I remember how utterly unproblematic I thought all this was.

He looked completely puzzled. "What are germs?"

"Germs," I replied, "are little tiny things you can't see, that break into your body and make you sick." There I was—totally new to the place, all of twenty-nine years old, in my bright white cassock—telling this old man who had lived his whole life in that vicinity about something of which he could only think me utterly ignorant.

With a hint of tolerant bemusement, he said to me, "Do you really *believe* that?"

He then tried with typical Teduray goodwill to point out to me the real facts of life. He patiently explained that spirits are everywhere, and that you can't see them or converse with them unless you are a shaman. So, even despite all the best of intentions, you can offend them. Then they may become angry and make you sick.

It was clear to me that I had to marshal my most incontestable argument. "Well, have you ever *seen* a spirit?"

"No," he said gently, but a bit triumphantly. "Have you ever seen a germ?"

I smile when I think back on that little exchange. Of course I hadn't ever *seen* a germ. I believed in germs for exactly the same reason he believed in spirits—because experts on that sort of thing had told me that they could see them and because "everybody knew" that germs cause disease. When I was very small, I had learned that "fact" as part of learning what the world was like, just as several decades later Miliyana was learning the "fact" that colugos were birds. She had learned or would learn, in much the same way, that spirits make you sick. And it wouldn't seem to be anything debatable, just a matter-of-fact piece of "knowledge" about what the world is like.

The plain truth—though I didn't understand it at the time— was that the old man I chatted with outside the clinic and Miliyana in Figel both grew up in a literally different world than I had. I don't mean just different degrees of sophistication or technical know-how or scenery; I mean they were instructed by people with a whole different understanding of the nature of the real. Most people on the planet—those with lots of schooling as well as those with very little schooling—grow up with the understandable assumption that what they learn as "reality" *is* reality. But many philosophers and most anthropologists realize that this is not so, that our various cultures indoctrinate us in very particular realities. The Teduray world and my world were fundamentally different "takes."

Figel Teduray found it exotic and a bit bizarre that there were actually people who doubted the existence of environmental spirits. When I first arrived, I felt the Teduray were the exotic ones, but I eventually came to appreciate their vision as simply different.

Even if all social and cultural worlds throughout the planet were the same, with a ready one-to-one equivalence between one language and another, learning the world would still be work and discovery for children. But learning a second language would be a far easier thing for adults to do. The fact is, though, that our various cultures and languages divide up and organize reality in different ways. We saw this in Mo-Udow's teaching his daughter that colugos are birds. For us, the bird kingdom doesn't include bats or colugos, and we have our reasons for classifying them separately. The Teduray, however, have *their* reasons for grouping bats, colugos, and birds together: all are warm-blooded and fly, a point that Miliyana learned effortlessly and immediately.

Similarly, Miliyana learned that in her language, in her world, shrimp and leeches were "fish" and snakes and insects belonged to another category, one that I roughly translated into English as "creatures." I could, I suppose, just as well have translated that class of critters—which includes both pythons and honeybees—as "bugs." But I settled on "creatures," because I was hard pressed to call a snake an "insect." For the Teduray, however, the association was perfectly natural, even obvious.

Another important difference that often tripped me up was that words which seemed to translate quite straightforwardly could in fact have a vastly different connotation. A good example is the word *bobò*, "fat." When Teduray said that someone was fat, they meant it in a thoroughly positive way: that person looked healthy, serene, flourishing. "My you are getting fat!" was a compliment, as it certainly is not in English. I have a lifelong tendency to weight and girth, but did so much strenuous exercise hiking in the forests and hills around Figel that I was quite slim. On occasion, I would show some Teduray person a photograph of myself taken earlier in the United States. Inevitably she or he would exclaim, "How fat you were, Mo-Lini!" I did not feel complimented!

Miliyana also learned—and so did I, eventually—about the many spirits with whom the Teduray shared the cosmos. Spirits, to them, were "people you cannot see." Some were smaller than humans and some were giants, but in general they were like humans, except that only a shaman could see and talk to them. Though present, they were invisible to everyone else. One type was the Swamp Spirit. These spirits were short, black people who wore black clothes and lived in swampy places. They were guardian spirits of wild pigs but tended to be mischievous in their dealings with humans, lusting after them sexually and occasionally attempting to seduce individuals who were in the forest alone. Furthermore, they had the ability to change their appearance to that of a visible, attractive human; this meant that casual sex in a swamp area was especially risky, because intercourse with these Swamp Spirits was generally fatal to a human being. So Teduray were wary of them and, in particular, warned their adolescent children strictly to avoid any situation where an incident involving them might occur.

Novel beings of this sort—not to mention complex grammatical differences—made learning Teduray much more difficult for my English-grooved brain than it was for little Miliyana's. I not only had to learn thousands of new words for familiar items, and learn to place them sometimes in utterly unfamiliar classifications, but I had to familiarize myself with things—emotions and feeling states, cosmological beings and places, legal and spiritual concepts—that simply don't exist in my Euro-American reality.

I never became as fluent in Teduray as Miliyana would be by the time she was six, but I worked diligently to internalize as much of that linguistic world as I could pile into my head and onto my tongue. It has long been a given of anthropological study that field research be done in the language of the place, and the good sense of this was immediately evident to me. To try to translate Teduray reality into the English-language categories that express my reality would have been to twist and squash it into something utterly different, something unrecognizable to the Teduray.

I had learned a few words and phrases of Teduray when I was at the Upi mission, but when I arrived to do my anthropological studies I began to work on the language in earnest. Although I got started in Mirab when we were gearing up for the forest, real progress began after I arrived in Figel and was surrounded by the language every minute of every day. I followed people around, pointing to things and asking their names. I gestured and grunted, squeaked and played charades—anything to discover particular words and how they were put together. Especially, I worked with Mer and Aliman, trying to keep it all straight, to systematize the babble into language. I knew many tricks from earlier experience learning other languages, and I knew that language learning required the same sort of discipline a ballet dancer or an athlete exercised. I had to practice daily, stretch my abilities constantly. Sometimes I got so tired mentally and linguistically that I just hid out in my house for a while, but I knew that if I did that too much I would never get anywhere.

Gradually, then, through seemingly endless efforts, I reached a point where the Figel folks and I were actually talking.

I didn't have much published material to go on. In the nineteenth century, Padre Guerrico Bennasar, a Jesuit priest at Tamantaka, a Spanish mission between Cotabato City and the Teduray mountains, had learned Teduray and written a short grammar of it, in which he tried to squeeze the Teduray language into the thoroughly alien categories of Latin and Spanish grammar. We know better than to try this exercise today, but it was standard linguistic practice in his time. So that work was not really much help. On the other hand, Ursula Post of the Summer Institute of Linguistics (another name for the Christian evangelical Wycliffe Translators) had spent a couple of weeks working on Teduray, and had just published a preliminary analysis of the sound system, what linguists call the "phonology." This did help me make a start. Beyond those two things, nothing had been written on the Teduray language.

I think it was knowing some Tagalog, which I had used as a mission priest, that helped me the most in the early months. Tagalog and Teduray, along with the more than one hundred other languages of the Philippines, form a subgroup of the large Malayo-Polynesian (or Austronesian) linguistic family. The Philippine languages are not mutually intelligible, but they have many cognate words—words quite close in form and pronunciation—and they share a similar grammatical structure, one markedly different from that of English and other languages of the Indo-European family.

From acquaintance with Tagalog, I was prepared for one of the most significant characteristics of the Teduray language: the fact that gender is not grammatically marked. "I," "you," and "they" are as in English, indicating person and number only; but the third person singular—"he," "she," and "it" in English—is just a single pronoun in Teduray. Likewise "he" and "him," "she" and "her," are all expressed by one ungendered word. The same is true of the possessive pronouns.

Knowledge of that feature of Philippine languages made Teduray easier for me. When I spoke, I was not forced to make all the gender distinctions we face in English, and the matter of gender bias in language—the subtle but ugly way in which half the human race is discounted linguistically—just never came up. I found that speaking Teduray was and *felt* much more egalitarian. It was a liberating characteristic, and I delighted in the emancipation.

One major grammatical difference between Teduray and English, however, proved much less user-friendly for a learner like me.

In Mirab, my small sons had a splendid time romping around and playing with the farm animals. Suppose my boy, Will, had tried out the accuracy of his throwing arm at the expense of some hen. In English, I could say the same sentence, "Will just threw a stone at the chicken," in several different ways. For example, it could be a reply to the question "Who just threw a stone at the chicken?" If, however, I answered the question, "What did Will just throw at the chicken?" I would stress the words in my response slightly differently. And likewise for a third question, "What did Will just throw a stone at?"

In English, my sentences would have different intonation and stress—"*Will* just threw . . ." or "Will just threw a *stone* . . ."—but the words themselves would not change. In Philippine languages, in contrast, words themselves change. Grammarians call this "focus." To express who was doing the throwing versus what was being thrown versus what the target was, three quite different sentences are needed, each with a different verb form and a different little word, called a particle, before each of the nouns. The situation becomes even more complex if you include additional information, such as that Will threw the stone with his left hand. In every case, the right verb forms and the right particles are critical, or you won't be understood. This was no problem for Teduray, because they grew up with focus, but it was extremely difficult for me.

Fortunately, focus was an aspect of Tagalog too, so it was at least not completely new to me when I went to learn Teduray. Other aspects of Teduray grammar, however, were tantalizingly different from Tagalog, and some I never did quite sort out. Even a linguist who came to Figel and worked with us for a while on Teduray grammar was stumped in certain areas. Although I got the hang of saying things more or less right and I understood Teduray speakers with no problem, I never did reach the point where I could explain why certain words, especially some of the particles, went where they did.

Learning Teduray, like learning Tagalog before it, made many calls upon my sense of humor. I remember with some embarrassment—and my family remembers with sheer delight—the first full Tagalog sentence I ever attempted. At lunch, instead of asking a young woman friend of ours to "please pass the bananas," I got a sound wrong here and there and asked her to "please stick the bananas up your ass."

She looked at me in some astonishment, said, "Yes, Father; excuse me, Father," and ran breathlessly off to tell about the bizarre new priest to gales of laughter.

Learning a new language and a new culture, if nothing else, teaches humility. If you can't laugh at yourself, you are lost.

One time, after I was in the forest a month or so and had crammed lots of words and grammar into my mind, I was walking on a trail when I met a fellow I knew slightly coming the other way. A week or so earlier, Mer and I had been caught by dusk—"nighted," as the Filipinos say—in the forest some distance from Figel and had come across this man's home. Although we were strangers, his family immediately made us welcome, gave us some warm food, and cleared a place for us to sleep. I remembered, on meeting him again, that the man's wife had been slightly ill, so I wanted to ask how she was doing. Using perfectly good Teduray words in a perfectly clear and straight sentence, I asked him, "How is your wife?"

He looked at me rather strangely and said, "She is still slippery." Then, quickly, he uttered the traditional departure formula, "You go that way, I'll go this way," and off he went.

As I pondered his odd answer and tried to make sense of it, it dawned on me what had happened, and I think I must have turned a bright enough red to light up the forest. The problem was that those words, in that order, aren't the way you ask that question. A Teduray would have said, "How is your wife's *falas* [lit., face = appearance or situation]?" or possibly, "How is your wife's gall bladder?" I had been taught that, but had not yet fully taken it in. The question I asked made literal sense, and of course that is how he understood it; for better or worse, he assumed I was asking about her physical, sexual qualities!

I still blush to think of what he made of my innocently intended question and wonder why he supposed I was so curious.

Another such incident occurred when I first arrived in Figel and was still concentrating on learning the language. I initiated a demographic survey of the community, for which I formulated a series of questions aimed at finding out people's age, family relationships, special skills, and the like. But when I asked people in Teduray, "How old are you?" I received some unexpected responses.

One of the first people of whom I asked this question was a wily old legal specialist called Mo-Anggul. Reputed to be a real character, with a gift for colorful conversation, Mo-Anggul looked at me, somewhat puzzled, then, stretching his arms out and flexing his leg muscles a bit, said, "Well, I'm still pretty much all right. I'm doing okay."

I said, "No, grandfather, how *old* are you?"

He replied, "Yes, I still feel quite fine, as though I were a young man. My wife will tell you that, too."

Mo-Anggul was clearly taking my Teduray question "How old are you?" to mean "How dilapidated—worn out, used up—are you?" When I switched tactics and asked him how many years he had been alive, I could see that this was not something he had ever given any thought to. He told me, "Oh, probably about two hundred."

I said, "Perhaps that is too many, grandfather."

He quickly revised his estimate and offered, "Yes, more like fifteen or twenty."

Mo-Anggul was apparently in his seventies or eighties, so I knew I was doing something wrong and there was more going on here than I was aware of.

The problem turned out to do with how forest Teduray thought about time. They were, of course, perfectly aware of the passing of time, and they knew that each year a certain cycle of seasons—rainy, dry, then hot—would unfold. They knew that each year they would perform their cultivation activities in their forest gardens in the same sequence and at roughly the same time of the year. Their calendar was the night sky, and they always knew where they were in the year from the position of the various constellations of their zodiac. But what they did *not* seem to do was count up the number of times these annual cycles occurred with regard to themselves. Wondering how many rainy seasons had happened since they were born or since they had gotten married never seemed to cross their minds.

To learn a person's age, therefore, I had to determine some key events in recent history which the Teduray knew about, such as the Japanese arrival in the area during World War II, a smallpox breakout about 1917, and a period of drought around the turn of the century, when many people died. Then I had to match these events up with age categories in their language, such as a baby that is still sucking, an infant that has been weaned, a girl or boy at puberty who is not yet married, one who is married but still childless, a parent, and a grandparent. So I finally learned, when taking census data, to say things like, "Were you married but still childless when the Japanese came?"

They would answer, using such concepts, with something like: "No, I was at puberty but not yet married." In this way I could pin chronological ages down fairly well.

Mo-Anggul was seventy-six.

I found the forest Teduray way of referring to the time of day different and charming too: they would simply point with outstretched arm and hand to the sky, to the place where the sun would be at whatever time they were referring to. "I will meet you tomorrow morning," Mo-Emét might say, pointing to the place the sun would be at about ten.

This approach is much less exact than clock time, of course, and could not be used for making a date for 9:45 in the morning, say, but forest Teduray saw no need for such precision. Indeed, I doubt that it would have occurred to any traditional Teduray, prior to encountering a clock for the first time, that time even *could*—let alone *should*—be reckoned in such tiny units as minutes, much less seconds. In this—as in many other respects—the forest was a more humane place.

Teduray measured objects in an interesting way too. In their way of reckoning, the size of something was figured by comparing it to a body part. For example, an eel might be described as the circumference of one's wrist—not in words, but by a gesture in which the wrist is encircled with thumb and forefinger. A large bamboo might be likened to the size of the speaker's thigh or a tree trunk to a circle of his outstretched arms.

Much of what was gracious about the traditional Teduray way of life had to do with, of all things, people's gall bladders. Not literally, of course. Literally, their gall bladders did what all gall bladders do—they stored bile manufactured by the liver—and Teduray were well aware of this. When they cleaned fish or animals they caught, they knew not to nick the gall bladder and release bitter bile into the flesh they wanted to eat. The gall bladder was, at that level, understood simply as an organ of the body, like the kidney or the heart. Figuratively, however, the gall bladder was the center of human life, emotion, will, and consciousness. Much like our "heart," but more so, the gall bladder was what housed one's state of mind and rational feelings, one's desires, one's intentions, one's delight or misery.

When I discussed anything in Teduray, the gall bladder would inevitably enter the conversation. In the evenings, after supper, Mer and Aliman often asked me, "What is your gall bladder regarding tomorrow?" And I might reply something like, "Tomorrow, my gall bladder will be to go with Mer and all the Figel men to the felling of the big trees for Balaud's garden, while Aliman remains here to interview Mo-Bintang."

For forest Teduray, the gall bladder figured in a precept that was absolutely central to their notions of how to live their lives: it was *"Don't give anyone a bad gall bladder."* The "gall bladder rule," as I came to call it, had two sides. First, you should do everything you could to help each other. Second, you should never do anything to wound another person in body or sensibility; you should never make another person angry or hurt. The Teduray in the forest lived by this rule as faithfully as they could, and they regarded it as the very foundation of good life and good society. Like all human beings, Teduray often fell short of their ideal, but it was remarkable—at least to an outsider like me—how much they honored this precept and truly did live it.

It was to respect my gall bladder, you see, that those Teduray men moved so quickly and risked so much to carry Len out of the forest—even though they "knew" that what he needed was quite different from what I thought he needed. The mere fact that I wanted him to have my kind of medical help was enough for them. In their minds, needing each other was a given reality of this world, and helping each other was the only rational way to live.

There are two other terms, *fiyo* (good) and *tété* (bad), that were, like "gall bladder," ubiquitous in Teduray life and of such importance that I want to define them carefully.

Something was *fiyo* when it was just right, exactly the way it ought to be. A man or woman who was good looking by Teduray canons (light skin, shiny long black hair, thick ankles, a narrow waist) was, with regard to appearance, *fiyo*. More generally, a person who worked hard and was kind and modest was *fiyo*. The weather was *fiyo* when it was clear so that one could do one's work. A decision was *fiyo* when made with sensitivity and sense. One who was sick was *fiyo* again upon recovery. A tool that was sharp and sturdy was *fiyo*. As was a meal that tasted good and was filling. The word *fiyo* in Teduray had the sense of "in harmony with all things," and it ranged over a huge number of connotations for which English uses separate words, such as proper, delicious, healthy, attractive, adequate, convincing, right, and, of course, good. In English, I render *fiyo* often as "good" but even more often as "just-right," and hope that the slight strangeness of that expression helps recall the great range of meaning of *fiyo*.

Its opposite, *tété*, was just as common in Teduray discourse and just as widely applied as *fiyo*. It connoted anything that was bad, wicked, ugly, defective—in short, anything that was not as it should be, anything that was fundamentally and profoundly amiss, that was not just-right. I render it in English sometimes as "bad," but sometimes as "not-right," so that its complex references can be readily noticed.

The sorts of feelings that were referred to the gall bladder were those that involved active thinking and conscious mental processes as well as mood states, visceral feelings, and emotional conditions. It was a mind at peace with the immediate surroundings and circumstances and, especially, free of anxieties or anger, a consciousness in harmony with the world, that manifested a "just-right gall bladder." On the other hand, a mind that was distracted from practical day-to-day concerns and troubled with some matter—whether lightly with apprehension or greatly with anger or hatred—was expressed in terms of a "not-right gall bladder." And when a person's gall bladder had been made not-right, its restoration to balance was the work of Teduray legal, spiritual, and medical specialists.

The good world for Teduray people, then, was one in which as much as possible was just-right. They realized, of course, that there are limits to the human capacity to bring about the good and that not every aspect of life can be just as it should be at every moment. Good weather is bound to alternate with foul weather. In a forest existence, there would inevitably be times when the stomach was empty and the muscles were weary. They knew that death would bring grief and that childbirth would bring pain. Such hardships of life were simply beyond human control. But many of life's misfortunes were not; they were seen as having a personal cause. And behavior that caused misfortunes to others was not-right, was *tété*.

I studied the Teduray language with great diligence, but never in my two years at Figel did I become more than a halting speaker of it. I could ask questions and do interviews, and I was understood well enough in that sort of conversation, but I was far from fluent, let alone articulate. It was a chastening experience for an educated, intellectual person like me to realize that I had to express myself in adult conversation with a preadolescent's command of the language. I came to the point where I understood what I *heard* with considerable fluency, but right up to the end of my stay among the Teduray I could not hold up my end of a discussion of any complexity without a great deal of help from Mer or Aliman; I just didn't command the quickness and the subtlety needed. I had a huge passive vocabulary, but a far smaller active one. For one who has spent his life relying on verbal agility, this was not easy to accept. But I endured the unaccustomed verbal clumsiness with all the grace and humor I could muster.

People occasionally likened me, in my Teduray abilities, to Captain Edwards, who is said to have spoken Teduray only clumsily but understood it well. It was probably a fair comparison, and certainly more accurate—if less flattering—than what I usually heard when I met Teduray people for the first time. Being polite, and perhaps a bit surprised, they would pronounce me fluent and praise my Teduray with extravagant generosity. But I knew better; I knew if I waited long enough, someone would say, "Mo-Lini speaks our language just like Captain Edwards."

Teduray were generally exceedingly polite, but the same was not true of people outside the forest.

One afternoon I was chatting with a young man named Beliyo, and I asked why he and some of the other younger men had their hair cut short. The traditional custom among the Teduray was for both males and females, once they were a year or two old, to stop cutting their hair. Women then gathered their hair into buns in the back, and men wrapped theirs around their head and secured it with a bandanna.

"Did you get a haircut at the market?" I asked him.

"Yes, very short," he smiled. He seemed slightly embarrassed.

"I thought Teduray men let their hair grow long."

"That's right, Mo-Lini. But it is shaming, because sometimes other people laugh at us when we are at the market."

The phrase "other people" meant "non-Teduray."

"They call us 'primitive' and 'natives.' Some of us feel ashamed, so we have the barber cut our hair. I also like long hair; it is our custom. Good long hair is better than this. But Mo-Lini, it is shaming to be singled out and laughed at. I always wear market clothes, too, when I go to the coast."

Who on this earth does not know that feeling? It is no fun anywhere or at any age to be shamed and laughed at. I sat in my house that evening working on my notes from the day, which were about legal concepts, but Beliyo's words kept coming back to me. His short haircut revealed something important about Teduray relations with people from outside the forest. The lowlanders did indeed think of the people from the forest as "primitive natives" from the hills, and they smugly ridiculed not only their hairstyle, but their traditional dress and their accent when speaking to the vendors in Maguindanaon or in the simple "bamboo Tagalog" language of trade. The ridicule was a regular "in-their-face" reminder to the Teduray of the social snobbery, arrogant power, and emotional violence common outside the forest. It was their encounter with racism and elitism.

I sat at my little desk, drifting in my reverie far from the notepad before me. One of the names Beliyo said the "other people" had called him was *ngengu*, which literally means "ignorant of some particular body of knowledge" but had been thrown at him with the sense of "uncivilized" or "primitive." Yet those were not just words used by "civilized" Filipino lowlanders to describe hill people they thought of as inferior, for I knew that the same words were very much alive in my own culture as well. People often used them when I would explain that I was becoming an anthropologist: "Oh, you'll be studying primitive people!" or "I just love to read about primitive tribes!" For a long time "primitive" was a common term among professionals in the field of anthropology, and I knew it was still used occasionally. At the University of Chicago the course on traditional religions had been renamed "Comparative Religion" from the older "Primitive Religion," but many of the most renowned anthropology books written before the middle of the twentieth century had titles like E. B. Tylor's *Primitive Culture* and Paul Radin's *Primitive Man as Philosopher*. Few anthropologists were as esteemed as Bronislaw Malinowski, and he wrote books with titles like *The Sexual Life of Savages* and *Crime and Custom in Savage Society*.

Those scholars thought highly indeed of "primitive" people and had no awareness whatsoever that they were slurring them with their terminology. But anthropologists today have entirely dropped the term, because we have all finally realized that, like "savage" or "barbarian," it is a pejorative, reflective of Euro-American assumptions about Western cultural and technological superiority. I am glad such terms are gone. There was no way anyone who truly knew the forest Teduray could conceive of them as "primitive" or "savage." They were highly sophisticated in the ways of their environment and the requirements of the life they led. They could survive and thrive, through a huge repertoire of skills and local knowledge, in a forest where, if left on my own, I would surely starve or be killed by venomous snakes or insects in no time at all! So I was not prepared to call the Teduray, or anyone else, primitive. Besides, with our serial killers, our ethnic wars, and our minuscule concern for the impoverished and hopeless among our own people, who are we to call anyone else primitive?

But there is another reason I never use the word "primitive" in discussing people like the Teduray. It gives an impression that Teduray life in the rainforest was directly linked to some primal original state, settled and unchanging, and that only when people from outside showed up were they forced to change. For years much anthropological writing gave this impression. Accounts of tribal life were written in the "ethnographic present"—they "do" this and they "do" that—as if some classic and unchanging social equilibrium held sway. But it was all just an illusion. No society has ever stayed simply frozen over long periods of time. It may seem so to the participants, because change is generally slow and subtle, but it doesn't really happen.

I once read that if you look at the Crab Nebula, a striking gas cloud in the constellation Taurus, you will not discern any change in its size: it looks completely stable. And yet astronomers say that it is expanding at a rate of seventy million miles a day. The Teduray were like that. Like all human societies—all things—they were changing and had been since they became a society, at perhaps the equivalent of seventy million miles a day. But I was looking at them during a nanosecond in their history and couldn't see the change. Whatever their long story had been, it is lost to us now, as frozen into an illusion of changelessness as the Crab Nebula.

The Teduray were like many people were before things went wild in the world with colonialism and the industrial revolution. They had no written language and they did not preserve much in their oral tradition about changes in their lives or ways. Forest Teduray did, however, have stunningly precise memories about things they felt a need to remember: just what goods were given in a wedding exchange made fifty years before, or the words of their immensely long cosmological epic, *Berinarew*. These they remembered perfectly. As for life in the forest, they seemed to assume it had always been pretty much the same as it was when I met them.

This was certainly not true. At some point, for example, they stopped pounding out bark for clothes and began buying yard goods or blue jeans in the market. At some point, they began buying iron tools, because they had learned of their practicality for cultivating gardens in the forest. These and other innovations must have had transforming effects, but the story is now lost. I can only describe how the people I knew lived and thought in Figel when I was among them, when they were living in what was often referred to by others as "the old way." Although Teduray outside the forest were changing rapidly, the forest people were also feeling the effects, if much more gradually, of advancing Western technology.

From the day I began learning Teduray until the end of my stay, I gave great effort and careful attention to the precise meaning of Teduray words and expressions. I would have long conversations with Mer and others about this word or that, often pursuing its particular connotations late into the night or throughout an entire day. Many that sounded like ordinary terms would turn out, under close inspection, to open up subtle but crucially important aspects of the Teduray world.

I remember a day when Mer, Aliman, a couple of Teduray friends, and I scrutinized the word *adat*. We spent hours at it. It is a common term, originally borrowed from the Arabic of the Muslim Maguindanaon, and used in just about all Malay-family languages to mean "folkways" or "customs." Numerous scholarly treatises have been written about "*adat* law," meaning the various tribal systems of custom and dispute resolution in Malay societies.

In Teduray terminology, the *adat* of a people was the sum of their proper ways, the things they usually do, the activities that mark them as a distinctive cultural entity—in short, their "customs." Every ethnic group has its own *adat*, and Teduray often asked me about the *adat* of my people concerning this or that. Indeed, I took it as a compelling obligation to do my best to describe the thinking, folkways, and social institutions of my people, in grateful return for all the hours Figel people spent trying to clarify theirs for me. It was not easy. What went on in Chicago, my most recent home, or in Los Angeles, where I grew up, was so different in every conceivable way from what people did in this tiny clearing in a Philippine forest—or from what they could imagine. But I tried. I recall one time when I attempted to describe the game of baseball to a group of bewildered Teduray men. After ten or fifteen minutes I just gave up. Anyway, it would have been hard for me, who loves baseball and sees it as a kind of American artform, to have dealt with the disapproval they would surely have felt about its being competitive.

As I was learning, Figel people did not think competition was a good thing.

Early on, in talking to Teduray, I realized that questions like "Why did you do that?" or "Why is this like it is?" would not get me far. They would simply reply every time, "It is the custom, Mo-Lini."

I knew I had to pay attention to minor details that might seem irrelevant but that sometimes held the key to understanding. As we were talking that day about this word *adat*, and looking with care at a number of comments by people and at stories that used the term in various contexts, I began to recognize that the word carried an additional fundamental meaning. For Teduray, *adat* was not only "customs"; it was also "respect," in both the noun and the verb form. "To do *adat*" was to pay respect to someone or something, to treat others with respect. This turned out not to be merely a second definition of the word; it was, rather, a core aspect, a distinctive Teduray coloration of the concept that I had not expected, given my understanding of the word in other languages. For Teduray, all customs aimed at the showing of respect, and such respect was why customs existed. I thus began to see the force of the idea that a person's or family's *adat* could have a definable, measurable quality. It was not enough simply to follow Teduray customs—all Teduray people did that—but an individual's or family's characteristic behavior had to be aimed at respecting the feelings of others. One could evaluate people's *adat* in terms of the general respect they showed for the gall bladders of everyone with whom they interacted.

"This will be a difficult marriage," a man had once confided to me when we were at a wedding celebration, "because the groom has bad *adat*." Although he came from a family with good *adat*, he was known to have a foolish tendency toward hot temper. The notion of *adat* suddenly became clear to me: it was not that the groom did not act according to the basic customs of his people; he did. But with his quick temper, he didn't act as respectfully as a proper Teduray should.

In my discussions with Mer and the others, I began to see that *adat* was not synonymous with another Teduray word meaning "custom," *tufù*. *Tufù* was custom in the sense of habit or idiosyncrasy. I wore a mustache in those days, and that was seen as my *tufù*. If a woman went at a certain time each morning to tend to her pigs or chickens, that would be her *tufù*. Families or communities could have this kind of habit as well. But *tufù* did not include that important dimension of respect or obligation. So although *adat* was, like *tufù*, what Teduray folks did and how they did it—their customs with regard to weddings, hospitality, labor exchange, and the like; it was also, unlike *tufù*, what they ought to do and how they ought to do it. *Adat* set standards of interpersonal respect and the honoring of each other's gall bladders, and in this sense it stood at the very center of Teduray life and thought.

Before I returned to the United States Mer and I—with lots of help from countless Teduray in countless conversations—put together the makings of a dictionary of the Teduray language. We had some fifty thousand different words on 3×5 cards, and when we reduced those to root words—from which verb declensions, adjectives, and the like derived—we were left with about six thousand entries. Of course, not all of those words had complex, uniquely Teduray, meanings—but many of them did. The task of getting those right meant sustained commitment to the careful probing of Teduray reality that alone could open up their semantic mysteries. I cannot count how many hours of the two years I worked in Figel were spent exploring the specifically Teduray sense of hundreds of terms, expressions, actions, and stories. None of my work, not just the dictionary, could have been done through reliance on a translator, and to have tried to do so would have cut the heart (or gall bladder?) out of my research. I could not have arrived at the detailed and culturally nuanced understanding of the language which my analyses of Teduray thought and action required.

Our efforts paid off majestically. I was able to apply their fruits to my speaking, hearing, and understanding, and day by day I grew increasingly confident and felt closer and more in touch with the way Teduray thought.

Gradually my consciousness achieved a kind of immersion in that Teduray world. Little Miliyana wasn't born knowing the Teduray reality; she learned it bit by bit, word by word, assumption by assumption, as she matured incrementally into full adult understanding. The same sort of process was now going on in me, right there in Figel. I arrived as ignorant as a newborn of the forest Teduray take on the world and what kind of behavior made sense in it. My perceptions and my consciousness had been shaped by a very different set of native understandings of what was sensible and meaningful, ethical and beautiful, absurd and obviously not so. The difference between my reality and the Figel Teduray reality was perfectly reflected in my original inability to converse with Teduray in their language. Like Miliyana, I had to learn to inhabit Teduray reality piece by piece. And in the process of learning their language, I began to learn the nature of their reality.

"What we call reality is not the same everywhere." This abstract fact was coming alive for me as I lived and spoke and interacted. I had known it, had studied it in graduate school, but the truth was that it had all been merely intellectual and remote from my experience. Sometimes in Figel, my mind would just spin. There I found myself *living* what, until then, had just been *thought.* The question "What is real?" stopped being theoretical and became crucial to the very fabric of my surroundings and my day-to-day life. Everything around me was proclaiming, "There truly are other worlds, other realities. Whatever is out there— the buzz and boom of sensory input, the raw material of perceptions—is being organized by these people in a very unfamiliar way. Stu, you are *in* another reality!" I felt this truth only faintly at first, like a whisper. And it felt odd, a part of the exuberance of the adventure but at the same time a bit scary. Where was all this going?

My task seemed straightforward but daunting: to formulate these people's reality as best I could construct it based on the evidence of their words and actions—through attentive observation and sustained participation in their conversations and activities—meanwhile striving to be misled by my own cultural understandings, blinders, and anxieties as little as I could possibly manage.

I was helped in this task by many advance warnings, by wariness, and by a variety of "tricks of the trade." Still, having said that, I must also state that anthropologists have come a long way since the days when it was believed that a "properly trained" and "theoretically armed" ethnographer could simply observe and write down a massive set of rigorously "objective facts" about how another people thought and behaved. The most I would want to claim for what I saw, and for what I am telling you in this book, is that it is my best "take" on their "take."

Nonetheless, I think my formulation of their reality, their thinking, and their actions is far more than just some fable I concocted out of my imagination and cultural preconceptions. Just as Miliyana would become better and better at internalizing the Teduray world as she grew into adulthood, until she would see things largely, if not exactly, the way others around her saw things, so did I, over the course of my time in Figel, become increasingly able to converse intelligibly with people about realms of reality that the Teduray took for granted. By the time I left, my take on their take was at least close enough that we could sit and talk about all sorts of things for hours on end without them correcting me. I feel completely sure that if the Teduray men or women I knew in Figel could have read and understood this book, they would have recognized the picture I paint and felt it was truly about them.

I do not in any way mean to imply that I "went native." My clumsy grammar and my accented pronunciation in and of themselves immediately gave me away as the outsider I was. I was also too tall, too white, too blond, and much too fumbling with things Teduray to pass for anything but a stranger among them.

"Going native" just can't be done. One can, of course, fit in. One can act as inconspicuous as possible. One can come to deep empathy with the cosmology and the moral understandings of a people. One can, over a very long time, learn the local language with remarkable fluency. But it takes years and years, often generations, before an immigrant comes to seem at all "native." Just think how hard it is for immigrants to the United States to adjust linguistically and culturally, how huge a task that is. The Teduray were hospitable and kind to me; they took me in and made me feel completely welcome. But I was never invited or expected to seem Teduray.

I have spent major periods of time—years on end—in several foreign cultures that I loved and felt empathy for, including Japan during my navy years and Indonesia later in life. I have strained to learn their languages and to fit in with their ways. I loved the chance to learn, to broaden my vision, to push the edges of my spirit out into new experience. But I always knew that in venturing into these foreign cultural waters and in tasting the flavor of other people's lives and spiritualities I was inevitably confronting my own limits. I was not Japanese, Filipino, or Indonesian. There was always a certain sadness in knowing that I would necessarily remain an outsider, that in important respects I would always be marginal to the worlds I was enjoying and the people I was admiring; nevertheless, that was the truth.

Still, having said that, I am amazed at the ways in which continuous inundation in an alien world of thinking, talking, living, and being—an alien reality—affected my mind. Among all the places I have lived, Figel was special in this regard. For years afterward, I continued occasionally to dream in Teduray, and I still have powerful moments in which pieces of that experience are recapitulated within me.

4 ❧ Mirab Interlude I

In mid-May, after eight weeks in Figel, Mer, Aliman, and I hiked, launched, and bused our way home to Mirab. Full of stories to tell the Conchas in Lebak, we sat talking late into the evening, until it was time to go to the beach and wait for the launch to leave for Cotabato City. It arrived at Lebak from the south and picked us up along with five others around midnight, docking in Cotabato shortly after 6:30 the next morning.

We had a bite of breakfast at Mariano's and decided to hitch a ride to Mirab on a passing logging truck rather than wait for the noon bus. The first truck to come by stopped for us; it was carrying no logs on its return trip into the mountains, so we joined the dozen or so other women and men sitting and bumping about on the empty truck bed. About half the passengers were Maguindanaon, and most of the rest were lowland homesteaders, originally from other parts of the Philippines; only one other man was Teduray, and we chatted with him all the way up about life in the forest. He was keenly interested in what Mer and Aliman had to say, as his own family came from Awang, near Cotabato City, and had had little direct contact with any forest Teduray. I listened intently and said very little; they were conversing at a speed that was still well beyond my nascent ability to follow.

We got down from the truck in Mirab a little before eleven, and I carried my pack joyfully up the slight slope from the road, past the Edwards house to my own. I had, of course, not been able to give anyone any warning of when I might be showing up, so I was greeted with great whoops of excitement by the boys and a big hug from Audrey. The coffee pot was put on at once, and we all sat around the kitchen table, we Schlegels and Armenia and Fernando, two young people Audrey had hired to help her with the work of keeping house. Len and Will babbled joyfully, Audrey informed me about a few things when she could get a word in, and the two young Filipinos sat shyly saying nothing on their own and answering queries only with a quiet "Yes, Father" or "No, *manang*." *Manang* is the Ilocano word used to address an older sister, and Audrey had asked them to use that rather than "Mother," a title foisted on her by mission tradition which she hated. I pleaded that they not call me by my old mission title either, but just use the traditional Teduray "Mo-Lini." But since I came to Mirab so seldom and Armenia was accustomed to addressing me as "Father," I was never very successful in this quest.

Proudly opening the door to a new kerosene refrigerator, Audrey offered me a San Miguel beer. She had bought the refrigerator in Cotabato and hauled it up on Hammy's truck, and it gleamed new and white. "It was a real extravagance, but living without it was just too hard," Audrey told me. "We can keep meat and leftovers. And we can have cold Coke and beer, even ice cubes for some rum before dinner." Will was especially excited by some crystally ice cream that he and his mom made by mixing canned condensed milk with mango fruit, beating it well, and freezing it in an ice cube tray. The homemade version didn't rival Magnolia ice cream—the principal commercial brand sold in the Philippines, which we got in Cotabato—but it was quite tasty and deliciously cold. It's a good thing the refrigerator was so helpful and popular: it had cost us five hundred dollars, exactly as much as the entire rest of the house, with all of its furnishings and other equipment!

From then on, we called our home the "Mirab Hilton"!

I soon learned that the kitchen was the real sitting room of the house, not the little living room that seemed to function more like a hall between kitchen and bedrooms. Len and I sat around the kitchen table one afternoon, while Audrey took a nap and Will had disappeared with a Teduray chum from the farm.

"Mom tells us a story every night about Peewee the Elf," he told me.

I smiled. "Who is Peewee the Elf?"

"He's an elf. He does a lot of fun things and gets into trouble, but he always gets out of it. Sometimes he goes to Figel and comes back; he tells us what you're doing and that you are okay. Sometimes he is in California with Grandpa and Grandma." Len looked at me quizzically, "Don't you see him? He sees you."

Peewee the Elf turned out to be a brilliant creation of Audrey's, and she told the boys a bedtime story about him every night when she tucked them in. He was a naughty little guy, whose pranks and mischief got him into lots of trouble and even danger, but who always ended up learning important lessons about how to be safe and good. Len related to me the story from a recent night when Peewee took some cookies without asking because he didn't understand he shouldn't do that. "But his elf mom told him, 'All you have to do is ask.'"

"Len, I had a book about some kids called 'the Gumps' when I was a boy. They were all a lot like Peewee."

"Were they true, like Peewee?"

"They were real, Len; just like Peewee."

One evening after the boys were asleep, Audrey and I sat at

the table in the dim light of a small kerosene lamp (although we had Coleman pressure lamps, they put out too much heat to sit very close to), and she told me how helpful Fernando and Armenia were to her. Fernando was about sixteen and Teduray, from one of the Edwardses' tenant families. Armenia was also Teduray, a few years older; the daughter of a poor sharecropper family near Upi, she had graduated from St. Francis High School a year or so before and knew us from when we had been at the mission.

"I just couldn't do everything by myself," Audrey said. "Everything is so much more difficult here; like at the mission, only harder. I'm just beginning to learn how to cook on the woodstove, and thank God for Fernando, who cuts the wood." She gestured toward Armenia, who was dozing in the cool evening air on our little front porch. "Armenia and I do all the washing by hand, and since we don't have any water in the tank from our roof—the rains haven't started yet—we have to haul water from the Edwardses' hand pump, not just for drinking and bathing but for all our laundry too. Often, we just do the wash down by the creek."

I had not thought much about how tough the day-to-day domestic chores would be for Audrey, and listening to her describe some of them made me wince. "I'm glad you got the two of them," I offered rather lamely. Audrey did not seem to be complaining, exactly, but I know she wanted me to learn a bit more about *her* life in Mirab in addition to learning about the Teduray life in Figel. And to care a bit more.

She sensed I was embarrassed and quickly changed the tone. "Look at the cake pans I made!" With a big smile, she got a pair of two-and-a-half-inch-high tin pans from the cupboard and set them proudly before me. "Look! Ta dah! I cut off the bottom part of two kerosene cans. Mrs. Edwards showed me how. They work great, once I got the oily smell out of them. But be careful: the edges are really sharp. I'll bake a cake for us tomorrow; I got some chocolate in Upi."

The following morning Audrey was up early to get breakfast started. We were going to have some eggs from the Edwardses' hens and some pork sausage that Audrey had made herself with meat from the market. "You can get sausages in cans," she told me, "but this is so much better. I learned to make it before we had the refrigerator. The spices help the hind leg of pig I buy at the Saturday market last all week."

Will came quietly into the kitchen, rubbing the sleep from his eyes. He sat, as he often did first thing in the morning, on the steps running from the kitchen down to the side yard, where the outhouse and bathing hut were. I was doing one of the daily chores: I took an empty gallon-sized glass jar, mixed some water in it with a virulent poison—I think it was Dieldren—and poured the concoction down the one-holer privy. It killed bacteria and insect life in the muck below and kept the outhouse from becoming smelly. (Who knows what horrors it did to the ground around and the water table. I never thought about those sorts of questions then.)

When I came back into the house I passed Will sitting on the step. I showed him the bottle, which we kept hung on a spike high on the wall between the door and the woodstove.

Will said, "Daddy, watch out."

"Why?"

"Because there's a terrible poison in that bottle to keep our outhouse from getting stinky. If you drank out of it you could be dead."

I smiled. "Thanks, hon, I will be careful."

Will pondered his mental picture for a moment, and asked me, with a solemn four-year-old curiosity: "Who would be our daddy then?"

"Don't worry. I'm careful."

But for him it was probably a considerable worry. I was already proving quite convincingly that I could not be counted on to be around day in and day out. I can still hear that question in the memory of my mind, and it often translates into the uncomfortable issue of *where* was his daddy so much of the time.

On that visit to Mirab, and on subsequent ones, I learned how much Audrey was handling in her domestic half of my research adventure: how many things there were that were not easy for her. She was young and strong, but as she told me, everything was so basic, took so much effort. I admired her grit and resourcefulness, but I never truly questioned the way our division of work was arranged. This period in our lives took place well before either of us heard about the women's movement, let alone had internalized its critiques and wisdom, and I just took for granted, far more than I ever would today, that Audrey was dealing with "her" job, just as I was doing "mine." I think she shared at least some of those same assumptions.

I had much to talk about with Audrey, and she with me, and I had fun roughhousing with my sons and hearing about all their projects, pets, and activities. Hammy and I had long talks about what I was experiencing. I had missed them all so much—my wife and boys, the Edwardses, the familiar surroundings—in the past two months. But I felt an insistent call to get back to my work in Figel, and after a few days I realized I was constantly distracted by thinking about that work. So I loafed in Mirab for a little less than a week. Audrey, Len, and Will were disappointed that I stayed such a short time, after having been away two entire months, and I think at some level I understood their disappointment. But I was just not fully present with them; I needed to get back to my fieldwork.

I returned to Figel with a mind whirling from pleasure at seeing my family again, but also with a certain melancholy that picked away at the edges of my joy. Audrey's hard work and loneliness spoke softly but urgently to me, as did little Will's question on the kitchen steps. I sensed in my heart that all was not completely well with me and my loved ones.

I was learning splendid things in Figel about how to treat people, but had little idea how to put them into practice in my own family. And at that point I wasn't ready to face such matters squarely.

5 ⚘ We Were Created
to Care for the Forest

Often at night I would stretch out on my back with Mo-Baug, one of the older men in the settlement, in the cleared area in front of my house while he patiently described the Teduray star constellations and their stories.

"Look, there," he said on a particularly lovely evening. "Those three bright stars. That is Seretar, the hunter. And those two smaller ones, they are the jaw of a wild pig, called Bakà, that he killed."

I was learning about their zodiac because forest Teduray used the night sky as a calendar. They believed that, like all of nature, the stars in the sky were put there for them, a gift to help them live. People carefully noted the movement of the constellations as the months passed, and from their position they calculated when the rains would come, or the dry season, or the best time to plant. I wanted to know how they did it, and little by little Mo-Baug told me. He was a fine old man of the forest and a specialist in storytelling.

On this particular night the sky was a deep black and the stars shone more brightly than I had ever seen them shine before. In Figel there was no smog, no luminance from nearby cities—just the quiet of night and the incredible brilliance of the star-filled sky. Mo-Baug's Teduray diction was a bit hard for me to understand because the old storyteller had very few teeth left, and his mouth was always full of betel quid. "And that one, that bright star with its three little cousins, that is Fegeferafad, a man known as a brave defender of his family's honor." Fegeferafad was made up of the brilliant star we call Procyon (his head) and stars we in the West consider part of Orion's dog and the twins, Castor and Pollux (his arms). My friend now began recounting the stories he knew about Fegeferafad, just as so often before he had spun out the myths associated with the other constellations.

As Mo-Baug was talking I saw a satellite crossing the sky. I interrupted the old man in midsentence and, using the polite kin term used for relative and nonrelative alike, said, "Grandfather, do you see that star that is moving?"

He watched the bright dot move slowly across the sky for a few seconds, and then said in a hushed voice, "Yes, I see it."

I was just delighted. I thought to myself that surely I was about to be told an "instant myth." I was going to see the myth-making process in its very inception. He would tell me it was a young man going to his forest garden or, perhaps, a hunter chasing a wild pig. I said to him with great anticipation, "What is it?"

"Mo-Lini," he said softly, "it is a satellite."

Mo-Baug had learned about satellites once when he was at the Lebak market and heard a launch described over a vendor's radio. He had no idea how—or why—people would put a star up in the sky, and he assumed that it carried a pilot, which it more than likely did not, but he knew the English word. I was totally astonished and must have grinned from ear to ear—it was the first English word I had ever heard from him. But I merely replied, "Oh, yes, it is a satellite, isn't it."

Traditional stories—myths about nature and the spirits and the beginnings of the world—were something everybody in Figel delighted in. And everyone above adolescence was aware of the general outline and thrust of the most common creation and nature myths, even though there was lots of variation in the particulars of how different people remembered them. Knowing them in detail and telling them with verve and suspense and humor was a specialty. Mo-Baug was a specialist in "the old stories," as were Mo-Bintang and Mo-Sew, the two principal Figel neighborhood shamans. During my stay in Figel I spent many a fascinating evening in the big house listening to them and other storytellers visiting from other communities tell their tales. But it was not just the specialist storytellers who spun yarns; almost everyone knew some stories and enjoyed telling them.

In the local version of Teduray creation stories, Tulus, the Great Spirit who created all things, actually made human beings four different times, but in each case the purpose was "so that they could take good care of the forest."* In the fundamental Teduray cosmic scheme, the forest—or nature in general—was created to supply humans with abundance of life, and they were here to live harmoniously with it and to see to its well-being.

I never heard how the Great Spirit originated. Whenever I would ask, people would say something like, "Well, I have no idea. The Great Spirit was just there at the beginning of things." But most people in the Figel area seemed to know the following version of the story of human creation, which I first heard told by two fine storytellers, Mo-Bintang and his wife.

First of all, the Great Spirit created the forest (the world) and then human beings ("the people you can see") and the spirits

---

*In what follows, wherever a Teduray spirit or cosmic realm does not have a translatable name I have assigned it an appropriate English title for simplicity—as I have done here with Tulus, whom I subsequently refer to simply as the Great Spirit.

("the people you can't see"), both out of mud. The Great Spirit was without gender, neither male nor female, and in making the first man and woman the Great Spirit made them somewhat different, in one key respect, from people now: the man had a penis like men today, but he was the one who gave birth to babies. To keep his penis from bursting in childbirth, therefore, he had to wind it many times around with rattan lashing. But childbirth was, of course, still horribly painful for him. So it was not long before the man who birthed the babies and the woman who suckled them agreed that the situation was unworkable. How could the men care for the forest if they had to endure such agony and indignity?

Because both of the first humans were shamans and so could see and speak to spirits, they pleaded with the Great Spirit to change the way babies were born. The Great Spirit wanted to help them out, of course, so, gently packing the two of them and all their children back into one big mud ball, the Great Spirit tried again. The Great Spirit made two persons, each with a head, body, two legs, and two arms just like before, and then thought the situation over carefully. Finally the Great Spirit took a bolo and put a mighty slash between the woman's legs, such that henceforth she would have the babies. But the handle flew off the bolo and stuck to the man, between his legs. So that's how we got to be like we are now. Childbirth was still somewhat painful for the woman, but much less so than it had been for the poor man. That was the second creation.

Then there were four people: a "black" man (meaning the color of the Teduray) who was married to a "white" woman (the color of Chinese and Europeans) and a white man who was married to a black woman. They were very careful to respect the spirits and honor nature by scrupulously caring for its well-being. But one day the white man eloped with the white woman, and they sailed off in an outrigger and went to Sung-Sung. (Sung-Sung was often identified with Hong Kong by Upi Teduray when I was there, but originally it was just some vague place "far across the sea.") The remaining black man and woman therefore married and became the ancestors of the Teduray. When she eloped with the white man, the white woman was pregnant by her previous husband, so her first child, born across the sea, was dark. From then on, all her children were white. The firstborn became the ancestor of all black people, and the others multiplied into the Chinese, the Spanish, and the Americans.

One day, after the Teduray had grown to be a numerous people, a great shaman named Lagey Lengkuwos visited the Great Spirit "beyond the sky to the east"; he returned deeply impressed by the great beauty of the Region of the Great Spirit. In fact, he decided that it was much nicer than the forest where he and the Teduray lived, and so Lagey Lengkuwos led all the Teduray people on a great journey to relocate in the land of the Great Spirit. This journey was described in a long epic poem called the Berinarew, which in its entirety required some eighty hours to chant. That evening, though, Mo-Bintang and his wife sang just one short section. It came from near the end of the epic, where the Great Spirit welcomed Lagey Lengkuwos and his people and gave them a place to live beyond the sky. This state of affairs, however, meant that no one remained to care for the forest, so the Great Spirit once again created a new group of Teduray.

This was still not the final creation. There needed to be one more, after Lagey Sebotan, another great shaman, used the Berinarew as a guide to replicate Lagey Lengkuwos's feat of leading everyone beyond the sky. Once again the Great Spirit had to create more Teduray, and these were the ancestors of the people alive today.

These myths were consistent with all I knew of the Teduray people of the forest. The Great Spirit created people to enjoy and care for the world. When the first creation didn't work well, like a good helper the Great Spirit made the humans another time, in a way that allowed them greater contentment. It was a quintessential Teduray myth, with no hierarchy, no coercive power, no violence. How unlike our Judeo-Christian story of Adam and Eve being driven from the Garden of Eden by an offended monarch God!

The world the Teduray believed they were created to care for did not "belong" to anyone. It was a kind of grand public domain, there for everybody to use and enjoy. To illustrate this, I need to explain a word that named a very common concept in their thinking. The term is *géfê*.

To be *géfê* of something was to have exclusive rights over its present use. A couple was said to be *géfê* of their house, the man *géfê* of his wife, and the wife *géfê* of her husband. People were *géfê* of their tools and indeed of any object, person, or even any ceremony over which they had legitimate personal use and interest. Although the word could be loosely glossed into English as "legitimate owner" or, more simply, "owner," the essence of the Teduray concept in fact suggested nothing more than present right-of-use. Thus a forest garden site "belonged" to the couple who were its *géfê* only from the time it was first chosen and publicly marked until it was completely harvested. After that, they no longer "owned" it—were no longer its *géfê*.

To steal something to which a person had this right-of-use was, of course, wrong and would cause a bad gall bladder. But that seldom happened. Teduray didn't compete to own things any more than they competed over anything else. The world that sustained them was simply too full of fine things for everyone. The main stealing that took place involved other spouses. That was commonplace, and I will be discussing this situation later on. Making off with anything else, however, was rare. I saw no sign of greed in this community, no urge to enhance one's own property at the expense of another person's, and no gloating about having more than someone else. Competition, greed, and self-promotion were simply alien to how Teduray understood the good life.

The intimate interaction with nature that traditional Teduray enjoyed was reflected most clearly in their economic practices. One evening in May, just a few days after we had returned from our first trip home to Mirab, Mer, Aliman, and I were eating some dinner with Ideng-Emét and Mo-Emét, the young couple who fed us and helped us out in many domestic ways. Mo-Emét said to me, "Mo-Lini, come with us tomorrow to our garden in the forest. We are all going to plant rice."

"Yes, just-right," I told him.

I was delighted because I knew that rice planting was one of the most important—and most festive—events in the annual cycle of forest gardening. I had already been to Mo-Emét and Ideng-Emét's forest garden several times since Mo-Emét first claimed and marked it off some four months earlier. "Swidden" is the technical term for the field cleared in the forest for a family's annual cropping. Every year, Mo-Emét, like the other Figel men, chose a new swidden site while out hunting in the "off season" following harvest. He would scout for such positive factors as suitable kinds of growth, availability, and soil type. Each family's site from the previous year was then allowed to return to forest, not to be cut and burned again for many years.

Earlier, in January, all the Figel men had gone with Mo-Emét to mark his choice of site. This event involved their doing a small amount of ritualized clearing of undergrowth, but, most important, it was the occasion when Mo-Emét formally expressed his respect for the spirits of the forest and asked them for permission to work that site. At that time, the men erected a small bamboo rack at one corner of the proposed swidden, while Mo-Emét listened carefully for the call of a small forest bird believed to communicate omens from the spirits to the humans. The moment he heard the sound of the omen bird, he was to point in that direction and interpret whether the spirits wished to let him use the area for his garden. After several minutes we heard a sharp cry from the bird, and Mo-Emét pointed directly in front of him—one of the directions that meant the spirits were agreeable. If he had heard the call behind him, or in front of him but at an unfavorable angle, everyone would have gone to a different corner and tried again.

Each man now lashed a tiny tube of cooked rice from which he had eaten a single grain to the little offering rack. This was to honor the spirits, whose cooperation throughout the coming swidden cycle would be important to the success of everyone's site. Mo-Emét's site was the first one to be ritually marked that year, because by watching the stars he had chosen the earliest day of any of his neighbors. All the neighborhood men join in on the first ceremony, waiting until the next day to go off and mark their own sites individually. They would not make any offerings to the spirits, but they would carefully attend to the call of the small bird.

The cooperation of all Figel neighborhood men in marking Mo-Emét's site was just the first of many times they would work together in neighborhood swiddens in the months to come. The next step was to slash the underbrush, and the Figel men did that as a group, proceeding day by day from one new plot to the next until all of the neighborhood's swiddens were slashed. Then they made the same one-after-another rotation to cut down the large trees on every family's site. The size of the swiddens, about one hundred yards square, was too large for any one man to have done the hard work of cutting the underbrush and then the big trees himself; but by working together, they got the job done in good time. Each man then burned the cut-down debris on his own field. When the burned swiddens had all cooled down, the neighborhood women went from one to another and planted corn.

After the corn was in the field and growing, each family spent time studying the sky to determine the best time to plant rice. This was the most sensitive calendrical decision of the year. Mo-Emét had reckoned the position of the constellations with great care and chosen what he believed was the most auspicious day by interpreting the phase of the moon.

At daybreak on the designated morning, the entire Figel neighborhood—women and men, adults and children—gathered at Figel settlement. As we headed down the trail to Mo-Emét's plot several people played gongs, partly to alert the spirits to what was happening and partly because the Teduray loved music and played it often, especially when, like today, they were engaged in a jovial and communal activity. Mo-Emét and his brother, Mo-Tong, carried baskets of rice seed from the previous year's harvest of Mo-Emét's swidden. Ideng-Emét and several other women carried some chickens and other foods destined for the day's feasting. Planting rice was a hard but happy job, and there was much joking and laughing and, especially among the young people, erotic teasing.

As soon as we arrived at the site, everyone formed a circle around what would be Ideng-Emét and Mo-Emét's ritual plot in the center of the field. About twelve feet square, it had been marked off with poles that were decorated with many items having spiritual meanings. A small saucer with some rice seed from the previous year's ritual plot was placed in the middle to signify the continuity of people's need for food. A comb was hung on one of the poles, representing the wish of all that the rice stalks would grow neatly and abundantly like well-cared-for hair. A mirror ensured that the spirit-guardian of wild pigs would see his own reflection and be too frightened to encourage any pigs to attack the maturing grain. The last item to go on the poles was a necklace that symbolized womanhood and fertility. The gong players led everyone in single-file procession around the ritual square four times, then continued playing as Mo-Emét and Ideng-Emét planted the seed from the little saucer in the plot. The rice that would grow from that seed would provide the saucer seed for the following year.

When the ritual-plot ceremonies were finished, all the planters prepared to sow the swidden with rice. The rice the forest Teduray cultivated was dry rice and went directly into the ground, in contrast to the wet rice varieties grown in the lowlands in flooded paddies. The men cut six-foot-long sticks from hardwood poles found among the burned debris on the field and sharpened one end to a symmetrical point. These "dibble sticks" were then used to poke a hole in the ground so that the rice could be planted. Each woman hung a woven rattan basket from her left shoulder by a carrying strap. Along with the seed, the women carried a few small wisps of kapok (a cottonlike substance) in their baskets, so that the load would magically seem as light as the kapok.

Starting at the top of the field, Mo-Emét and his male companions went first, roughly abreast, back and forth across the entire width of the swidden, driving their sticks into the ground every foot or fifteen inches. For a little while—for the fun and companionship of it—Mer and I put down our notebooks and joined in the dibbling. "You'd better watch out, Mo-Lini! The spirits will take your books!" someone called out. Awkward though I was, dibbling was fun.

Ideng-Emét and the women followed, also forming a flanking line, dropping seeds into the holes. Ideng-Emét told me later that fifteen to twenty seeds are generally placed end up in each hole, but that expert seeders could place fewer than ten, a highly appreciated talent. I had often seen young girls, back at Figel, being trained by their mothers to plant rice and corn seed. They devoted many hours to practicing with small pebbles or sand. I noticed, however, that in the actual seeding of a field no one criticized anyone for doing a poor job.

As the planting proceeded, no one stopped during the sweeps across the swidden to urinate, prepare betel, or resharpen a stick. But every so often, a break was called to take care of such necessities. All through the planting the atmosphere was festive, with much playful shouting. The men called out encouragement to each other, such as "Hurry up!" or "Watch out! You will be overtaken by the women!" The women would respond with, "Don't be slow. We're coming up on you!"

I was always somewhat surprised at the bawdy humor of the Teduray. Ideng-Emét once yelled at Mo-Emét, "Husband, the way you are poking that stick into the ground reminds me of last night, when you did some splendid thrusting and poking as well!"

And he shot back, "Wife, if you had as much seed in your loins as you have in that basket, we would surely have too many children!"

Another woman chided her husband that she wouldn't mind if his erections got as big as his dibble stick, and he promised her that she would soon be surprised and happy. This lively repartee went on all through the day. Everyone had great fun, and the time passed quickly.

Throughout the planting, some prohibitions were scrupulously observed. Workers never husked a rice seed with their mouths, for fear that rats and rice birds would do the same thing to the coming crop. They didn't blow mucus from their noses, since seed-stealing insects are sensitive to that sound and could be attracted. They never picked any of the small weeds growing along the planters' path, as the rice might be similarly uprooted by wild pigs. And they never ate anything within the swidden's boundaries, lest rats, pigs, insects, and birds do the same to the rice. Several of the children were given the task of broadcasting sesame and millet seeds around all four edges of the swidden. A good portion of these grains would grow and be used for food, but the main rationale for the practice was that it provided a distraction to ants and lured them away from the newly planted rice seed.

About midmorning, Ideng-Emét and several other women were replaced on the planting line so they could prepare a simple but hearty meal near the perimeter of the swidden. She and Mo-Emét had brought all the food for this meal from home, and they shared it with all the workers. In subsequent days, when helping the other families plant their fields, Ideng-Emét and Mo-Emét would be similarly fed by the owners of those swiddens.

The field was fully planted by late afternoon, when everybody again gathered around the ritual plot in the center. Led by Mo-Emét and Ideng-Emét, each man poked one hole and each woman planted a few seeds. The men then left their dibble poles stuck in the ground within the ritual plot; Mo-Emét took some of each of the various types of rice seed that had been planted and set them aside to use for reseeding areas that "took" poorly, while Ideng-Emét divided up all the remaining seed among those present. This rice was taken home, where it was pounded, cooked, and eaten that night so that, even if someone who had helped in the planting were to die before harvest, she or he would still have eaten from this field.

Mo-Emét and his wife then cleared away all the ceremonial items from the ritual plot. The procession formed and, as a familiar tune was hammered out on the gongs, everyone walked four last times around the center plot and headed back to Figel. From there, the families from other settlements in the neighborhood went home.

This working together on one another's swiddens defined the "neighborhood." The twenty-nine households in seven settlements that made up Figel's neighborhood referred to each other as "people of Figel" or "people of the same *inged*"—a word that in general means "place" but specifically refers to the home territory of those who share in swidden work and associated rituals. Neighborhood cooperation in shifting cultivation activities didn't end with planting rice. Although Ideng-Emét and Mo-Emét went on by themselves to establish a great variety of secondary plants in their field, amid and around the sprouting rice—fruit trees, root crops, vegetables, spices, and the like— and Ideng-Emét and her son would work on their own to keep it as weed free as possible, the whole community would return in early September to harvest the mature rice. At that time again, each family's swidden would be harvested one after the other by the whole neighborhood.

Harvesting was characterized by sharing. The reaping of the rice itself was done by the women, who cut off the panicles and gathered them into bundles while the men stacked the accumulating bundles in piles beside the swidden. Before hauling the rice back home, each participating woman received one-fifth of all she harvested as her personal share. Such sharing was an insurance policy assuring that, even if their own swidden's crop failed or was totally eaten by rice birds, every family would end up with plenty of rice from other fields they had worked on, rice they needed both for food and for seed the following year. The numerous other crops that the swiddens yielded were not formally shared in this way, but no one would have considered letting a neighboring family go hungry, so informal sharing of just about all kinds of food was common practice. The attitude was clearly that there was always enough for everyone.

Ritualized sharing happened four times during the year, when all the families of Figel neighborhood came together for a sacred meal called *kanduli*. These ritual meals marked significant points in the cultivation cycle and were characterized by every family eating some rice from every field they worked on and serving some rice to everyone who worked on their field. I will be discussing *kanduli* in a later chapter; here I want only to note that these simple community meals gave powerful expression to the interdependence and mutual aid of everyone in the neighborhood and to the necessary help of the spirits, who were given food offerings as well. Figel people had no other major communal rituals: the *kanduli* testified eloquently enough to the essence of their life together.

Once the principal crops of rice and corn had been harvested, Ideng-Emét and Mo-Emét's swidden would continue to yield fruits and tubers and other foods for many years, but it would not be recut, reburned, or replanted. People knew that any additional cropping on the plot would put it in serious peril of transformation into savanna grassland, which could never be cultivated, and they did not want that to happen. So they allowed their harvested swiddens to lie fallow, gleaning what continuing bounties as they could while the forest reclaimed the land and restored itself. True, the forest would not come back just as it had been—the huge trees of the primary forest took centuries to grow—but within a decade it would become mature second-growth rainforest with much the same general structure and ecological characteristics it had had before it had been worked. There was no set rule about how soon an old swidden might be cultivated again, but in practice no one ever returned to work one for a long time.

The various tasks associated with swidden work were only one part of the total economic activities of my Figel forest Teduray friends. While the Figel people were swidden cultivators to be sure, they were at the same time accomplished hunters, expert fishers, and keen gatherers of wild food and other necessities from the forest they knew with such intimacy.

During my stay in Figel one of my neighbors, Mo-Santos, kept hunting dogs, and I became fast friends with one of them. He had no name—the Teduray didn't give names to their dogs or cats, which they thought of mostly as hunters, guards, and mousers. I somewhat furtively—I didn't want to cause trouble—began calling him "Datu," but stopped speaking to him entirely when Mer reminded me that it was against the customs to give animals human names or to speak to them as though they could speak back. In Teduray logic, to do so was disrespectful of their true nature and would bring serious punishment upon the disrespectful person. I honored that, but I did think of my little chum as Datu in my mind and wordlessly fed him scraps of food whenever I had a chance. He, in return, lavished on me the sort of affection that his species gives with such abandon.

In addition to Datu and Mo-Santos's other hounds, there were a few dogs and cats in the Figel settlements. Several families kept pigs for the meat, and just about every house raised chickens for food and eggs. With the exception of these few domesticated animals, however, it was wild animal life that occupied people's attention.

All the men hunted regularly, and in certain seasons—notably from June to December, after the major work of clearing the swiddens was completed—hunting and fishing constituted their main activities. Even I took to going hunting almost daily. I believed in those days that I needed some meat each day, so the first thing I usually did each morning was make a brief trip into the forest or along the river to shoot a monkey or large bird with a .22 rifle Hammy Edwards had loaned me. I would feel no such compulsion today and, indeed, would be quite content just to eat the splendid array of fruits, grains, fish, and vegetables that Ideng-Emét regularly prepared for us. But I remember, as a colorful part of my two years in Figel, that I hunted for some of my own food. The problem is, I didn't really have the stomach to be a hunter. The meat tasted just fine, but monkeys were too much like people for me to face up to the hunter's task of cutting them up and cleaning them. I left all that to my research assistants, something I doubt very much they had expected to be part of their job description.

The most prized game animals for the Figel men were wild pigs and deer, but they didn't turn down smaller catches like monkeys and a variety of fowl. A kill was always accompanied by a short speech to the appropriate spirits, in which the hunter respectfully asked their permission to kill that particular animal and expressed his gratitude for its role in sustaining him and his family. I made the same little speech to the spirits myself, whenever I shot any game. It seemed the right and respectful thing to do.

Much of the hunting was done at night, when many kinds of prey were most vulnerable. The darker the night, the better—except that hunting was forbidden on the nights when there was no moon at all, at the request of the spirit caretakers of the forest animals. The first three nights of a new moon were thought to be great times to hunt, and the fourth night the best of all, a time of especially good luck. The sixth night after a full moon was also held to be particularly auspicious.

Figel men had a wide range of hunting techniques, from bow and arrow or blowgun to group hunts. They knew how to erect numerous kinds of cleverly devised traps and snares. Many of the more technologically complex methods, such as spiked pits, log falls, and spring spears, were considered, like storytelling, to be specializations. Although women seldom participated in hunting, which often included running hard through the forest, the men were on the whole superb and resourceful hunters who knew the forest and the habits of game intimately.

People enthusiastically augmented their diet with fishing, too. A number of relatively large rivers flowed down from the mountains, and all traditional Teduray neighborhoods were located within easy reach of some stream rich in fish, eels, crustaceans, and other aquatic foods. Because the watercourses were slow, shallow, and clear during the relatively dry season from November through April, and often flooded during the times of peak rainfall in July and August, there was a certain seasonal quality to the dozens of fishing techniques the Figel people used. Some methods required clear water, while others, like large stationary fish traps built right in the middle of the Dakel Teran, depended on the river being swift and flooded.

Men and women both worked the streams and brought in significant catches. People ate most of what they caught, whether meat or fish, fresh, although large catches could be preserved by salting and drying or by smoking. As with hunting, so too with fishing: good luck was generally shared with settlement mates. No strict rules applied to fish, in contrast to the requirement that wild pigs or deer be equally divided among the entire neighborhood, but I saw lots of informal sharing. It just seemed to come naturally, one more piece of the mutual help which Teduray valued highly and practiced earnestly.

It would be hard to overstate the extent to which Figel families looked to the wild plants of the forest as a major source of food and other necessities. Even when blessed with superb harvests on their swiddens, a sizable portion of what they lived on came from gathering wild resources. The forest provided starch staples such as wild sweet potatoes, manioc, and taro, a vast assortment of vegetables, seeds, nuts, and pods, and a multitude of wild fruit for snacks as well as meals. Moreover, occasionally men but especially women—for gathering was one of their specialties—would bring home all sorts of goods needed in daily life, from construction materials to firewood, from medicines to a cosmetic oil for softening dry skin. For the plants that came from the forest, as for the catches from hunting and fishing, the spirits were always sincerely respected and thanked.

Just as women occasionally hunted, so men would cheerfully join in foraging for wild plant foods from the forest when needed, but gathering was primarily a specialty and expertise of women. Children of both sexes often went with their mothers to gather, and women taught the young ones from an early age to recognize edible fruits and plants. They showed them which barks served as soap and which could be pounded into barkcloth, as well as the materials best suited to weaving baskets and traps, the plants that yielded beauty aids and pillow stuffing, and those that could be made into water containers. Children learned to identify and cut firewood, and came to know the best bamboo for house or trap construction. They learned to recognize and prepare rattan and suitable vines for lashings, to know which saps provided lamp fuel and which were effective in poisoning fish. The time spent gathering food also served as school. The years of childhood, and especially adolescence, were the principal time when traditional Teduray attained their easy and deep familiarity with the forest—their *friendship* with the forest. The forest was by no means just the scene for making swiddens; it was itself, like the river, regularly and richly harvested. The Teduray all believed what Mo-Emét once told me: "When we work with each other and with the spirits, there is plenty for us all." Much more than the market in Lebak, where they occasionally trekked for needed iron items, cloth, salt, or various sorts of exchange goods required in legal settlements, the rainforest all around them was the Figel people's true provider.

Actually, there was precious little they needed from the outside world. Other than certain items that had symbolic legal significance, such as necklaces, gongs, and betel boxes, the most important things Figel people got from the Lebak market were their iron tools. They didn't use money themselves, or know much about it, so they would take with them on the hike to the coast just enough rattan or other forest or garden product to sell to a vendor for the cash they needed to make their necessary purchases. Everyone knew how much rattan or tobacco was required to be able to buy a bolo or an ax blade. They would simply sell what they needed to sell, buy what they needed to buy, and go home. This limited relationship with the market, where they often were treated with little respect anyway, was part of a nearly total ignorance of the marketplace as an institution for maximizing advantages or profits. Economic competition was simply outside their experience and their taste. When they went to market it was not to "do business," but to meet the few needs of their family that nature did not supply directly.

On balmy evenings when most people had stopped working for the day and there was still light enough to see, the men of Figel often played *sifà*, a game similar to hackysack, in the clearing in front of the big house. Standing in a large circle, using the inside of their bare feet, six or eight men would kick a woven rattan ball about the diameter of an American baseball from one to another. The idea was to keep the ball off the ground for as long as possible. I watched many a game of *sifà* and was always amazed at how expert Teduray men were at kicking the ball high in the air so that it came down in perfect position for another man, across the circle, to kick it further on its way. A number of women would generally watch, visiting with each other about the events of the day and cheering the men on. *Sifà* was a game of skill, but it was a *cooperative* skill, not a competitive one. Teduray did not compete with each other in any aspect of their life; it simply was not seen as respectful. As the Teduray would say, "That's no way to live." Cooperation, in contrast, was part of the good life and highly valued. "The important thing," I heard many times, "is never to give anyone a bad gall bladder. That is what makes life good. Help each other live."

One evening, I sat on the little porch in front of my house watching a game of *sifà* and pondering how well it symbolized a huge difference between the Teduray notion of how to live and the one I had grown up with in the United States. *Sifà* was a splendid metaphor for Teduray life, because the way to win was for everyone to win, and the object of the game was to help all the other players do well. *Sifà* was a homey little drama of cooperation. On the other hand, I thought to myself, the game that best captured American life would have to be football, where competition and winning are everything. With its exalted stars, its institutionalized violence, its military vocabulary (quarterbacks throw "long bombs" and "march" the "offense" down the field to "victory"), and its ever-repeated drama of winning and losing, the NFL is "as American as apple pie."

Games reflect culture. American children may play hackysack, but much of our adult world is the setting for relentless, grinding competition to achieve and maintain what society holds to be good, a struggle for the highest of stakes, in which the aim is to defeat the opponent (as in warfare and similar rivalries) or to put the opponent out of business (another sort of warfare). A sense of scarcity, not abundance, underlies all we prize and do; that's "simply the way the world is." Indeed, for many of us our understanding of fundamental economic reality starts from the premise that there is not enough to go around. The resources for success and happiness are limited, so people cannot thrive equally—and many, our leaders tell us, don't deserve to anyway. In our society, worrying about someone else's feelings or being indiscriminately helpful might be nice, but "everybody knows" that nice guys finish last; for many Americans, a gall-bladder rule would seem like "no way to live."

There are many excellent sides to being American; I love my country and would not choose to live anywhere else. But we tend to be an NFL, not a hackysack kind of country. As I watched the *sifà* ball lofting back and forth, I thought about how uncongenial the forest Teduray would find my native culture.

To Mo-Emét and Ideng-Emét, to Balaud and Mo-Baug— to all the Figel women and men—the forest was not just their "environment" or some "eco-zone." It was their world, their home, the place where their lives took place. They knew it intimately, and they knew from their old stories that they had been created to care for it. That notion was the context for—and a fundamental part of—their spirituality, their understanding of what the world was like and how they ought to live in it.

They didn't own any part of nature the way their Maguindanaon neighbors believed they owned their land; they were merely user-owners, *géfé*, of whatever part they needed for however long they needed it. They shared the wealth of existence, but they didn't possess it. Their lives were simple, but not poor, and life was a journey, not a battle. One of the women shamans once told me that the Great Spirit was the real owner (in our sense) of the world, but most forest Teduray would not have said even that. Such proprietary rights and privileges were so foreign to Teduray ways of thinking that she had to use the Maguindanaon word for "owner." Rather, they saw themselves as stewards, as caretakers of all that was.

This stance was manifest in every aspect of their lives. People took meticulous care to preserve the forest environment, even, as we have seen, to the point of laboriously clearing mature forest to make new swiddens rather than recropping the previous year's. As a result they had lived untold generations in the forest— since "the beginning of time," they believed—without its becoming destroyed and replaced by grassland. They carefully protected certain forest trees, which they valued for fruit or other potential gifts. They avoided overcutting bamboo stands that they considered particularly useful. Hunting, fishing, and gathering were all carried out with care not to overexploit the natural resources on which human life depended. The traditional customs contained rule after rule of respect for the integrity of the environment: "Don't foul the river with excessive (fish) poison"; "Take only what you need from a fruit tree"; "Never cut or burn a swidden two years in a row, so that the forest can grow again." The forest was home and would always be home. It had to be guarded and conserved for future generations, even if that meant greater expenditure of labor in the present. But care of the forest was, after all, what the Teduray believed humans were created for.

6 ❦ Mirab Interlude II

In mid-August of that first year in the forest, my little crew and I again headed for Mirab. As I swung down from the rickety old bus that had carried me up the Upi road from Cotabato City and deposited me at the Edwards farm, I felt again, and acutely, the loneliness of being away from my family for so long. I had sorely missed Audrey and the two boys those last three months in Figel.

I walked past the Edwardses' farmhouse and closed in on our front porch, shouting, "Hey, I'm home. Where is everybody?"

I heard Len's voice call out, "Daddy's here!" and he and Will tore around the side of the house and grabbed me. They had been working in a little garden Hammy's grandmother had fixed up for them behind the house, near the privy. As we hugged each other and the boys, both talking at once, chattered at me furiously about their adventures, Audrey appeared at the door to the Edwardses' kitchen. I held her close to me with joy but also with some guilt, a little uncertain about my place and role in the family.

Perhaps in part that's why Len and Will's little garden fascinated me so much on this trip home: there with them I could avoid facing Audrey. The garden was about one yard wide and two yards long. Hammy's elderly Teduray grandmother (the boys called her "Grandmother" too) had cleared the grasses and broken up the hard soil. I was amused to see my boys, squatting comfortably like a couple of native Mirab folks, working away in the dirt, weeding around the small onion and bean shoots that were coming up and watering each one from a metal teapot. I noticed that the plants were arranged in neat rows, and thought how different the little plot was from a diverse scatter-seed Figel swidden.

Len did most of the gardening, since Will, less able to concentrate on relatively solitary tasks for any length of time, would quickly be off looking for someone to play with. It was readily apparent why Will was making so much more progress learning to speak Teduray than Len was.

Both boys were clearly happy to be living on a farm. They loved pets and had collected a whole menagerie of chickens, guinea pigs, dogs, cats, and even a little frog. Of course, being American, they gave them all names and spoke to them constantly. Audrey told me that the Teduray around Mirab didn't seem to like them doing that; she had no idea why, but people became upset and agitated. Still, though repeatedly cautioned about such Teduray sensitivities, the boys seemed unable to refrain from calling their animals, scolding them, and talking to them in a whole variety of ways.

Each time they did this within earshot of the Edwards home, a short ritual would take place: Hammy's grandmother at once dropped whatever she was doing and rushed into the house, grabbed a wok from the cooking area, and ran back to where the animal had been addressed. With visible urgency and concern, she picked up the puppy or guinea pig and dipped it into her wok. Then the old woman gently but firmly advised the boys not to be foolhardy. Later I learned that pretending to cook the offended animal was a way of preventing harm from striking the boys for breaking the Teduray taboo against speaking to animals.

I had been in Mirab several days when I was forcibly re-minded that improper dealings with pets were not the only dan-ger to be faced. We were reasonably well protected by the Ed-wardses and their armed tenants from bandits, even though from time to time small groups of brigands would pass through the Upi Valley. Like all rural people, however, nature and some of its potentially hostile creatures were a constant concern. There were numerous types of snakes around, including several species of grass snake and even boa constrictors, which would occasion-ally make off with a small farm animal, but these were all harm-less to humans. One type of snake, though, could be lethal: the Philippine cobra, a nonhooded but highly venomous variety. And lately one or more were being seen near our Mirab cottage almost every week.

One of Hammy's tenant farmers had built Len and Will a little bamboo playhouse, roofed with woven leaves, behind the Mirab Hilton, and the boys loved to spend time in it. Sometimes it would be a fort and sometimes a store; occasionally it was a truck or bus. On this particular morning the quiet of the dawn was shattered by loud, throaty squawks of distress coming from just outside our bedroom window. I jumped out from the mos-quito net to see what the racket was. It turned out to be a frog, screaming in terror, halfway down the throat of a good-sized boa in the rafters of the playhouse. It was no real crisis for us, just the balance of nature playing out one of its individual dramas, but Audrey and I were shaken. We both realized all too clearly that the snake could very well have been a cobra attacking one of our sons.

As it was, the boys were sobbing, thinking it was their frog Poncho being swallowed (this turned out not to be the case). The racket brought Hammy and our helper Fernando running, and Fernando killed the boa with a mighty whack of his field knife. After breakfast, Audrey and I gave the boys another stern lecture about avoiding snakes, and especially about looking out for the cobra. They had heard this many times before, but this time they listened very soberly. To reinforce the message, for their bedtime story Audrey told them about the time Peewee the Elf had nearly been killed by a cobra.

That evening after the boys were asleep, I finally asked Audrey about my being away from them all for such long periods. How were they doing? Did the boys miss having a father on hand? Were Will and Len too much of a burden on her, with no other parent there? Was she as lonely for me as I was for her? She assured me that they were all doing fine. The Edwardses were a big help with anything that came up, and the boys were busy all day. She missed me too, and although each day was demanding, they were enjoying their stay in Mirab.

Her reply seemed genuine and reasonable. After all, we had discussed our plans at length and she had always agreed that this was something I had to do, and had to do away from the family. I heard Audrey's words with great relief and took them at face value. I wish I had been more aware then of what I would learn little by little and only with the passing of years: that confrontation over conflict and candor about deep feelings were extremely difficult for her.

Decades later Audrey would tell me that although in many ways it was a delightful time for her, she often felt frustrated at being left alone for those long periods when I was in Figel, and she had carried some resentment ever since. I am not sure what I could or would have done if she had told me in Mirab how she felt; we were by then committed to the Teduray work, supported by a grant, and halfway across the world from home. We had a huge stake in what I was doing and little option but to see it through. Nevertheless, I wish I had been more conscious of the weight I had left on Audrey's shoulders. I know the Figel people would have given far greater attention to the needs of Audrey's gall bladder than I was able to do.

On the way back to Figel I slept in the sun for most of the launch ride. The following day as I hiked through the forest I fretted a bit about the snakes, my family, and other problems, but soon my mind was drawn back to my studies and to some troubled thoughts that were pressing for attention.

Especially I pondered the striking difference between the Teduray approach to life and nature and that of my own people. The little frog and the boa constrictor in my boys' playhouse were engaged in a genuine life-and-death struggle; their battle seemed to encapsulate the way so many of us Americans, with our glorification of competition, think about life and act in it. We characteristically take the world to be *inherently* competitive, a field of combat over the mortal stakes of who will win and who will lose, who will succeed and who will fail. But is that not simply our "take" on reality, the way we *choose* to structure our social and economic lives? The Teduray of Figel rejected out of hand the sort of competition that most Americans consider normal and good. They called it "no way to live" and put their stress on radical cooperation among all life forms. Nor did they concern themselves with individual rights, as we tend to do. Theirs was an ethic of *care*, not of *rights*. Sustenance and social justice were achieved not by everyone being able to assert personal rights in the struggle of daily competition, but by everyone looking after each other and working cooperatively.

What would it be like, I wondered, if all people began to share and work together for one another's good? If we all took it as a moral imperative not to give anyone a bad gall bladder? Might we escape from some of our imagined or self-imposed scarcity, from some of our obsession with ourselves, our numbness toward others? Might our politics be less harshly adversarial, our political leaders less narrowly given to their own special interests?

My mind also struggled to take in that great forest I was hiking through. What would happen if we all came to see nature as sacred? I wondered what our environment would be like if we could feel the terrible shock the Teduray would feel to see us filling the oceans, streams, soil, and atmosphere of the planet with life-threatening pollution.

I was feeling increasingly unsettled; something was happening that I had not bargained on. The more I mulled over the forest Teduray's fundamental assurance that the fullness of being human—the possibility of joy and zest in life—was a *gift of nature* and an *achievement of community*, the more that conviction seemed clear and true to me.

7   Everyone Needs
to Be in a Pot

Mo-Santos had several of what the Teduray called "specialties."
One was that he hunted wild pigs with dogs and spears. When
he came to my house early one morning and asked me if I wanted
to go hunt a pig, I had no inkling of what I was about to witness.

We left the Figel clearing at midmorning and headed at a
brisk pace directly into the forest. Mo-Santos took nothing with
him except two spears. His three trained dogs ran ahead of us,
circling back from time to time as if to urge us on. After about
an hour a sudden frenzy of excited barks and yips told Mo-Santos that his dogs had sniffed out and cornered a pig. He broke
into a dead run, following the sounds, while I did my best to
keep up.

The dogs had cornered a boar between a couple of big trees.
Their teamwork was impressive, but not nearly as impressive as
the size of their quarry. The animal was huge, about twice the
size of a domestic pig—much larger than I had expected. It was
frightened, and it was enraged. I felt a surge of fear, and my in-
stincts hollered at me to cut and run. But I was too fascinated to
do anything so sensible. My knees shook and my body was saturated with adrenaline, but I stayed, standing so near I could actually smell the animal.

Mo-Santos ran right up to the beast, and when it was distracted for a second by the snarling dogs, he dropped his ordinary killing spear to the ground and took quick aim at the enormous pig's belly with the special hunting spear, the blade point of which was sharply barbed and detachable, fastened to the midpoint of its shaft by a short vine rope. Without even a second's hesitation, Mo-Santos plunged the spearhead into the guts of the boar. The shaft broke loose immediately from the blade. The animal, screaming with pain, tried to run, with gory and frightening results. The spear's shaft caught in the forest undergrowth like a dry-land form of sea-anchor and the barbed blade was ripped from the boar's belly, virtually eviscerating it. At once, Mo-Santos snatched up his killing spear, ran over to the panicked and frenzied beast, and thrust the spear into its heart.

The entire drama happened in seconds and left me trembling. What Mo-Santos did took almost unbelievable skill and courage. I had witnessed his specialty and could easily see why, among the men of Figel neighborhood, he was the only one who practiced this particular technique.

We left the pig where it had fallen and hurried back to Figel for help; meanwhile, the dogs showed off more of their careful training by leaving the body alone but keeping potential scavengers away. Two men returned with us to the kill site and carried the carcass home, slung between the ends of a stout bamboo pole. For their efforts they were given the boar's head. Teduray prized pig's head for several delicacies: the brain, the tongue, and especially the meat on the cheeks, which was said to be the tastiest part of the entire animal.

I watched while the rest of the flesh was carved up and divided into thirty-two packets, one for each family in Figel neighborhood, including one for Mer, Aliman, and me. The packets were identical, each with an equal portion of leg meat, rib meat, belly meat, and so forth. All that Mo-Santos got as the hunter and killer of the pig—aside from admiration, gratitude, and his family's single portion of meat—was the tiny strip of flesh that covered the animal's sternum, valuable not as food but as a symbol of the boar's strength and courage.

Such division of the meat was, of course, entirely practical. Mo-Santos's family could not have eaten that large amount of meat before it spoiled in the tropic heat. I suppose they could have made jerky out of most of it and preserved it that way for their own use, but they would not have done that. The equal division of the boar revealed a significant characteristic of the Teduray understanding of a person's specialty: Mo-Santos's efforts were not just for himself, but for the whole community.

The notion of "specialist," or *furong*, was central to forest Teduray society. I have already mentioned that expert storytelling was also a specialty, and there were many others. Everybody had areas of particular expertise, which they offered for the well-being of all. I mentioned that when I first arrived in Figel and my language ability was still too spotty for free conversation, I started by compiling a demographic census of all the families and individuals in the neighborhood. I soon learned that people understood their specialties as an important part of who they were, and I added to my survey the question "What are your specialties?" A person might say to that, "I am a specialist in fishing with poison," or "My specialty is basket-weaving." Everybody had at least one specialty; many had several.

People learned their specialties as they were growing up, simply by watching their elders. I often saw small children playing at one special skill or another—a little boy building a toy fish trap using bits of straw to represent the wood or bamboo poles, or a young girl practicing the speech of gratitude to the spirits her mother used in ritually commemorating the first cut of new rice. They watched and they practiced, and the day eventually came when they were making real fish traps and real rituals. Many young people played at rudimentary basket weaving. They blew rice kernels through little make-believe blowguns. They sat in circles and pretended that they were legal sages, settling a conflict that threatened their society. As they grew older they grew more skillful from all those years of watching and imitating. Almost imperceptibly what had been play became real, as the children grew to be adults with special skills to offer for the good of the community.

Specialties were not full-time professions. Even the most esteemed legal specialists engaged in the same economic and social activities as all the other women and men. They farmed their forest gardens and helped in their neighbors' fields; they hunted, fished, gathered wild food, raised children, and participated in rituals. Spiritual specialists—shamans—were people who could see and speak with spirits, and thus could help with wisdom and healing, but they were otherwise just like anyone else. And so it was with all specialties. Women gave birth to babies, legal sages to justice, shamans to the restoration of harmony with spirits. All were equally important and valued gifts to the community.

Most specializations did not have such spectacularly communal results as Mo-Santos's divided-up pig, however. A basket weaver, for example, didn't weave a basket for every family, but only for someone who asked and, generally, who traded something in return. Nevertheless, all specialties were felt to have a distinctly communal purpose. Basket weavers were contributing their expertise quite explicitly to enhance community well-being. As with everything else in the Teduray world, specialties were not ranked; all were valued equally as contributions to the common success of the group and the harmony of their life together. A specialist in playing the zither played for all, and a shaman dealt with spirits for the good of whoever in the community was sick. The women and men who were legal sages were specialists in finding the just solution to issues that threatened social harmony. Specialists did not do what they did for personal gain or merely for their own enjoyment.

And certainly they did not engage in their specializations to achieve coercive power. The very idea would have been foreign to them. Domination was seen as nothing but a tool of ranking; its only use was to enforce some hierarchical pecking order—and that was "no way to live." Forest Teduray were well acquainted with hierarchy and power among the people outside the forest, but Teduray men didn't seek such power and they didn't try to wield it—not over women and not over each other. If politics is "the institutionalization of power," as it is sometimes defined, then the Teduray would have to be called a society without politics. They didn't even have "leaders," as we think of leaders. What they had were "specialists."

In fact, there was no hierarchical ranking of any kind in their entire view of reality. Absolutely fundamental to their understanding of "the real" was the belief that everything in the cosmos was equal in rank and value. All human beings, whether men or women, whether adults or children, whether the finest shaman or the most ordinary basket weaver, were considered of equal worth and equal standing in society. All the various spirits were equal to each other as well. There were, to be sure, differences in esteem and prestige. The Great Spirit, who created the world as well as all the humans and other spirits, stood high in *prestige* among the spirits, just as Balaud, the legal specialist in Figel, was greatly renowned for his judicial wisdom and skill. But the Great

Spirit was nonetheless precisely equal in *rank* to all the other spirits, and Balaud was not considered any greater a person than any other man or woman in the community. It was the same with all of nature. Humans and spirits were no greater than any animal or any plant; there was no species hierarchy any more than there was any other kind of ranking. The Teduray of Figel were, in all respects, radically egalitarian.

Women and men were clearly different—and the Teduray delighted in the difference—but they were not ranked. I need to stress this, because it contrasts so fundamentally with what we in America experience: among forest Teduray *neither gender was thought superior to the other in any way.* Men and women related with empathy and an ethos of interdependence, with a mutual sharing of life's problems and joys. Although women were specialists in childbearing, both men and women carried around young children, nurtured them, and helped raise them. There was no sign of anything like a "battle of the sexes." Rather, an abiding spirit of harmony existed between the sexes, and both men and women saw each other as equal participants in the great dance of life. Once I became accustomed to it, I found gender equality to be one of the Teduray's most endearing characteristics.

This egalitarianism carried over into working life. Although men, being stronger than women, tended to do heavier work, such as cutting down the large forest trees when making swiddens, this work was not seen as more valuable or more honorable than, say, weeding, which task tended to fall to the women. And in areas of activity that did not involve physical strength, men and women were on equal footing: both could be and were legal specialists or shamans, for example; both worked at gardening and gathered wild foods. Greater male strength was recognized, but it did not in any way suggest the supremacy of one gender over another, nor did it provide the rationale for any form of social oppression, organized warfare, or concentration of private property. Weeding and felling trees, weaving baskets and hunting for wild pigs, giving birth and fathering children—all were really just different but equal specialties.

Not only were the genders unranked in forest Teduray society, but they were held to identical values as well. Common American phrases such as "Isn't that just like a woman" or "He's a real man" would have been utterly puzzling to a resident of Figel. In general, the forest Teduray didn't view gender, in itself, as decisively affecting a person's disposition, potential, or personality, as is common in more hierarchical and male-dominated societies. Thus, absence of gender marking in the pronoun system—no "he, his, him," no "she, her"—was characteristic of the entire language. There was only one word for spouse, not different words for "husband" and "wife"; there were no gender distinctions between siblings: no words for "sister" or "brother." Like any society, Teduray made gender distinctions, of course— men and women were clearly different from each other in dress, hairstyle, and reproductive role as well as in such physical attributes as strength—but when it came to positive and negative values of human behavior, the same criteria applied to men and women alike.

Such values as caring and nonviolence, warmth and nurturing, sharing and empathy, which were considered "feminine" in the world I grew up in, were held to be quite general and proper for both genders in Teduray society. Likewise with bravery and assertiveness, intellectual calm and rationality, sexual and conversational boldness—these were not masculine qualities in Figel but equally valued and fostered in everyone, in women every bit as much as in men. Far from being gender-specific, they were panhuman ideals. By the same token, a great many of the traits that Westerners tend to see as masculine glories—such as emotional toughness, conquest, and domination—were roundly condemned in Teduray society for *everyone.*

Along with specialists, the other fundamental social building block—the "home base," you might say—of Teduray life was the family, and again equality was the rule. The word for "family" also meant "cooking pot," from the idea that people who formed a family all ate out of the same pot. In almost all cases, a family consisted of a married couple and their prepubertal children. Occasionally a dependent elderly person past the age of childbearing or economic work would be included in "the pot," but since most people worked on into older age, such expanded families were relatively few in number.

These nuclear families were considered fully independent and self-determining units. When children married, they no longer ate from the same pot as their parents, but formed a new household and a new pot, at which point they were on their own socially and economically. There were no larger kin groups such as clans or descent lineages, not even family surnames. A family could reside in any settlement its members wished, though the location chosen would necessarily be one of a group of settlements that cooperated in economic activities and did rituals together. Sometimes a bride and groom built a house in the settlement of one of their parents, but no rule required them to do that, and when it happened everybody was clear that the new family was now economically associated with the parental family merely as neighbors.

Teduray believed that the husband-wife relationship that created the pot was critical in two ways. For one thing, it meant that every adult had the partner she or he needed to survive economically. Individuals could not make it on their own. The ways in which the abundance of the forest was tapped—especially the work of gardening, but also hunting, fishing, and gathering—involved huge amounts of cooperation. Women and men both had to make their necessary contributions to the family's keep. The conviction that neither would have been viable on their own ran deep in Teduray consciousness.

The second reason that the marital partnership was deemed crucial was that it produced and raised children. Every child—like every adult but more so—had to be part of a functioning pot for survival and well-being. Procreation and child-rearing were a fundamental piece of what families were for.

Because families were understood as utterly essential to life, Teduray expended vast social effort in creating and maintaining them. As we shall see, however, men and women could fall short of their moral ideals, and the forest Teduray legal system had an important role to play in keeping the society peaceful and stable, particularly because there was a high incidence of elopement with each other's spouses. Well over 95 percent of the cases that legal specialists considered had to do with some aspect of making family units, or remaking them when they were broken by death or divorce, or settling disputes that dealt with who was married to whom.

In addition to being part of a pot, all Teduray had well-defined sets of relatives who did not form an actual social group but who were very important to them and were referred to as *segedet*, "close together." A person's "close" relatives consisted of everyone descended from his or her eight great-grandparents. Anthropologists refer to such a set of close kin as a "kindred."

The kindred included parents, grandparents, and great-grandparents, plus any of those people's descendants—aunts, uncles, cousins, children, nephews, and nieces. They were called "close" relatives in contrast to those who were unrelated or were more distant blood relatives, all of whom were "far." Women and men who were "far apart" could marry, but any sexual union among "close" people was incest and so forbidden.

Beyond setting the boundaries for incest, the kindred played other significant roles in a person's life. It was held responsible for that person in *all* moral and legal contexts. Marriages were formed and dissolved by agreement between the kindreds of the couple. And if anyone became the focus of a legal dispute, that person's kindred immediately emerged and, if the person were found at fault, all members of the kindred were held responsible for collection and payment of the fine. Moreover, if people whose gall bladder had been wounded refused to settle the matter peacefully through law but instead decided to seek violent retaliation, they would not necessarily go after the actual offender. In Teduray social logic, revenge might be taken on *any member* of the offending kindred, just as, in response, countervengeance might be launched against anyone in the avenger's kindred. This is one of the reasons Teduray abhorred violence and moved against it with such fervor. It could diffuse out from actual disputants into the larger society quickly and devastatingly.

Making marriages and settling disputes through law always involved the passing of a collection of legal exchange goods, called a "security settlement," from one kindred to another. These exchange goods were a class of items that, aside from their practical everyday usefulness, had great symbolic meaning. An example of such goods is the brass gongs that were played each morning and evening in Figel. Gongs were not made by the Teduray, who did no blacksmithing or other metalwork; they came into Teduray society by trade with the coastal or lowland Muslims. Other kinds of exchange items were krises (wavy-bladed swords), glass-bead necklaces with gold ornamentation, fancy working knives, china plates, elaborate brass boxes to hold betel quid ingredients, sarongs, and hunting spears. What they all had in common, aside from the fact that they came into Teduray society through trade, was that they passed hands from kindred to kindred over and over again throughout the years as marriages, divorces, and other legal issues were settled.

Traditionally, Teduray women and men first married soon after they reached puberty, and the proper way in which this initial marriage was made was through prior negotiations between the kindred elders of the couple. A wedding united two persons as spouses—it created a new pot—but it also brought all the people in the couple's two kindreds together as in-law relations, with responsibility for the continuance of the new family. Thus the process of making the marriage began with complex negotiations between the two kindreds, and the wedding itself was just a brief episode in a long series of transactions. Throughout it all, exchange goods were used to symbolize the relationships that existed and that were being established.

I witnessed a wedding not long after my arrival in Figel, and it and the events leading up to it were quite typical of the process for making first marriages. Kufeg, a sixteen-year-old boy from Timanan, a settlement some eight hours away from Figel by foot, married Layda, who was fourteen and came from Megelaway, a settlement of Figel neighborhood.

The proposal of marriage was initiated by Kufeg's parents and several other kindred elders, who, without telling Kufeg what they were up to, came to Megelaway, along the way watching very carefully for good or bad omens. Forest Teduray interpreted many occurrences as omens, such as seeing certain birds fly over-head or hearing the sound of the little house lizards as one left on a hike, and took these signals very seriously.

I was not present at this negotiation, but I know that the vis-itors would have announced their purpose in a metaphoric and oblique way. They might have said, for instance, that they had come to inquire whether Megelaway was a nice place to live. If interested, the girl's parents might well have replied that there were many fine house sites in Megelaway. If not interested, they could have said that it was not a very nice place and they were thinking of moving themselves. Approaching the matter in this roundabout manner left open the possibility of a refusal without anybody suffering open embarrassment. Since the response of Layda's parents was favorable, Kufeg's party was able then to speak openly of its purpose and offer two exchange items—say, a kris and necklace—to symbolize the engagement. In all of these and the further negotiations, the wishes of Layda, like those of Kufeg, were never considered. Indeed, neither of them was aware of what was taking place.

When Layda's parents accepted the two items, the kindred el-ders of both young people arranged a meeting to discuss all the exchange goods that would be given by Kufeg's side to Layda's side as the "security settlement" and to set the date for the wed-ding. This meeting, called a *tiyawan*, took place in the Figel big house. *Tiyawan* were "sessions" held for the formal negotiation of agreements by legal specialists, of which a marriage was the most common. They were also the forum for the nonviolent set-tlement of disputes. Kufeg's kindred would give some of the set-tlement during this session and the rest at the wedding ceremony itself. The security settlement agreed upon was quite typical: eight necklaces, eight krises, twelve spears, five brass boxes, two sets of gongs, and several other lesser legal exchange items. Collected from the various members of Kufeg's kindred, they would then be distributed to the various members of Layda's kindred. The exact contents of the settlement would be remembered by all involved for years, because, although the items themselves would have long since been scattered about on other occasions of giving and taking by Layda's kindred, an identical number of items would have to be returned someday if the marriage were to break up—if, for instance, Layda eloped with some other man.

The legal specialists, in particular, would remember. While I was in Figel I witnessed time and again the ability of a legal sage to recite the precise composition of a security settlement—how many of this item and how many of that, what was given by the time of the wedding and what was given at the wedding, the physical characteristics of each item—and all this twenty or thirty years after the settlement had been accomplished! The first time I observed this happening I thought, "Oh, sure, this old guy is just making it up," but I wrote down the details to be polite. A year later, I listened as a different legal specialist who had been at that same wedding listed the identical settlement to the last detail. Figel Teduray were illiterate, and so there were no written records of such transactions, only the memories of the participating legal sages. Such spectacular feats of recall were intrinsic to their work, and they were impressive to witness.

The session to establish the security settlement finished, thoughts and efforts turned to the wedding itself. The nuptial ritual and feast for a first marriage is very elaborate. Should the couple not stay together, their subsequent weddings would contain most of the same ritual elements but would be much plainer and simpler.

On the day before the wedding of Layda to Kufeg, her kindred gathered at the Figel big house. Layda herself didn't know that she was the one to be married, having been told that she was keeping the secret from a cousin. In the early evening, the people were all chatting after eating, when a middle-aged woman— one of the legal specialists in Layda's kindred—suddenly stood up and announced in a loud voice, "Now Layda will be married to Kufeg!"

Layda, startled and embarrassed, began to cry and to struggle to run away, as was expected of her in this situation. Her relatives grabbed and held her and shouted out four times the traditional Teduray wedding cheer: *"U u efri!"* She was then covered completely with a handsome silk sarong, and once her worst crying had subsided she was placed in a specially constructed enclosed room. Layda had to stay there, covered from head to foot in the sarong and guarded by some of her young unmarried girlfriends and a few of the older women. She was not permitted to talk or to allow her head to emerge outside the cover.

On the same day, while all this was going on in Layda's community, Kufeg's kindred in Timanan also gathered at the home of one of their legal specialists, where that evening they shocked the boy with the same shouts and much the same procedure, giving him no more chance to decline the marriage than Layda's kin had given her. He, too, was covered with a handsome cloth and kept from talking to anyone, though he was not put in a separate room. The following morning, Kufeg folded the sarong neatly and wore it across his left shoulder for the trek to Figel and the ensuing wedding ceremony. Before leaving, the men in his kindred fashioned a canopy held aloft by four poles for the groom to walk under, and they conferred informally to be certain they had all the exchange items they had agreed to give at the ceremony.

In Figel, on the morning of the celebration, Layda's people were busy preparing many things. Some were for ritual aspects of the ceremony; others were more practical, especially great quantities of rice and chicken wrapped in banana leaves in meal-sized packets. These, along with similar packets containing rice cakes and candy, were for the groom's kindred to "purchase" at the wedding for greatly inflated prices, such as a blouse and a sarong or its equivalent, their number and price having been negotiated in advance as part of the whole settlement. These food packets were, in a sense, an exchange on the part of the bride's side for the security settlement from the groom's side, so it was important that there were enough.

Kufeg and his party arrived in Figel, dressed in their best clothes, about an hour before dark. As they drew near they began playing gongs, and when they came to the big house, they shouted out four times, "U u efri." Those waiting in the house responded with the same call, and under the cover of his canopy, Kufeg and his kindred entered the house. There was a certain amount of ritual giving and accepting of various exchange items, and then the meal followed.

When all had eaten their fill, the evening was well advanced. Sleeping mats were brought out and mosquito nets hung. Couples talked quietly between themselves, and soon one of the men and one of the women present began to take turns chanting some of the many subplots of the *Berinarew*, the great Teduray epic that, as we have seen, tells of the adventures of Lagey Lengkuwos, who led the second creation of humans to the Region of the Great Spirit, beyond the sky. On that particular evening, they chanted the story of Lagey Lengkuwos and his companions coming to a cosmic realm where there were many spirit Giants, and how he brilliantly tricked them into letting his people go by and on toward the Realm of the Great Spirit. Meanwhile, legal specialists gathered in a corner of the big house and chatted about old legal sessions. Ideng-Amig, one of the women among them, recalled at length how a particularly difficult situation had been brought to an elegant resolution.

The following morning, after breakfast, the remainder of the security settlement was formally given by Kufeg's side to Layda's people in a wordy and tedious set of speeches that lasted several hours. I should say that they seemed wordy and tedious to me, with my then still sketchy understanding of the language; the Teduray seemed to relish every word. This speechmaking lasted the rest of the morning and well into the afternoon, whereupon everyone broke for lunch.

When all had finished eating, the actual wedding ceremony began. Layda was brought out from her seclusion, and the sarong was removed from her head. Kufeg was similarly led to join her on a mat, where he sat on Layda's right. Both faced east, so that their lives together might increase in joy, just as the sun rises from the east to its zenith. Two legal specialists, one from each side, came and stood before the couple, the person from Kufeg's kindred standing before Layda, and Layda's standing before Kufeg. Each mother prepared a betel quid for chewing and gave it to her legal specialist, who, in turn, passed it on to the woman's new child-in-law, who chewed for a few moments, then placed the chewed quid on a bandanna. At that point the two legal specialists moved behind Kufeg and Layda, again standing behind the one from the other kindred, and began to comb their hair—Layda's first, then Kufeg's. As they combed they gave speeches, urging the newlyweds to be virtuous, faithful, and hardworking and not to cause trouble to the marriage and thus to their families. This done, the elders exchanged their combs and gave them to the new mothers-in-law. A single plate containing some rice and a hard-boiled egg cut in two was then brought to the couple, each of whom, turning to face the other, ate a bit of the rice and some of the egg.

That concluded the marriage ceremony, and the guests began to leave. Several of the legal sages lingered on to discuss legal problems, but the wedding itself was finished. Layda and Kufeg were now a new family, a new pot. They could settle anywhere they wished, and they chose to build a house in Megelaway near Layda's parents. Whenever I saw them, they seemed happy together.

An aspect of these first-marriage procedures puzzles and disturbs me still. I feel that I know, from observation and countless conversations, that traditional Teduray did not, in general, see adults as ranked over children. They let them participate in all aspects of life that they showed interest in, and there were no rules such as our "Children should be seen and not heard." Adults knew that they had responsibilities toward young people, and they understood that youngsters needed to mature into adult wisdom, but they didn't, as far as I could see, relate to them as underlings in a hierarchical or controlling way. And yet here was this striking behavior where they did not ask adolescents at puberty whether they wanted to marry at a certain time, did not give them any choice of spouse, did not even allow them to opt to wait a bit, although the bride and groom wept and struggled. I wish I had investigated more thoughtfully the seeming implications of what I saw done to those young people, but although I was surprised and startled at the time, I couldn't say anything then and somehow never later followed up on it and inquired further. I was told that the weeping and struggling were expected and virtually ritualized, but still all this denial of the young people's autonomy certainly seems to me in retrospect coercive, emotionally and spiritually violent, and thoroughly inconsistent, not only with the gall bladder rule but with just about every other aspect of Teduray principles of respect and egalitarianism—a glaring anomaly.

Somehow, though, the harsh treatment of the bride and groom must not have seemed to the Teduray an exception to their usual graciousness. Young people were not thought to be adults until their first child was born. Perhaps the elders considered children too immature to make such a socially important decision as choosing their own first partners. Or maybe the practice was simply an inconsistency; no society is immune from illogic, and I discovered lots of other less troubling inconsistencies when I was trying to grasp their cosmology. In any case, no graduate student doing fieldwork today would fail, as I did, to explore the thinking behind that behavior, and I regret that I didn't look more closely into the matter.

I leave this wedding scene with one final comment. What I am calling a security settlement is generally referred to in anthropological jargon as a "brideprice." But that term, conventionally defined as a sum of money or property given by a husband or his family to the father or family of the bride, is not suitable for the Teduray. Forest Teduray did not purchase anybody, and women did not have a price. The gift exchange was meant to symbolize the fact that the woman's kindred had given her to the marriage and that the man's kindred had secured the marriage with legal exchange items. If the woman were to cause the marriage to break up, her kindred would have to return the items. If the breakup were the man's fault, the woman's side would simply consider the items theirs to keep and no longer part of a remembered security settlement. Any given settlement was thus not an enduring collection of actual exchange items, but a mental "list" that represented the relationship between the couple and between their kindreds; it linked many people to a given marriage and stood as a token of their ongoing responsibility and concern for the good health of that marriage. It was not understood as a price paid for a woman.

I will describe in a later chapter how legal exchange items, in the form of fines, brought a peaceful end to interpersonal disputes of all sorts by representing symbolically that the fault had been accepted and the disrespect had been recognized. Legal exchange items were not just a class of valuable things that people passed from family to family; they were much more. Legal exchange items were artfully employed as a tangible metaphor for social relations. They were the symbolic "coin" of the Teduray social realm, standing for and supporting a state of social justice, equity, and equilibrium.

In Figel neighborhood, two of the twenty-nine married men, Balaud and Mo-Sew, had two wives each, and thus each was part of two separate pots within the same household. I was speaking with the two of them one day, and I asked what it meant that each had two wives. The issue concerned me because the idea of a wife as property to own or to hand from man to man is very common and does damage to women in the parts of the world where it holds sway. I wondered if, perhaps, patriarchy was peeking through the egalitarian curtain, much in the way adult dominance had seemed to sneak into first weddings.

It was not.

"We have two wives so that the women will not be alone after their husbands die," Mo-Sew told me. "It is their wish, too, not to be left alone. I got my second wife, Nayaan, when my brother died of pneumonia many years ago. Our kindred had given a security settlement for his marriage to Nayaan, so when my brother died my kindred just arranged with her family for Nayaan to be married to me. She wanted a husband, and her children needed a father."

Balaud told me a very similar story about "inheriting" his brother's wife.

I asked the two men if they had greater standing in the community because of having two families, and they both laughed.

"No, Mo-Lini, we just have more work. A widow's kindred will usually marry her to an unmarried man, if possible, because they know keeping two families is difficult," Balaud said. Both he and Mo-Sew saw the practice as hard but necessary to the well-being of some, especially older, widows. "We don't mind. Our wives are good to us, and they and their children needed to be in a pot to survive."

When I asked women about this matter, I got the same response. They also said that, if they wished, they could remain widows and not remarry; they could join a brother or sister's family. But most women preferred being a co-wife and thus living in her own pot. Inheriting women may be an issue of oppression in many societies, but it apparently was not here.

The traditional Teduray of the forest had no Judeo-Christian tradition to instill shame in them about their bodies, and they were tremendously earthy and lusty. Many people told us that sexual pleasure was a gift to be given and received with joy, and countless observations of interacting couples confirmed that view. As in all social relations, the rule never to give anyone a bad gall bladder was a guiding principle in sexual matters as well; coerced sexual relations were spoken of as immoral, indeed inhuman, and certain to result in violence. But freely consensual erotic pleasure was a forthright delight.

According to the rules of custom and respect, sexual relations between women and men were supposed to be restricted to marriage, even though that was not necessarily the case in practice. The thought was not that sexual pleasure outside marriage was intrinsically bad, but that it often and predictably led to social disruption—a bad gall bladder—and thus to potential violence. If a dalliance were to become known, it could lead to a shift in commitment and thereby break up families, infuriate spouses left behind, and cause enmity between a couple's kindreds. It led to disagreement about who the father of a child was. And therefore the rules were clear: rights to sexual access were to remain exclusively between marriage partners; adultery was not supposed to happen.

This is hardly the way things were in actuality, though. Sexual matters caused some very real tension among the forest Teduray. As I mentioned before, a huge percentage of the cases that had to be settled by the legal system concerned the repair or rearrangement of broken marriages. Relationships outside marriage did occur, and even though most lovers were careful and discreet, often their feelings grew stronger for each other and weakened toward their legal spouses. And so they would make their relationship public by eloping. The most common misbehavior that the legal system confronted, in its efforts to prevent violence by people with abused gall bladders, was running off with someone else's spouse. Three or four elopements in any woman's or man's lifetime were standard. No wonder the arranged first marriages, however much protected, were accepted; they were not very likely to last!

There was a man I liked very much named Mo-Ligaya. He was a splendid storyteller and an accomplished legal specialist. When I first met Mo-Ligaya and interviewed him for basic information about himself, I asked him, as I had learned always to do, what his specializations were. He told me he was a legal specialist. After we'd talked about that for a while, I asked him if he had any other specialties. I didn't yet know, at that time, that there were such awesome specialties as doing hand-to-hand combat with gigantic wild boars, but I also wasn't prepared for his reply. He laughed and said, "Yes, another of my specialties is elopement!" He had, it turned out, run off with someone else's wife six times. Or perhaps I should say he'd been run off with— because elopement worked both ways in this egalitarian society. Affairs involving married people were very common, but six of them may well have been enough to qualify Mo-Ligaya as a specialist, at least in his own mind.

Whenever elopement occurred, the legal system would spring into action to divorce the previous couples, to marry the new couple, and to get the myriad exchange item arrangements back in order—all before anyone did anything violent. So there was always a degree of anxiety between partners, never knowing for sure when they might be abandoned, and considerable social tension surrounded actual elopements; however, except, perhaps, in the case of the deserted persons, who were predictably furious, this tension was not about breaking the sex rules as much as it was about the need to keep society in good, safe working order.

Following an elopement, all the involved kindreds expended immense effort to sort everything out and get everybody once more into a properly married state. This was to prevent bloodshed, to be sure, but also to ensure that all adults and children would be in pots, where Teduray believed they needed to be to survive in the world. And since almost everyone married, divorced, and remarried numerous times in their adult life, it is no wonder that the legal system had developed such elegance and that the most effective legal sages were highly regarded by everyone.

I spent many evenings going back and forth over my field

notes, lost in thought about these matters. Why were elopement and sexual affairs so rampant among Teduray? I think it was, in part, because sex was seen as such a marvelous thing to give and receive, and because the gall bladder rule conditioned people to want to please each other in every possible way. Then too, the high incidence of sexual straying from marriage must have been partly due to the legal system being marvelously effective in picking up the pieces.

But surely the picture was more complicated than simple erotic *joie de vivre*, kind gall bladders, and effective dispute resolution. The real context was the total picture of a society where equality among all people—all beings—was taken for granted; where people gave what passed for leadership in a given area because they had something to offer, a particular specialty, not because they were anointed; where Mo-Santos's providing meat to one and all was a gift, and such gifts, not some hierarchy or some concentration of coercive power, were the basis of the social order; where marriages brought people and kindreds into positions of parity and equity, for the good of the couple, not into positions of superiority and inferiority symbolized by bread-winning on the man's part and domestic subservence on the woman's. Little by little, I began to see that sexual relations between Teduray men and women took shape within particular understandings of social order and human relationships, understandings that inspired Mo-Santos to risk his life for the good of everyone, that underlay the complicated negotiations leading to Layda and Kufeg's marriage, that let Mo-Ligaya take delight in his sexual attraction even when he knew he was causing a degree of social harm and legal effort by his repeated elopements, and that gave Teduray the understanding they had of gender role, gender equality, and gender behavior—all the aspects of social interaction I have been discussing in this chapter.

8 Mirab Interlude III

November came, the rains began to slack off considerably; I had been missing Audrey, Len, and Will with what seemed like a visceral ache. Moreover, it was just a few days until my own American "native feast" of Thanksgiving. So I decided to head again for Mirab and some rest and recreation. Aliman, Mer, and I left Figel early on a Saturday morning. The paths were muddy in many places and the river still seemed swifter than usual.

All along the hike and through most of the long next day on the coastal launch, my thoughts were troubled, as they had often been lately in moments of solitude. On my previous trip to Mirab a sense of dislocation had begun to stir in my mind, and since then I had frequently reflected on the sharp contrasts between Teduray and American culture. Now, perhaps underlined by the prospect of rejoining my family for several days, my own people's ways of living seemed to press on my thinking with new urgency.

In Figel I had been working intensely trying to understand family and social arrangements, gender role conditioning, and the Teduray attitude toward sexual pleasure and sexual responsibility. Inevitably perhaps, the contrasts in this area between "them" and "us" filled my imagination. I could see that it would be difficult for any society to accommodate such a high incidence of elopement, but as I rolled around in my mind the events and relationships I had been tracking in the forest Teduray social order, and as I increasingly began to see the logic that held everything together, I realized that many aspects of this radically egalitarian side of forest Teduray life had a deep human appeal to me.

My thinking kept flashing from Figel to California and Illinois, where I had most recently been living, and to Pennsylvania, where I had spent my boyhood. Was the United States, seen in the light of Figel, really such a beacon of equality as I had been reared to think? Was it inevitable that many people were *up* (men, Caucasians, the wealthy) while many others were *down* (women, African Americans, poor people)? Were our marriages any more stable—or any more joyous? Was sexual experience as happy and delightful, as unoppressive, for us as it was for these forest lovers who, in and out of marriage, freely offered and freely accepted gifts of physical pleasure and who held in contempt any effort to force those gifts? Were Mo-Ligaya and Balaud, Mo-Santos and Mo-Bintang, any less "real men" because they honored and respected women as their equals in every way? For that matter, were Ideng-Emét and the other women any less "feminine" because they were strong-willed and shared with men most of the key specialist roles?

Such questions swirled around in my head all the way to Mirab.

The big event of my week home, which I was glad not to miss, was Thanksgiving dinner. Captain Edwards had taught his family all about this annual festival, and they observed it with zeal and delight. I arrived on the scene late in the day on Monday, and the Edwards family and Audrey were already busy preparing food and the decorations. The next morning I saw that sweet potatoes were piled outside the Edwardses' kitchen door, and dozens of eggs had been collected and saved for Helen Ruth, Hammy's unmarried younger sister and a great friend to Audrey, to use in making that rich custard which carried the Spanish name of flan. Chickens had been caught and, in place of their accustomed free-ranging around the house, penned in a little wire corral, from which they were due to join canned sardines on crackers as finger food with drinks before dinner. I noticed a case of Tanduay Rum and several cases of San Miguel beer piled on the porch, and I knew that the old grandmother would soon be picking a large crop of vegetables from her garden.

At our house, Audrey was baking cakes in her cut-down kerosene can cake tins. She even proposed to make an "apple pie," although there were no apples anywhere around; she had a recipe for making pretend apples out of soggy Ritz crackers, of all things, drowned in the appropriate spices and a mountain of sugar. She also had heaps of other fruit—papayas, breadfruit, *marang* (a sweet sticky fruit that grew on trees next to our house), pineapples, several varieties of bananas, and oranges— ready to be peeled and sliced for dessert along with the flan. I was dispatched to Upi in the truck to buy a Chinese ham, some roasted peanuts, and a few other last-minute necessities.

For most of Wednesday and early Thursday, while the cooks in the house did their final chores, the men, earnestly assisted by Len and Will, prepared what would be the centerpiece of the meal. Months before Hammy had obtained some turkey chicks from Mr. Mamaril in Upi, an old man who years ago had been principal of the agricultural school there and who had somehow managed to round up some exemplars of this utterly nonnative bird. The chicks had grown up on the Mirab farm, making, by all reports, rather disagreeable neighbors to the humans there. Only one had survived, and its destiny, of course, was to be the main course on Thanksgiving.

Hammy and his sharecrop tenants dug a pit in a small clearing beside the Edwards house. They filled it with kindling and larger pieces of cut wood, and over it they erected a spit. It was exactly the way people prepared to roast a suckling pig for the much-prized and very occasional delicacy of *lechon*. Hammy told me that they had prepared their Thanksgiving turkey this way for years: by slowly turning it over a fire, its body skewered on a long bamboo pole. The pole had to be continuously dampened with water to keep it from burning; meanwhile, the turkey was basted with its own drippings collected in a pan suspended just below the spit.

While Will chatted excitedly in Teduray with a little farm boy, kibitzing the whole production, Len explained every detail to me in solemn tones. This was a major event, and both boys knew it; like budding anthropologists they asked a million questions each step of the way, all of which were politely and carefully answered in the typically gracious Teduray way by one or another of the men. It was all very sociable; the party was clearly under way for these men. As they constructed the barbecue pit and rigged up the spit, they downed many bottles of beer and ate a steady supply of fried potato and taro chips which were issuing from the kitchen to keep up their gall bladders. They told stories, sang songs, and fondly recalled other turkeys and pigs from days gone by. By late afternoon, when Audrey called our sons, protesting and pouting, to get cleaned up for dinner, the group was still gathered around the hole laughing and telling tales, and the men had switched from beer to rum.

Dinner in the Edwards home was, by any standard, a memorable feast, and it was recognizably in the classic genre of American Thanksgiving dinners. There was no wine; the only wine available in that area was church sacramental wine, and it was regarded as unseemly to drink that at a meal, however special. But all the other typical ingredients were on hand: turkey, white potatoes and gravy, candied sweet potatoes, tinned cranberry sauce, bright fresh vegetables, even pickles and olives. Little *pan-de-sal* breakfast breads served nicely as rolls, and of course rice was on the table for those who, like most Filipinos, never felt full without some rice at every meal. Several bowls of *felàfà*, which I particularly loved, were provided; *felàfà* was a Teduray hot-and-sweet condiment, made by frying shredded and dried coconut with chili peppers. The desserts were delicious, even the Ritz cracker pie. We took a long time to eat, everyone enjoying the food and each other. Compliments were awarded to all who had cooked, and now the women were a lively part of the storytelling. Seven of us sat around the table: Audrey and I and the Edwards adults. The youngsters, both Schlegels and those of the Edwards extended farm family, ate in the kitchen and, in the manner of children, soon finished and ran outside to play. Tenant families from the Edwards farm sat on the floor throughout the house, joining in the eating with enthusiastic pleasure.

I don't know how long we might have continued, perhaps long into the evening, but about an hour after the desserts had been cleared away we suddenly heard the raucous sound of a shrieking chicken. One that had survived the holiday ax was now manifestly in a state of misery and terror behind the house. We all ran out the kitchen door and found Len and Will peering into the Edwardses' outhouse looking both delighted and a bit guilty. Just for the fun of it, they had thrown a hen into the toilet! The poor bird had virtually disappeared into the muck at the bottom of the privy pit and was frantically thrashing around and screaming. The other Teduray children were nowhere to be seen; they had obviously cleared out as soon as they saw what the little white boys were up to. Hammy was in a controlled rage, and the rest of the Edwards family were, to say the least, not pleased.

Hammy very sternly lined up our two naughty sons and gave them the most vigorous scolding I think they had ever received in their young lives. He warned them about disrespect to other life, lectured them on the monetary value of a good hen, expressed disbelief that anyone would do such a thing, stated his disappointment in them as friends and relatives. Len and Will both looked at the ground through the entire session.

They seemed ashamed of themselves, but when Hammy finished his harangue and we all settled back down at the dinner table, Audrey and I were astonished and humiliated to hear our naughty son Will whisper distinctly to Len: "Let's do the cat!"

On the morning of our departure to return to Figel, I learned that Mer and Aliman had gone ahead and would meet me at the launch in Cotabato. Hammy claimed illness from a bout of dysentery—or perhaps from too much rich food at the recent Thanksgiving feast, combined with a couple of boys whose naughtiness exceeded his tolerance. So, laden with a large supply of turkey sandwiches in my backpack, I drove down the hill with Audrey in the Edwardses' truck; she would see me to the boat and then drive back up to Mirab.

I felt glad to have those hours on the road alone with Audrey. I tried to describe Figel social organization to her, and I wanted to ask her how she felt those ways compared with ours, but I got nowhere. She seemed uninterested, bored by the whole topic, as she generally seemed now when I talked at any length about my work. Perhaps I was simply too new and too close to it to give my research any clarity at that moment, or my mind was too perplexed; perhaps Audrey had her own preoccupations and wished I would talk to her about them; perhaps she was simply resentful about my being in Figel so much and in Mirab so little. Or possibly the whole topic was just more threatening to her as an American woman than she wanted to admit on a bumpy road with a husband she seldom saw those days. We soon switched to a more congenial subject.

Forest Teduray ways, even to me, threatened easy composure. What began for me as a graduate school fieldwork requirement, an extended social science exercise, was becoming something far more serious, something risky and deeply personal, a matter not only of writing a dissertation but, just possibly, of reshaping my whole approach to life.

9 🌿 The Woman Who Was Born a Boy

In the evenings, when it got too dark for *sifà*, families usually gathered under their houses to eat and talk. Before long, musical instruments were brought out and the air began to fill with the sound of gongs, flutes, drums, and zithers of several sorts. People danced and human voices lifted in song. I loved the music of the Teduray, and they clearly did too.

One of the instruments that I particularly enjoyed was an eight-string zither, carved from a piece of large bamboo and often decorated with brightly colored bird feathers. When played by an expert, the bamboo zither made a sound similar to that of a harp.

One evening I was listening to my next-door neighbor, Ideng-Tong, play her zither, and I commented to Mo-Tong how lovely I found his wife's music. He said to me, "Mo-Lini, you should hear Ukà from Lange-Lange [a place several mountain crests away from Figel]. She is the best of all Teduray zither players. Perhaps she will come and play for you, and you can put that on your *radio*." He used the English word, but was referring to my tape recorder.

I said, "Just-right, cousin. I would love to hear her play."

I might have known when I made that reply that word would get to Ukà and she would come when she had a chance. About two weeks later, one of the Figel men told me he had been in Lange-Lange and that Ukà said she would come play for me.

Not long after that, the celebrated musician came to Figel, and we had a most memorable bamboo zither festival. Ukà stayed for ten days, every evening playing for a couple of hours to those of us gathered around the still-burning cookfire under the big house. Ukà played several different kinds of pieces. Some were slow tunes of well-known love songs; others were fast, intricately repetitive traditional melodies. Some were her own compositions. Other people played their zithers or other instruments from time to time, and there was a bit of singing and dancing, but for the most part people knew that they were hearing the finest zither player of their day, and they urged her to play piece after piece. I made tape recordings and took some photographs, but mostly I just joined my companions in total enjoyment of her music.

One evening as Ukà was playing I asked the man next to me if she was married, because she had come to Figel accompanied by her brother, and her name didn't indicate any children. He replied, "Oh no, Mo-Lini, she can't be married. How could she have children? She is a *mentefuwaley libun.*"

I had never heard that term before, but it was perfectly clear Teduray and meant "one-who-became-a-woman." I said, "Oh, so she is really a man?"

"No," he said, "she is a genuine woman!" His word for "genuine" was *tentu,* which means "real" or "actual."

But if she were *really* a woman, what did it mean that she *became* a woman? I was confused. (Remember that this whole conversation was in Teduray and therefore was without pronouns like "he" or "she," "him" or "her.")

I asked my companion, "Well, then, when she was born was she a boy or a girl?"

When he replied, I detected a slight incredulity that I could be so dense concerning a perfectly clear situation. "She was born a boy, Mo-Lini. Don't you remember? I just said that she is one-who-became-a-woman!"

"So then, cousin"—I, the dense stranger in his world, forged bravely on—"she is *really* a man, just dressed like a woman!"

My friend's disbelief at my inability to see what was right before my eyes seemed to go up a notch, edging toward a puzzlement equal to my own. He said, "Can't you understand? She is *really* a woman! She is one-who-became-a-woman."

So I played my trump card, sure it would clear up all this silliness: "Well, does she have a penis?"

"Yes, of course she has a penis," he said. "She is one-who-became-a-woman."

Finally I stopped quizzing him. In my world what identifies a man as "really" a male and a woman as "really" a female are their genitals, but evidently this was not so for the Teduray. In the months following this revelation, I asked several people about this phenomenon. I learned that in their view of things, what made you *really* a certain gender was the social role you played: how you dressed, how you wore your hair, what you did all day, how you were addressed by people, what gender you thought of yourself as being. And as far as Teduray were concerned, you could be whichever one you pleased. I later met a man who had been born a girl but who had chosen to be male and had lived a long life as a man. Most boys grew up wanting to be men and most girls grew up wanting to be women, but if anyone didn't and wanted to switch, nobody cared a whit. He or she was not thought of as strange or eccentric and, except that marriage was considered inappropriate, was treated just like everyone else.

Seeing my interest and opacity with regard to these people who changed gender, someone asked me, "Mo-Lini, didn't you have ones-who-became-women and ones-who-became-men in America?"

"Well," I said, "we have women and men who wear the other's clothing, and we have men and men who would like to be the other gender."

"So, you see," he said, "it's just the same with you."

"No," I had to reply. "Many Americans give such people a bad time. They despise them and consider them bad people."

"Just because they want to be a different gender?" he asked, amazement on his face. And his next question still rings in my ears: "Why is that? Why are you people so cruel?"

This willingness to let people decide on their own gender took me completely by surprise. The whole notion that gender is a matter of social and cultural definition and not a biologically given fact began to be considered and discussed by feminist anthropologists in the mid-1970s, and today has become a commonplace within the discipline of anthropology as well as among feminist women and men. It is now clear that in every society being "male" or "female" is a question of who is understood to be what and for what reason—a piece of a given society's take on reality—rather than a straightforward question of anatomy. But I met Ukà almost a decade earlier and had never heard of such ideas. If I had, I would have been much less naive about gender.

Through persistent inquiry, however, I did come to some conclusions about gender in forest Teduray society. The reason the Teduray could casually and happily allow people to choose their own gender was that being a man carried no higher status than being a woman; men had no power to protect and defend.

When I first encountered this attitude on the occasion of Ukà's zither festival, it struck me as truly odd. But as I discussed

it with many people over the following months and thought an-
alytically about what they told me, the notion of freedom to
change genders began to seem quite logical. So many features of
Teduray life—their very positive attitude toward erotic pleasure, their concern for families as the context for economic via-
bility, their strong commitment to the bearing and raising of
children, the often-stated belief that people who chose to change
genders were excluded from and irrelevant to marriage *because
they were irrelevant to procreation,* and the total absence of gender
politics—provided a social and cultural climate in which anxious concern about gender role-switching had no need or reason
to exist.

I knew that in my culture, transvestites and transgendered people
were sometimes homosexual and sometimes not, but I was curious whether Teduray ones-who-became-women and ones-who-
became-men might be gay. Ukà had a family because she was
part of her brother's pot. But did her choice of gender mean that
she was cut off from physical love? I tried to ask about that
too, but with less success. I concluded, though, that since they
were considered irrelevant to the conception of children and
thus didn't marry, and since persons who changed gender surely
would not be denied love partners, ones-who-became-a-woman
like Ukà probably had sex with men.

I made several attempts in different ways to get at the matter
of sexuality, and in every case I was met with a complete lack of
interest in the issue. I thought that perhaps I didn't know how to
ask the question, but I eventually discovered, when Mer and I
were doing concentrated and systematic work on the dictionary,
that the Teduray language simply had no terms for homosexual,
heterosexual, or bisexual. They knew such categories existed in

other Philippine languages but, as with the distinction of spouses or siblings by gender, had apparently never thought them useful or necessary for their own culture.

I didn't think to study homoerotic behavior in Figel; like gender, it was not something I had been sensitized to in my training. I never learned—never asked very clearly or directly—whether women had sexual relations with women, or men with men. I think they did, and I would be willing to bet that people considered erotic pleasure between persons of the same sex as fully acceptable.

10 ⚘ Cebu Interlude

My family and I spent Christmas of 1966 in Cebu City, a lovely spot in the Visayas, the central islands of the Philippine archipelago. Tree-lined streets and old Spanish colonial homes were everywhere, the dwellings of the Filipino urban rich and the largely Chinese middle class interspersed by the consulates of nations related diplomatically to the Philippines. There were a great many poorer homes too, of course, but they didn't seem to dominate as they did in Cotabato and Upi. Cebu had some interesting restaurants with good food, which provided a welcome change from Mariano's Chinese place where we always ate in Cotabato. It felt good to be in a "real city" again.

We had been invited to spend Christmas with some American friends, Frazier and Susie Meade and their children. Frazier was stationed in Cebu City as the American consul. I had met him while doing some special studies at the University of Michigan in Ann Arbor, preparing for my Teduray research. A career diplomat with experience in several other countries, he was sent to Ann Arbor by the State Department to get some orientation to Philippine history and government. We met at the home of David Steinberg, a fine historian who had specialized in Philippine-American relations during World War II, with whom we were both doing independent studies.

The Meades lived in a lovely, modern, air-conditioned house on a small hill in an elegant section of the city. Audrey and I were given a spacious bedroom with a private bath, and the boys were settled into a smaller bedroom next to ours. The cook made delicious meals and snacks, including many dishes whose ingredients and preparation went far beyond anything we could concoct on our woodstove or from the resources of the weekly market in Mirab. There was a garden behind the house, overlooking Cebu City and the harbor, and an expanse of lush green lawn where we played croquet each evening before the cocktail hour. The whole scene was a striking change from the Mirab Hilton, and yet very different from America as well.

What I enjoyed most about the four days we spent with the Meades, however, was not the comforts but the conversation. In their early forties, both Susie and Frazier were sophisticated and articulate people who had traveled widely and had come away from each new place with perceptive observations. They had interesting insights into Filipino politics and daily life in the cities, neither of which I knew much about. Frazier spoke with enthusiasm about American policy and trade and, when I raised the topic, with a somewhat defensive but dogged loyalty about our role in the war then raging in Vietnam. Susie and Audrey compared notes on helpers, markets, and raising children in a foreign land. Audrey was intrigued by the formality that obtained with the white-uniformed cook and housegirl of this house, while the Meades found fascinating the way we treated Armenia and Fernando in Mirab as virtually part of our family. Will and Len immediately made friends with the Meade children, a girl several years older than Len and a boy about Will's age, and we seldom saw any of the children except for meals and at bedtime.

On Christmas Eve we sang carols around an upright piano and admired the presents stacked beneath the Christmas tree, a real pine tree, decorated with tinsel and ornaments no different than we would have had in the States. Beneath the tree, in the midst of all those gifts, was a miniature village, complete with a train and station and several streets of houses lit by tiny street-lights. Since we were accustomed to life without electricity, the twinkling lights on the tree and in the toy village were particularly magical and nostalgic for Audrey and me.

The Meades were Episcopalians, and Susie and Frazier knew that I was a priest. Since there was no Episcopal church in Cebu, they asked me if I would celebrate a simple home Christmas Eve Eucharist for our two families. The request took me by surprise; I had not thought of myself in those terms for some time. In recent years, in fact, I had developed considerable confusion about the whole issue of Christianity and my priesthood. It would probably have been best if I had just taken a long sabbatical from the Church until I sorted my thoughts out, but for needed income during graduate school I had worked part time at a suburban parish, saying one of the daily masses and working with the youth. It had seemed somewhat dishonest and uncomfortable, and I was greatly relieved to be away from it all in Figel. Taking an explicitly sacerdotal role at that moment didn't feel right to me at all. So, without much explanation—I hardly knew what to say—I begged off. I know the Meades were disappointed and perplexed by my refusal, but they said no more about it.

The following morning, when everyone was up, we opened our presents. It was, in a way, a bittersweet moment. The Meade kids had piles of gifts, purchased at the U.S. military commissary or received from their American grandparents through the diplomatic pouch. Audrey and I, and especially Len and Will, watched in wonder as the trucks and the dolls, the games and the sports gear, were unwrapped and displayed by the children and as the adults opened their boxes of fine sweaters and other store-bought delights. We Schlegels had nothing of the sort to give the boys or each other. Aliman had made little bamboo whistles for each boy, and we gave them each a T-shirt from the market in Cotabato. Audrey and I had decided that our trip to Cebu—a considerable expense on our spartan fellowship budget—would be our gift to each other; all we had to put under the tree were two homemade cards we had written to each other.

It was not an easy situation for either family, but it was a memorable one. On a recent visit to Will and his family in Kansas City I saw that he still had that whistle. Perhaps in its own rustic way, having been made just for him by a dear friend and companion, the little bamboo noisemaker meant more to him that Christmas in Cebu than any shiny truck or Monopoly game from F.A.O. Schwarz could have. I don't know. I only remember the huge disparity in gifts at the time.

Christmas Day we had a festive and hearty meal, this time replete with two excellent wines from the commissary.

We planned to go home the following day. Christmas evening, Audrey and I went for a long, quiet walk through the Meades' neighborhood and into central Cebu. Predominantly Roman Catholic, the people had decorated their homes and stores with Christmas lights and especially with those little tissue-paper-and-bamboo lanterns that are such a part of the holidays in the Christian Philippines and that we knew so well from missionary days in Upi. The evening was balmy and much cooler than the day had been, so we walked, hand in hand, for over an hour.

As we strolled along, I spoke to Audrey about some of the things I was seeing in Figel and especially the remarkable story of Ukà of Lange-Lange, the one-who-became-a-woman. Like me when I was learning about the Teduray option of choosing one's gender, Audrey found the story both strange and compelling. "But it really is our bodies that tell us which sex we are!" she said, and I tried to explain the whole business of different "realities," different ways of carving up the world into meaningful chunks and naming them.

We talked about how different it was for us growing up, and how we had been taught by our family and peers to fear and despise people who were different, who were "queer." I recalled how I grew up amid tremendous concern about "fags"—an ugly word that described something I certainly didn't want to be, long before I had any idea what it meant!—with transvestitism even further beyond imagining.

I don't know that my wife and I had ever discussed these topics before at any length. She told me about her "discovery" that a friend was lesbian and the tangled feelings the revelation had brought up for her. I described to Audrey how one of my uncles in Pittsburgh, who I eventually realized was gay, had been obliquely referred to as "a bit strange." I told her about meeting the first men I knew to be homosexual in 1951 when I was about nineteen years old and in the navy, my ship stationed in San Francisco. I went to an Episcopal parish in the city for almost a year before I learned it was what we would call today a "gay church." Somehow I hadn't noticed that the men were all with other men, that there weren't many women, and that there was no Sunday school for kids.

Audrey found it hard to believe that it took me nearly a year to realize the parish was mostly gay, but I urged her to remember the times. Homosexual people were being very discreet. And I was just a naive teenager!

Every Sunday a group of us would go to Mass, then to one of the cafés in North Beach, where we'd talk all afternoon. I made some lifelong friends at that church, men who taught me many of my most cherished values about society and politics. I think they were among the first other men I ever connected with as true friends.

My church friends all knew I was straight long before I knew they were gay, and they liked me for who I was. One day, though, a visiting air force officer took me aside and propositioned me. He told me he could hardly believe I wasn't gay, since every single person I hung out with was! That was when I finally got the picture. It made me afraid at first, but I had made some powerful friendships by then, and I kept them.

Audrey asked me if I thought we Americans would ever learn to accept other forms of sexuality the way the Teduray do. Would we ever stop being so cruel to gay people? Could we, too, just live and let live? I told her I had no idea: our patterned way of seeing the world goes down so deep. But I now knew it was possible. I had seen it in the rainforest.

What I saw among the Teduray was no illusion. It was a society that had existed for untold centuries with just such freedoms, profoundly at peace with itself and with the world outside.

11 🌿 Justice without Domination

About a three-hour hike through the forest from Figel—not really far as the Teduray reckon distances—was a settlement called Keroon Uwa. This was the home of Mo-Sinew, a well-known legal specialist. Four months into my first year in the forest I accompanied a large group of Figel people, including Balaud and several other Figel legal specialists, to Keroon Uwa for an overnight stay. The people there expected us; there were to be several judicial discussions—what the Teduray called *tiyawan,* which I translate as "sessions."

We hiked at a relaxed pace, with singing and much laughing. I had no inkling at the time that a complex story was taking shape elsewhere that would bring Balaud and Mo-Sinew, and many others, into extremely serious legal discussions.

At Keroon Uwa, while many of the local people busied themselves with cooking, fetching wood and water, child care, and chatting, others from both communities joined the legal sages who had gathered in the house of Mo-Sinew. I had not met Mo-Sinew, though I had often heard his name; he struck me as a rather tired man of perhaps sixty. About five foot six—average size for a Teduray male—he wore the traditional pajama-like clothes and sported a brilliant purple bandanna around his head. When Mo-Sinew spoke, his voice was like gravel and carried a weariness that was reflected in his face. He emanated little of the fire or wit characteristic of Balaud and many other legal specialists I had seen.

The sessions themselves were to begin the following morning, but the legal sages talked late into the night about old cases, about illustrious and well-remembered legal specialists of old, about troublesome Maguindanaon outlaws from outside the forest, about the ways of the homesteaders in the Upi Valley area, about pending issues to be discussed the next day, and — of course — about me, the young American who had taken up living in Figel. I was hard to miss — I was whiter, taller, and incredibly awkward whenever I sat on a bamboo floor surrounded by folks who had learned as children to sit gracefully.

During the course of the evening Balaud spoke at length about a situation that concerned one of his brother's grandsons, a rather hot-headed young man from Figel neighborhood named Mo-Ning. He was not with us in Keroon Uwa, but Balaud was concerned about Mo-Ning's fears that his wife, Ideng-Nogon, might be sexually involved with Mo-Sinew's oldest son, Sinew. She had run off with him a year or so before, but soon regretted her act and returned to her children and husband.

"Ever since," Balaud said, in a soft and indirect manner, "Mo-Ning has been suspicious of Sinew. I'm afraid that he has good cause to feel that way. We all know that bad food can upset the strongest stomach. I am quite worried that if the situation continues, Mo-Ning's gut may hurt him and affect his gall bladder." Then, speaking straight and with feeling, he said: "My grandson's gall bladder could turn against Sinew and Ideng-Nogon. This could be very dangerous, because Mo-Ning can be a very explosive young man."

Mo-Sinew apparently knew of the possible affair between

his son and Mo-Ning's wife. He sat back when Balaud finished speaking and began to prepare betel. After a moment's silence he said firmly, "You are right; it must be stopped. It is very bad." The talk then turned to other matters.

Early the next morning, the legal sessions we had come to Keroon Uwa for were easily settled. In a happy mood, we left for home an hour or so after midday. Balaud's and Mo-Sinew's concerns about Mo-Ning and Ideng-Nogon seemed very remote.

The elders were right to be worried, however. Just three months later, in the middle of October, Ideng-Nogon left her husband and eloped with Sinew for the second time, taking her youngest child with her.

She and Mo-Ning had lived in a small house just across the Dakel Teran from Figel, about two hundred yards upstream, in a settlement called Birà. I knew him slightly, but had never spoken at any length with Ideng-Nogon. The women and men of Figel regarded her as a good mother as well as a great beauty.

Aliman and I were away from Figel the night the elopement was discovered. When I arrived back a few days later, Mer told us that people were upset and worried. Mo-Ning had gone directly to Balaud as soon as he discovered that his wife had run off with Sinew. Mo-Ning was something of a hothead under the best of circumstances, and everyone who knew him went to great lengths to respect and protect his gall bladder. That gall bladder was certainly bad now: Mo-Ning was furious. Balaud talked to him calmly, as he had almost constantly since the elopement. He persuaded him to eat something and to bring his bedding and his two remaining children to the big house, where he could calm down. Balaud assured Mo-Ning that his angry gall bladder would be well taken care of and that he would get everything that was coming to him. All the exchange goods that made up the security settlement would be returned to his kindred, and Sinew's kin would have to pay an appropriate fine.

Mo-Ning ranted nonstop for several days, going around from house to house in Figel, fussing and shouting about his bad gall bladder for Ideng-Nogon and her lover, and even occasionally picking up a spear and emphatically thrusting it into the ground. He spoke of the fierce revenge that he and his brother would surely visit upon the eloped couple's kindreds if his bad gall bladder were not well cared for by Balaud and the other legal specialists. Everyone empathized with his anger and desire for vengeance, even bloodshed, but they urged him not to do anything violent, which would be "no way to live." To the satisfaction of all, Mo-Ning, though agitated, stayed in Figel and did not attempt to pursue the couple.

By the third day Balaud had calmed Mo-Ning enough to begin the legal work, so he sent a message to Mo-Sinew urging that a session be scheduled so that the matter of Mo-Sinew's wayward son could be settled without delay. He also sent messengers to Terefunon, beyond Keroon Uwa, to find Mo-Nanah, Ideng-Nogon's father and a legal specialist himself, and call him to a session that would arrange the return of the security settlement given at his daughter's wedding. Balaud's two messages spoke sternly of his own anger at what had happened to his kinsman, as well as of Mo-Ning's rage at the insult he had suffered. Balaud also made known that Mo-Ning had trusted his gall bladder to his care and was not seeking blood vengeance. Both Mo-Sinew and Mo-Nanah sent word back that they would come to Figel for the sessions as soon as possible.

Mo-Ning returned to his home in Birà after eight days with Balaud in the big house, considerably calmed down.

Even though he was no longer present, his situation was the main topic of discussion among the Figel people and those who stopped for a rest when passing by on the forest trail. Late into the night, Balaud and others talked and shouted, alternating stories of how such an affair can lead to ruthless revenge with comments on the virtue of restraint, the foolishness of Sinew and Ideng-Nogon, and the absolute necessity of getting every bit of their security settlement back "home" to Mo-Ning's kindred along with a substantial fine. Most of the talking was done by Mo-Ning's kinfolk. People unrelated to Mo-Ning mostly listened, nodded in agreement from time to time, and asked an occasional question. Eventually, legal specialists from other places could be expected to join in the sessions and help seek a just outcome.

Mo-Ning stormed back to Figel in a rage the morning after he had gone home to Birà. When would his legal session be settled? If he didn't see his security settlement come home to his kindred soon, he would surely kill someone. As he strode around the yard in front of the big house yelling, his relatives and others gathered about him, softly urging him to calm himself. Balaud came down to the yard and cajoled Mo-Ning to trust him: "When you think we are not interested in fixing your gall bladder, that's the time to go killing people. Not now. Not as long as you trust us. You watch how we are doing this for you." Mo-Ning quieted down a bit and was again persuaded to stay in the Figel big house until his case was settled.

That evening a large group of Figel men and women gathered in the big house for a long and serious discussion of the situation. Balaud began with a lengthy lecture to Mo-Ning, advising him not to travel around the forest but to stay close to the house, so that he would not be blamed should any misfortune occur to relatives of Sinew or Ideng-Nogon. He could not carry any weapons or even tools that could be construed as weapons.

Above all, he should be patient and wait, trusting the various justice-givers who would be working to set things aright. The old man stressed that what they wanted was to get everything settled justly and to get the kindred's exchange goods back before anyone was hurt or killed. He recalled that Mo-Ning's grandfather, himself a legal specialist, had once been unable to contain his rage and had killed someone before a session could be settled. "That," he said, "was not the right way."

Then they discussed the various coming sessions, of which there would have to be four. In addition to the ones settling Mo-Ning's kindred's hurt and anger toward the kindreds of the two elopers, a session would have to take place to create the new marriage between Ideng-Nogon and Sinew and to establish a new settlement to secure that union. Finally, the fact that Ideng-Nogon and Sinew had grieved each other's kindreds by putting them at risk of possible blood vengeance would have to be adjudicated. These latter two legal sessions would not involve Figel people or Mo-Ning's kin.

A few more days passed, and Mo-Ning hiked half an hour downriver to the house of his mother and stepfather, both of whom happened to be important legal specialists. He said it had been almost two weeks since the elopement and that his gall bladder could not tolerate waiting any longer for justice. He would get his homemade shotgun, and he and his brother would "fix" the matter themselves. His threat had the effect he doubtless desired: his stepfather, whose name was Mo-Anggul, and his mother, Ideng-Amig, urged patience in the most serious terms, then hurried to Figel to confer with Balaud. Mo-Ning went too, as did some other neighbors—about twenty people in all.

Ideng-Amig was respected without qualification as a major legal sage, one who could be trusted and who knew how to speak with grace in the roundabout rhetoric of sessions. Her husband, however, was another story. Close to eighty years old, white-haired, foxy, and strong, Mo-Anggul was a man whose actions often belied the gentle look on his face when it was in repose. In 1927 he had lost his temper during a legal session and speared a man, for which the American colonial authorities put him in prison for several years. His reputation as a legal specialist was a curious mixture of admiration and contempt. On the one hand, his skill in oratory was known throughout the Dakel Teran area, and everybody agreed that he was an important legal sage. On the other, most also agreed that he was untruthful and self-seeking.

One of the principal features of the forest Teduray legal system was that legal specialists did not compete during a session to "win" for "their side." They all worked together to find the just outcome, to determine who truly had "the fault" and who had "the right." Although legal specialists represented their kin and stood ready to "accept the fault" when their kinsperson had done wrong, the proceedings were thoroughly cooperative and in no way adversarial.

Mo-Anggul, however, was known behind his back as a "cheater," one who seemed to contend for his own kinsman and not for the actual truth of the situation. More than that, he was considered a "liar": one who would make promises or agreements just to conclude a session, then not abide by them. People therefore seldom entrusted their gall bladders solely to Mo-Anggul, and other legal specialists would generally not agree to discuss matters in sessions with him unless he had companions to share responsibility for his side. Mo-Anggul was somewhat prickly about all this, so some people tried to avoid him in sessions, giving the most elaborate and carefully euphemistic reasons for not showing up. For these reasons alone, it was not surprising that Mo-Ning went first to Balaud for help and not to his stepfather.

The talk in Balaud's house was once again long and heated.

Mo-Anggul, offended that Mo-Ning had not approached him first, was bristling. "Mo-Ning now says that he will call his brother and they will settle this matter themselves." As if Mo-Ning was not in the room, he continued: "Do those two feel their elders are not doing anything? Don't they have any respect for Balaud and me? For his own mother? Can we elder legal specialists not talk well? Can he not trust us?"

At this point Ideng-Amig addressed her son directly. In a strong voice and with a tone of authority, she echoed her husband's concerns about Mo-Ning's open threats: "You keep talking such foolishness. If you and your brother cannot be stopped from revenge killing, even I can't help you!"

But Mo-Anggul was not finished blustering. "When Mo-Ning and Ideng-Nogon's security settlement was first arranged years ago," he said, "there were many disputes. I worked hard to ensure that there would be no bad feelings, even going so far as to confess an old, nonexistent fault in hospitality to Ideng-Nogon's father and giving an extra hunting spear to make it right." He looked around the room before continuing. "Now, after all that help, Mo-Ning should surely trust me with his gall bladder. Instead he talks about stabbing or shooting."

Ideng-Amig's approach was more direct. Looking deep into her son's eyes, she said, "It is not your security settlement but your kindred's. If you go stabbing anyone, you will not only put your elders in grave peril of counterrevenge, but you will cause them to lose all rights to their exchange goods. If you go to the place of your in-laws to stab someone, you should not expect any further help. You must be patient and hold the anger in your gall bladder. Do not threaten vengeance."

Mo-Anggul, unable to contain himself, jumped to his feet, something he would never do in an actual session. I thought his own gall bladder must have been so badly hurt by Mo-Ning that, if the younger man hadn't been close kin, he would surely have demanded satisfaction in a session himself. "It was only this morning, thirteen days after the foolishness, that you came to me. You have no respect!" The hurt was clear in his voice. "If you do not respect me as your father, I will forget you as a son and give you no help at all with your session." He would have gone on, but Balaud gestured to claim the floor.

The revered elder spoke softly to Mo-Ning, looking him directly in the eyes the whole time. "My grandson, you have already been wronged by Ideng-Nogon and Sinew once before. You should not now be this bothered by what those perpetually foolish people have done. You should cool down and permit your elders to get their exchange goods back and to free you from Ideng-Nogon." Balaud glanced briefly at Mo-Anggul, then back at Mo-Ning. "Once your stepfather, Mo-Anggul, killed a man, you know, and the municipal judge sent him to the provincial prison. I don't want that to happen to you." Everyone present knew that the shouting was now over. The room was hushed as he went on. "Moreover, grandson, you are young. All you have in this is the woman. The security settlement belongs to your kindred, not to you. If you will just hold your gall bladder, then we will see that Mo-Nanah and his kin return the entire security settlement or, if that isn't possible, that they urge another of their women to marry you to justify keeping it. But, my grandson, that can only happen if our side is calm, not if we go stabbing." He looked intently at Mo-Ning.

Mo-Ning looked down for a moment, then said quietly, "I am cooler, and I want the session. I want our exchange goods back."

Mo-Ning was far more concerned with those goods than with the loss of a particular woman. Though I had seen this time and again, it always seemed strange; I know that, if it had been Audrey who eloped, I would have been hurt and furious with *her*. But anger about the security settlement was the normal response in Teduray society. Among them, a man's or woman's honor didn't rest on a spouse's continued loyalty, but on everything being just-right with regard to the security settlement that his kindred had given and her kindred held. Mo-Ning was much more outraged over what had been done *symbolically* to his family's standing than over how Ideng-Nogon had betrayed him personally.

All three judicial sages had worked hard to redirect Mo-Ning's anger away from revenge. The same concern was being played out among Sinew's kin in Keroon Uwa and among Ideng-Nogon's in Terefunon.

Early the next afternoon, messengers came from Ideng-Nogon's father, Mo-Nanah, saying that he was sorry for the delay in his coming to settle the session. He fully acknowledged his daughter's fault (her lover's equal culpability was not his issue) and said that he intended either to return the security settlement or to seek another unmarried kinswoman as wife for Mo-Ning.

Mo-Nanah and a group of people, mostly part of his daughter's kindred but including some unrelated legal specialists who came to join in the session, arrived just before noon on the following day.

I was curious to meet Mo-Nanah, who had been the subject of such lengthy discussion. He was thin and bony and dressed in ragged shorts and a T-shirt. Although he had an appropriately serious demeanor, he did not look particularly aged, but neither did he seem strong physically.

The session began at once. It was what Teduray called a "hot session," in that it concerned Mo-Ning's angry gall bladder. Mo-Nanah came into the big house and, without the traditional handshake of greeting, immediately sat down on the floor, five feet to the left of Balaud. Mo-Anggul, Ideng-Amig, several minor legal specialists from Figel, and a couple of others from a neighborhood farther up the Dakel Teran sat down in a rough circle about twelve feet in diameter. Also in the room, just out of the circle with their backs against a wall, sat a number of other interested Figel and Terefunon people. There were several minutes of silence while everyone prepared betel. Then, speaking quietly, Balaud noted in an indirect way that Mo-Nanah had been a long time in coming. "You may be hungry," he said, "it is very late in the day."

This roundabout, often allegorical manner of talking in legal encounters was called *binuwayà*. It enabled participants to speak openly of sensitive issues, matters that could hurt feelings if they were addressed head on, and some facility in it was required of anyone who sought to be a legal specialist. Skill in using such rhetoric with insight and wisdom separated the great sages from the lesser ones and was a source of pride and reputation.

Using the same indirect speech, Mo-Nanah quickly replied that he had been held up trying to collect the exchange goods he needed to "send home" during this session. His actual words were "I would have come at once but the way was terribly grassy. I don't know why the way had to be as grassy as it was. My people are slow to cut. I finally decided to disregard the high grass. I knew I had to proceed."

The session was not long or drawn-out. Ideng-Amig and Mo-Anggul both made speeches recounting, in metaphorical stories, the anger of Mo-Ning and the patience of Mo-Ning's kindred. The speeches were stern, without being hostile. In both of them, indirect reference was made to Mo-Nanah's having said that he was prepared to accept the fault of his daughter. Mo-Nanah listened solemnly, and when Mo-Anggul finished he spoke out straightforwardly, saying, "I accept my daughter's fault."

All the other adjudicators said, "Just-right."

A typical hot session like this could readily take many hours to reach the point where one or more of the legal specialists accepted that their kinsperson had the fault. Even then it would still not be over until the other justice-givers present agreed that fault and right had been truly and justly determined. This case was sufficiently clear-cut that fault was acknowledged within the first hour.

There was a moment of silence, then Mo-Nanah began, in direct Teduray speech, to ask the patience of everyone present. "Here is my plan," he said softly and with evident anguish. "I intend to go to Keroon Uwa and ask Mo-Sinew to help me. His people must soon give us a security settlement, so that Sinew and my daughter, Ideng-Nogon, will be properly married. I will ask him and Sinew's kindred to give the settlement to your kindred instead, with an amount of items fully equivalent to the one which you gave us when Mo-Ning married my daughter." He studied the other faces in the room, but they were all still without expression. "I will then consider that to be Sinew's security settlement for Ideng-Nogon."

There was a dramatic pause, broken only by the voice of Ideng-Amig, who said softly, almost in a whisper, "Just-right."

Mo-Nanah seemed to catch his breath. He looked solemnly

at all the women and men in the judicial circle, and continued: "We cannot wait any longer for me to gather the necessary exchange goods from my kindred. This is the second time my daughter and Sinew have been the cause of danger and shame to us, and furthermore, I am ill. If you agree with my plan, I will show my good faith by presenting Mo-Ning's kindred with a *fegefefiyo fedew* [an exchange item designated as 'something to make the gall bladder good']." In a soft but dignified voice Mo-Nanah asked, "May this settle our dispute with Mo-Ning and his kindred? If so, Ideng-Nogon and Sinew will become Sinew's kindred's responsibility alone." Then he placed his kris in the center of the circle as the *fegefefiyo fedew.*

The others conferred and agreed. Balaud spoke for the consensus when he said, "Yes, well-planted rice can only grow if granted sun and rain." And, as all the other legal sages present said, "Just-right," he handed the kris to Mo-Anggul and Ideng-Amig.

Balaud's point was clear. With evident concurrence of other legal specialists, he had acknowledged Mo-Nanah's acceptance of his daughter's responsibility for Mo-Ning's bad gall bladder, he had trusted Mo-Nanah's assurance that the security settlement would be returned ("would come home") from Mo-Sinew, and he had recognized the kris as sufficient to satisfy Mo-Ning's and his kindred's immediate need for public vindication. In using the metaphor that he did, of benevolent natural elements offering life to well-planted grain, he was enunciating the opinion of all the sages that, given the circumstances, Mo-Nanah and his people had done all in their power to make things right. There was little more discussion; the other specialists assented to that judgment and endorsed it as their own. When Mo-Nanah asked if the session were finished, Mo-Anggul answered for them all: "Finished."

Mo-Nanah was served food, but ate only a few bites before he left with his group for Mo-Sinew's community. As he left the big house he exchanged the traditional handclasp with everyone present.

The first of the sessions brought on by Ideng-Nogon and Sinew's elopement was finished. Peace was restored between Mo-Ning and Ideng-Nogon and between their kindreds. Mo-Ning and his people harbored no more grudge toward her or her kin. His hurt was vindicated and his gall bladder healed, at least toward his ex-wife and her family. In the days following, Mo-Ning and his relatives were calm as they awaited the coming of Mo-Sinew for his session a couple of weeks hence. In the evenings, the Figel people gathered regularly in the big house to talk, but during the day they attended to their usual tasks.

There were still harsh feelings toward Sinew's kindred. Mo-Ning's anger would not be calmed in that direction until there was a fruitful legal session with them as well.

It was only some ten days later that Mo-Sinew sent word to Figel that he would come for his session in four days. At about one o'clock in the afternoon on the promised day, he and a number of close relatives and other companions arrived in Figel from Keroon Uwa. He and the Figel sages had sent word to several other legal specialists, including several who were from neither of the two involved neighborhoods, and they too began to arrive for the discussions.

When Mo-Sinew and his party arrived at the big house, many people were already there. They silently took seats on the floor and listened as Balaud and Ideng-Amig advised the younger men to leave this matter to their elders, who were less likely to get riled up. When there was a break in the talk, Mo-Sinew rose, went to Balaud and the gathered adjudicators, and gave the traditional handshake with elaborate exaggeration. He asked, "May I still come to this place?"

The others nodded, and Ideng-Amig answered somberly, "This is the place for our session."

Mo-Sinew sat down and looked all around the room. The actual session would begin later, but there were important things to say immediately. "I have been long in coming for this session because I have had to search among Sinew's kindred for help with the exchange goods." This was said in ordinary, straight Teduray, but it was not just a casual comment. Although the session had not begun, the metaphorical rhetoric had. As Mo-Nanah had done, Mo-Sinew was indicating obliquely but clearly that he was prepared to accept Sinew's fault and settle the issue at this time.

Somewhat coolly, in contrast to Mo-Sinew's ingratiating manner, Balaud said, "We who are Mo-Ning's kin have not found the long delay easy but we hope that, at last, the matter is going to be settled nicely." He fixed his look for a long moment on Mo-Sinew's eyes. "Mo-Nanah is being helpful. He is even willing to accept your return of Mo-Ning's original exchange goods as being Sinew's new settlement to his people for Ideng-Nogon." Balaud paused and there was total silence in the room as he took some betel, chewed a moment, and then spit carefully between the slats of the floor. "We have been very patient," he went on, "in not even considering taking our complaint to the municipal authorities, even though Mo-Ning, like the rest of us, has been angry now for many weeks."

Mo-Sinew answered immediately. "We appreciate your patience and we are fully prepared to accept my son's fault and make everything right. You—Balaud and Ideng-Amig—may speak for Mo-Nanah in our session." I wondered if the omission of Mo-Anggul was just because he was not present, or another subtle indication of his disfavor as a man of justice.

Balaud said slowly and softly, his words distinct in spite of a mouth full of betel quid: "Mo-Nanah was very clear. You who are Sinew's kindred should be the ones to return Mo-Ning's security settlement."

At this point, the conversation became much lighter. Everyone present, feeling clear with regard to the situation, relaxed markedly and spoke in a jovial manner. The initial encounter between the major legal specialists of the two sides was now finished. Mo-Sinew and his companions got up and went to sit with their own group. One of them said to the Figel people, "What happens to us now is in your hands, whether we will be killed or not, for we have come to your place."

Balaud replied, "There will be no killing. Tomorrow, when Mo-Anggul is here, we will finish everything nicely."

The session over Sinew's fault toward Mo-Ning began at about seven the next morning. Mo-Anggul, who had arrived early and had been sitting quietly drinking coffee, abandoned his placid face and began a long, heated speech. He talked on the surface about a time when he encountered hostile spirits in the forest, but everyone recognized that his account was really about the trouble Mo-Ning had had from his marriage to Ideng-Nogon, the many delays endured in settling this elopement, and the patience that Mo-Ning's kindred had shown. When his story was finished, Mo-Anggul laid out a series of small pieces of reed, naming them one by one as the items in Mo-Ning's security settlement for his wife.

Mo-Sinew studied them intently for several moments, then

said in plain Teduray, "My son has the fault for Mo-Ning's bad gall bladder, and I accept that responsibility."

All of the adjudicators present, including those from Keroon Uwa, agreed that the fault was Sinew's. Of course, everyone knew that the fault was shared by Ideng-Nogon, but that issue had been settled. The only concern now was Sinew's disregard of Mo-Ning's gall bladder.

Mo-Sinew and his companions placed on the mat, one by one, eight items: three krises, four necklaces, and a homemade shotgun. Each piece was carefully studied by those in the circle around the mat. Several metaphorical speeches by others reiterated the chronology and facts of the case. One of Sinew's kindred affirmed that he would return every item that had been part of Mo-Ning's security settlement for Ideng-Nogon. He asked, however—now in straightforward words—for an extension of time; they could not give everything that day. Balaud and Ideng-Amig agreed with the delay and suggested a period of three weeks. The other adjudicators quietly said, "Just-right." It was then about 10 A.M.

Three weeks later to the day, Mo-Sinew and a group of companions including some other Keroon Uwa area judicial sages arrived in Figel. Balaud, Mo-Anggul, Ideng-Amig, and three specialists from other places were waiting for them, and they began the session without delay. For this final meeting, Mo-Ning was asked to be present to receive the official "peace offering." Mo-Sinew began the session by asking Mo-Ning to accept a kris from Sinew and a brass box from Ideng-Nogon as their peace offering. By custom, this was the last thing to be given in an elopement settlement. Mo-Sinew politely asked Mo-Ning to accept it right away, in order to put a symbolic end to the danger felt by the people of Keroon Uwa. The others in the circle all nodded, expressing consent. Mo-Ning said that his gall bladder was now just-right, since the rest of the settlement was going to "come home."

Mo-Sinew then gave several pieces of exchange goods, equivalent to about two-thirds of the remainder, and asked that the adjudicators allow him another month to raise the rest from Sinew's scattered kindred. Mo-Anggul protested vigorously in a long speech, arguing that his people had accepted the peace offering in advance of the remaining exchange goods out of kindness—to end the danger—and that Mo-Sinew should keep his commitment without further delay. One of Mo-Sinew's kinsmen offered to give three more items of exchange goods at once, and another legal specialist, who was unrelated to either Mo-Ning or Sinew, said, "I myself will give two pieces to help end all this trouble."

As several in the sages' circle affirmed, "Just-right," they put two krises, two spears, and a brass betel-quid box down on the mat.

Two weeks later, Mo-Sinew and one of his cousins came to Figel and delivered the rest of Mo-Ning's kin's security settlement as well as an additional item of exchange goods for each of Ideng-Nogon's two children, who had been left with Mo-Ning. These pieces were called *bunù* (literally, "to place on her lap") and were customary whenever a mother ran away from her children. The *bunù* signified that she did care for them and established her right to visit them in years to come. With this last short, formal session, the matter was finished.

Mo-Ning and Ideng-Nogon were now officially divorced, and Ideng-Nogon was free to marry her lover, Sinew. The two of them still had to deal with the fact that they had shamed their respective kindreds, who would rebuke them for their behavior. The couple would feel humiliated at what they had done to their relatives, and they would surely act carefully not to cause further offense in the days to come. But they did not have to fear any violence from Mo-Ning and his kindred, all of whom felt fully vindicated and whose gall bladders were once again just-right.

Moreover, Mo-Ning too was now free to remarry. He found a new wife not long after—through appropriate negotiation, not elopement.

Sinew and Ideng-Nogon were still together when I left the forest. In their new marriage, the two of them enjoyed the full support and encouragement of their society and all its institutions. Divorced partners seemed to feel little or no resentment toward each other once all the relevant sessions were settled. Ideng-Nogon would be welcomed to visit her children living with Mo-Ning and would do so with delight; Sinew would treat her children as his own. The youngsters would love and respect both parents and stepparents.

The Teduray legal system, which I have portrayed through the case of Ideng-Nogon's and Sinew's elopement, was not competitive and adversarial like that of the larger Philippine legal establishment or that of the United States. Although some of the legal sages represented kindred, their loyalty was not to personal interests but to the restoration of just, public order. Their goal was not for either side to "win" but to achieve a genuine settlement in which all fault was determined and accepted and all hurt gall bladders were vindicated and restored. Sessions went on, often at great length, until all those in the circle could agree on the proper analysis of events, the proper outcome, and the proper fines or penalties. Whether there was one legal specialist present or ten, the situation was never "one against many." And when the settlement was reached, it was invariably regarded as the joint achievement of all participating adjudicators, not a personal triumph or defeat for anyone. The skill of legal specialists was understood in terms of their capacity to achieve justice, not their ability to outwit or otherwise overcome others. Even to appear to tend toward such a goal was to invite the severe censure of being called, like Mo-Anggul, a "cheater."

Legal specialists clearly had "authority," even though they did not have the slightest capacity to enforce their decisions by use of coercive force. They could not have anyone ostracized, beaten, imprisoned, exiled, or executed. They merely agreed on what should happen: who should pay whom what fines in the form of exchange goods. And, in all but the most unusual of circumstances, it happened.

A common definition of "authority" in Western jurisprudence is "power plus legitimacy." A state has authority, the great jurists have said, because it has the power of its police and army and the legitimate right to use that power to coerce its citizens. But I believe the Teduray showed conclusively that legitimate authority does not always need to come out of the barrel of a gun. Nothing makes authority *necessarily* rest on coercive power. Authority can be given for whatever rationale people choose to do it, and the Teduray gave their legal sages the right to make authoritative decisions not because they controlled any force but because they were acknowledged to be experts at restoring justice and thus at preventing social disorder.

The forest Teduray saw violence as a completely natural human response to anger, and their moral and legal systems sought to prevent violence as one of the society's most profound goals. Teduray would fight only to prevent outsiders, such as the Maguindanaon, from taking them as slaves or stealing their goods. Balaud once told me that forest Teduray men wore a kris to symbolize that willingness to defend themselves. But among the Teduray themselves, violence was abhorred. It was "no way to live."

Nevertheless, angry people were potentially violent, capable of exploding into bloodshed and vengeance. So Mo-Ning's fury and the rage of his kindred over Ideng-Nogon's elopement with Sinew seemed perfectly understandable to everybody on all sides of the issue. Mo-Anggul was furious with Mo-Ning for not respecting him, but no one doubted for a moment that he would restrict his anger to shouting out advice. It was axiomatic to Teduray that between families lay an arena of potential danger and bloodshed, while among close kin there was relative safety. Parents gave moral advice or even a mild scolding to their children, but, "the world being as it is," no one would scold a "far person" and risk the consequences of making that person's gall bladder bad.

Other people in other lands may not understand human nature in just that way, but to the traditional Teduray, those propositions about human and social reality were simply true. They were "objective realities"; they were Teduray common sense. To flout them would not merely show bad taste or upbringing; it would suggest a degree of madness. Therefore, the process of settlement that Mo-Ning and his angry kindred went through was not just some arbitrary set of legal institutions that had evolved in the society. Rather, it followed brilliantly a path of what might be called "natural healing."

First, Mo-Ning and, to a somewhat lesser extent, his kindred registered the hurt that had been done to his gall bladder. When a Teduray's gall bladder was hurt by the actions of another person, she or he made no secret of it. Teduray were expected to get hot about having been caused that bad gall bladder. Nobody tried to shame Mo-Ning for his rage; no one ridiculed him, or told him he deserved what happened or that he was wrong to feel the way he did. His pain was respected. Healing has to start there, and for the Teduray it did.

Second, the anger was expected to erupt in loud screams of protest. Mo-Ning shouted and fussed and paced around in terrible agitation, reiterating over and over his pain and resentment, while threatening dire retaliation. This went on for days. There could have been no doubt in his mind that his distress had been heard. And although constant efforts were made to calm him down so that he would not resort to violence, nobody criticized his lengthy ranting; rather, his companions gave it serious respect. In innumerable ways, his elders and his community supported Mo-Ning and helped him release his anger fully, even as they were leading him to reevaluate how he should respond.

Third, Mo-Ning was offered a socially honored way to deal with his distress: by taking it to a session. His family and his community, represented primarily by several legal specialists, made his pain public and handled it with great seriousness. *Mo-Ning did not have to internalize his anger and then act it out in some form of antisocial mayhem.* Balaud and Mo-Anggul and Mo-Ning's mother, the legal sage Ideng-Amig, took up his cause with all the skill they possessed as masters of their justice-giving specialty, and so did the several adjudicators who were not related to him. They all affirmed his inherent goodness as a human being and the appropriateness of his pain as they reminded him that he had choices about his subsequent behavior.

And fourth, the series of legal sessions that resulted in the full return of his security settlement did something public and concrete to address the source of the hurt and put it in its proper place. The kindreds of Sinew and Ideng-Nogon, bearing corporate responsibility for the two lovers, were given a peaceful forum for admitting fault and for making restoration through the return of exchange goods, the symbolic marker of Teduray social relations. By the time the several sessions had run their course, the offense to Mo-Ning and his kindred was past history. They had been publicly vindicated and restored to a sense of peace; they had been given, once again, just-right gall bladders.

In this therapeutic process, Mo-Ning's case was typical of how the forest Teduray dealt with offenses. It was an elegant system. It was a healing system, and a gracious one. And it did all that it did without employing either coercive power or organized violence.

The Teduray that I knew in the rainforest put great emphasis on repairing bad gall bladders as quickly as possible without violence through the legal system, and they put even more stress on never giving anyone a bad gall bladder in the first place. People made mistakes, of course, and did not always live up to that moral code, so there was need for the skills of the legal specialists. But Teduray, whether relatives or not, usually tried diligently to respect each other and to give one another a hand. They put serious effort, both social and personal, into avoiding *all* violence. Children were taught from an early age to scan their social world for what they could do to encourage and assist all other people, and they were taught most certainly never to inflict physical or spiritual injury on anyone.

This commitment to mutual aid, support, and respect gave these people a quality that is almost impossible to describe, a sort of peace combined with a palpable graciousness. For much of the time I was doing my research I didn't fully assimilate the drastic contrasts between my own cultural heritage and what I was seeing in Figel. Such insights, and the transformation they inaugurated in me, came slowly. But they did come, and they came with strength.

I will never forget the kindness with which the Figel people characteristically treated me and each other. And I will never forget the way their world valued interpersonal gentility and abhorred violence of any sort. Every time I went back into the very different world outside the forest, and especially when I returned to daily existence in the United States, I could not help but be struck by the overpowering contrast.

12 🌿 Mirab Interlude IV

One morning in Mirab—on a visit "home" from the forest in early March 1967, my second year there—Hammy and I decided to drive to Cotabato City for a day "on the town." We banged and bucked our way down the rough Upi-Cotabato road for two and a half hours and arrived at the coastal town just in time for a good lunch at Mariano's. Afterward, Hammy and I did some shopping at the hardware store, then went to a movie. The theater was, as always, a refuge from the heat and humidity of midday.

The movie let out in late afternoon and we headed back to Mariano's for a snack. We were enjoying a cold San Miguel—another of the joys of a town with electricity—and had just been served a heaping platter of deep-fried prawns, when gunfire erupted outside the front window, not ten feet from our table.

We knew instinctively that the Maguindanaon must be at it again. The two principal political and dynastic factions, the "lower valley" people and the "upper valley" group, had been blood enemies for centuries, and both treated Cotabato City as neutral territory. Adjacent to the café was a stairway going up to a second-story room that was as near as Cotabato City came to a nightclub. Apparently a young upper-valley datu and his retinue of bodyguards and other retainers, all armed to the teeth, had been up there having an impromptu party. Mellowed by rum and beer, the whole gang had just poured down the stairs and onto the street, where they were completely surprised to find a young lower-valley datu and *his* gang of armed thugs getting out of jeeps in the same short block. Immediately, both sides crouched down behind the jeeps and opened fire; in seconds, a pitched battle took shape.

When the shooting began, Hammy and I hit the floor underneath our table, taking our beers with us, to wait things out and, as far as possible, to be out of the way of stray bullets. Hammy was much more used to this sort of thing, and seemed much more casual about it, than I! His Teduray heritage was from Awang, where fighting with and occasionally against the Maguindanaon had gone on for centuries. He always armed his Mirab tenants with rifles and had several times told me colorful stories of tense standoffs he had had with bandit gangs who ranged around the Upi Valley and who periodically came to see if they could rustle his water buffalo working animals. After the first minute or two, he cautiously reached up onto the table and got our prawns; a few seconds later, he reached up again and got the hot mustard. I relaxed a bit. I figured we might as well try to make the most of our situation.

The shooting was intense and lasted about five or six minutes. When it subsided, the wounded on both sides were taken to the provincial government hospital, where they were placed in separate, heavily guarded wards, and the Cotabato City police showed up and made some official inquiries. One police officer came into the restaurant and spoke to Hammy in Maguindanaon. I don't know what they said, but they laughed a lot and seemed to think the episode was just some more young datu silliness.

We had a few more beers and some fried rice and chicken,

then headed home to Mirab before dark. Hammy was always eager to hear about the forest people I was getting to know so well in Figel. With the recent violence fresh in our minds, I related to him the story of Mo-Ning and his eloping wife. It had been a year since I had witnessed those events, and telling the tale got us talking about some of the questions that had been preoccupying me.

Americans, Maguindanaon, Awang Teduray—and most of the world—seemed addicted to violence. At home in the United States, the newspapers and radio news programs provided daily examples. People fought wars and revolutions, held hostages, went on drunken and violent rampages, beat and murdered their spouses, and enjoyed watching aggressive and violent sports. And most people seemed to consider all that as inevitable. Myths that ran through our various religious traditions portrayed violence as a part of the very beginnings of the universe: in Judeo-Christian scriptures, Cain murdered Abel at the dawn of human life; in many ancient myths from Europe, humans were created out of the blood of a slain deity; the earliest gods of the Aryans, sweeping into Europe several centuries before the present era, were vicious gods of war; and on and on.

In so much of the world, societies pitted good violence against bad to protect themselves and their institutions. How often had I seen that scenario depicted in comic books and TV cartoons, in movies and novels, even in our criminal justice system and our foreign policy. "Is good violence done against bad people really the only way we have to understand and settle our problems?" I asked Hammy. "Or is it just a cultural myth that justifies the very killing and bloodshed it describes by calling it good?"

"I don't know," he said softly. "I've never seen anything but violence! Like those guys shooting it out this afternoon."

Hammy spoke at length about how, in his observation, there often seemed little to choose from between the police and the army on the one side and the "thugs" and "troublemakers" on the other. "In countries like the Philippines, where all of us have guns, who is to say what violence is good and bad? And is it so different in the States?"

We both knew that when Hammy went to bed that night, he would check the automatic pistol he kept beside his bed to be sure it was loaded and ready. We had no illusions about our world, the world outside the rainforest. But for a magic hour or two, bouncing along that bumpy road, we found ourselves wondering whether it really had to be that way. The forest Teduray said it did not, and they would have none of it. Their myths and stories told of a different sort of world, a world of abundance for all, lived in cooperation, without ranking to divide us, power to oppress us, or violence to do us harm. One of their great truths was that reliance on "good" violence—physical, psychological, emotional, even bureaucratic—was just no way to live.

I was not through with the topic of violence on this Mirab trip. I planned to go back to Figel in another day or two, but then Hammy came by our house and asked if I wanted to go with him to an Alangkat village an hour's hike west of Mirab. I had heard of the Alangkat a few times; all I knew was that they were a group of Teduray who many years before had launched some sort of armed rebellion that had been squelched by Captain Edwards. I told Hammy I would love to meet some Alangkat and sent word to Mer and Aliman that our return to the forest would be briefly postponed.

The walk to the Alangkat village was pleasant, and the people there greeted us warmly. They were tenants of the Edwardses and had known Hammy his entire life. The story they told me of the short, sad episode that took place three and a half decades before moved me profoundly.

In the early 1930s, the changes launched by the impact of American rule in the Upi Valley were well under way. The forest was being cut back relentlessly. Outsiders, who had a different understanding of reality—Christian and Muslim homesteaders, American missionaries, and colonial officials with radically new teachings—were flocking into the Teduray area. Novelty and change were everywhere; to many people the world must have seemed as though it were falling apart. In the midst of all this cultural confusion, there were some outside the forest who wanted to give up, not by joining the new way but, looking back to the example of Lagey Lengkuwos in the *Berinarew* epic, by escaping "beyond the sky."

The Alangkat movement began with a prison break on the northern island of Luzon. A Teduray man in the Philippine Army, named Maw, lost his temper and killed another soldier, so was sentenced to serve a long term in the stockade. He and two other prisoners managed to escape after a few months, and Maw made his way back to his home near Upi, where he set up camp on a remote mountain, Mt. Perez. A bit crazed from his experience and apparently feeling he had nothing to lose, he proclaimed that he was a shaman and was ready to lead the Teduray people beyond the eastern sky to the Region of the Great Spirit, just as Lagey Lengkuwos had done long ago. He claimed a special relationship to the Caretaker of Avengers spirit and took red as his special color: he always wore a crimson bandanna and tied a bright red cloth to his kris.

Maw called for all Teduray to come up to his camp atop Mt. Perez and prepare for permanent departure from the Place of Humans. They should come with their whole family, armed and ready to fight if anyone tried to stop them. Maw further told them that he had a Maguindanaon charm that, so long as they wore red and were defending him, would render his followers impervious to wounds; bullets, arrows, or krises would magically bounce off their bodies without breaking the skin. Eyewitnesses described how Maw truly seemed able to strike his arm with a sharp kris yet not be cut. (In retrospect, they guessed he knew some sleight-of-hand trick.) Memories varied regarding how many people joined Maw on the mountain, but all agreed that the number of families was substantial, perhaps a fifth or more of those in the Upi Valley at that time. Many were Awang families from farms along the Upi road and long acquainted with violence. Others were displaced forest people, willing in their desperation to take on the violence of their peasant neighbors in a last try to escape a world that had changed beyond recognition.

Captain Edwards, who was then both provincial governor and head of the local contingent of the Philippine Constabulary, soon became concerned. He heard reports of acute hunger and sickness on Mt. Perez, where the Alangkat families were not planting crops because they believed Maw when he said they would all be leaving "very soon" for the Region of the Great Spirit. Edwards tried to convince people not to join the Alangkat, and he repeatedly sent messages to Maw, urging him to disperse his followers and come down peacefully. He warned Maw that if he did not, he would have to face Philippine Constabulary troops, who would force his surrender.

Maw grew, if anything, more agitated and defiant. A follower who had been close to him told me that Maw was convinced the government would eventually forget all about him, but if he believed that, he certainly underestimated Captain Edwards. Moreover, Maw began sending groups of Alangkat men down from their encampment to seize food and other needed supplies. Again and again, he postponed the day when the group would start their cosmic journey to the East. Before long, Maw announced that the Great Spirit wanted him to marry some of the women in his following, and then, growing bolder yet, he started dispatching bands of men off the mountain to grab women, even some married women, and bring them to him. They killed several people on their sorties, and once hacked a man to death because he refused to return with them to Mt. Perez.

With these escalations, Captain Edwards felt he could wait no longer for a peaceful end to the matter. He led a large group of constabulary soldiers to Mt. Perez and up to the Alangkat camp. Lookouts warned Maw of their approach, and when Edwards and his men arrived at the outskirts of his clearing, they found all the Alangkat men in a large group, armed and waiting for them. At their head was their prophet, dressed in crimson traditional trousers and bare to the waist. He kept shouting in Teduray, which the captain could easily understand, "Shoot me! Shoot me! You can never kill me. Your bullets will slide off! Go ahead! Shoot me!"

Edwards called through a bullhorn, "Lay down your arms. Only those who have killed people will be punished. The rest of you will be free to return to your homes. Lay down your arms." He tried to calm them: "There is no reason to fight. We are your friends. We are the law."

Maw just waved his red-festooned kris in the air and screamed even louder, "Shoot me! Your bullets are useless!" The Alangkat men, in their red bandannas, waved their krises wildly in the air. Every few minutes Maw turned to them and assured them that they were totally invincible, protected by his charm from any wounds.

Several more times, Captain Edwards pleaded with the Alangkat, with all the authority he had built up as a military conqueror, colonial governor, builder of schools, founder of courts of law, representative of a foreign and almighty God, and even a fellow Teduray by marriage. "Lay down your arms," he repeated. "You cannot overcome our guns. We do not want to fire. We do not want to hurt you. Give up your resistance, and only those who have killed will face trial."

Maw screeched hysterically, over and over, "Shoot me! Shoot me!"

Captain Edwards turned to the soldier next to him, the outstanding sharpshooter among his troops, and quietly said, "Shoot him."

The marksman hit Maw in the center of his chest and killed him instantly. He fell to the ground. His followers lowered their krises. They stood and looked in disbelief at the body of the prophet they had believed to be invincible. With that, the Alangkat movement was over. The constabulary soldiers arrested all the men who were known to have killed and put them in chains. The company cook began making a hot meal for all the others and their families. That night, in the Alangkat encampment, Irving Edwards told those assembled that he would take care of them.

Meeting a few weeks later in Mirab with representatives from every Alangkat family, Captain Edwards formally gave them half of a large land area he had originally secured for himself by title to assure his family's economic future. He said he would arrange, as soon possible, to give each family title to enough land for a farm. His only condition was that they give up their Alangkat dreams, settle back into normal life, and once again live in peace. It was a considerable gift, especially since Captain Edwards had already donated almost all the rest of his originally appropriated land to the Upi Agricultural School. Irving Edwards kept for his family only the relatively modest area in Mirab, where Hammy thirty years later let my family build our little cottage.

The captain was beloved and held in awe by every person who had known him—except perhaps by his relatives back in Boston, who were never able to understand what he was doing, far away from home, with a native wife and family. I think the Teduray were the wiser judges. They recognized that this was a person with a great and good gall bladder, who had given them the very best he knew.

I never met Irving Edwards. He died in the mid-1950s, a decade after having been released from a Japanese prison camp and a few years before I arrived at the mission. He was at the time of his death a virtually penniless citizen of the Philippine Republic, the nation into which he had toiled with such dogged effort to incorporate the Teduray. I have little positive appreciation for his dream of "civilizing" the Teduray; but if anyone was going to represent the push of American manifest destiny in the Upi Valley (and I believe that someone would inevitably do so, given twentieth-century Philippine and U.S. history), I am glad it was Captain Edwards. He was, quite clearly, an extraordinary human being, whose vision was marked by compassion and integrity. Unlike many Spanish before and Americans since, Irving Edwards did not come to the Philippines to get worldly goods; he came to give what he truly believed was a better world.

A day or two later I bade good-bye to Audrey and the boys and was on my way back to Figel. I planned to ask if any of the older folks there remembered the Alangkat movement, to gather recollections. But I knew already how they would answer the questions I was pondering: "Mo-Lini, all violence is bad. It is no way to live."

13 ❉ Shamans and Sacred Meals

For a long time after I settled into Figel, I left the subject of spirits and the spirit world strictly alone. I knew there had been some concern about my intentions—a few people were aware that I had once been "Father Schlegel" at the mission in Upi—and I didn't want to stir up fears that I was in the forest to convert anyone. I therefore concentrated my research on the Teduray legal system, economic system, and language.

I had learned a few words for spirits—I was aware that a whole host of terms somehow referred to them—but I hadn't a glimmer of what those words really meant. As time passed and I got deeper and deeper into the Teduray world, my avoidance of the work of the shamans became increasingly frustrating. There was a whole realm of significant thought and action about which I knew little.

I did learn about the healing work of shamans.

Not long after my arrival in Figel, Mo-Bintang, one of the two shamans in the larger Figel community, was called to the house of Mo-Tong, who was suffering from a long-lasting and terrible headache. The house was near mine, and Ideng-Tong invited me to observe the shaman at work.

Five people played gongs around Mo-Tong's house. Mo-Bintang approached Mo-Tong, who was lying on a sleeping mat with cool, damp leaves on his head. The two men discussed how long the pain had gone on, and Mo-Tong described his headache vividly, pointing to the base of his skull.

"Aha!" the shaman said. "It is no surprise! You have a stone in your neck!"

He began slowly and deeply to massage Mo-Tong's neck, soon concentrating on a particular spot from which he withdrew a moist, glistening pebble about the size of a hazelnut. Both Mo-Bintang and Mo-Tong knew perfectly well that removing the stone would bring only temporary symptomatic relief. The shaman would still have to deal with an angered spirit.

I watched the whole operation with fascination and with all the commitment I could muster to keeping an open mind. Mo-Tong recovered, and I tucked the incident away in my notes and memory until about eighteen months later. By then I had seen other objects removed from people's bodies, and I was more capable of asking the right sort of questions about the shaman's healing techniques. One day, I politely asked Mo-Bintang about the stone in Mo-Tong's neck. "Taking out stones is common among healers, nephew; it is a trick," he told me. "I had the stone in my mouth, concealed in my betel chew, and I pretended to pull it out of Mo-Tong's neck. He was fooled and it helped him get well. But of course, I also had a session with the spirit that he had angered."

Clearly, Mo-Bintang was adept at misdirection and sleight-of-hand. But he had not just performed some parlor trick in order to hoodwink his client or to puff up his reputation. As we talked about this deception, I realized that Mo-Bintang saw "taking out" stones and other foreign objects as a useful but ancillary technique in the healing process, a sort of placebo. The *crucial* healing work for Mo-Tong had to take place in spirit realms that only Mo-Bintang and other shamans could see.

Shamans—some were women and some men—lived in every forest Teduray neighborhood. Mo-Sew and Mo-Bintang were the two most prominent spiritual interlocutors in Figel. Their defining characteristic was that they could see and talk to spirits in their sleep, during what we would call dreams. Teduray had no concept of "dreaming," no sense that they were in a different consciousness while asleep. During sleep, their souls simply left their body and traveled about. It happened to everyone, although typically one retained only the slightest memories of such nocturnal journeys upon awakening. Most people couldn't see or talk to spirits while they were asleep any more than they could when awake. Those who had been given the gift to do so became the shamans.

Mo-Bintang, who lived in the nearby settlement of Erab, told me once about how he came to know he was a shaman. When still a small boy, he realized that when his soul went out at night he met different kinds of people that he never saw any other time and that most other people never met face to face. "I was frightened at first," he said, "but soon it became natural for me to play with spirit children and to talk and listen to the wisdom of spirit adults." As he grew older, he was sometimes accompanied by other, more experienced shamans on his nighttime excursions, and he told me, "I learned by watching them at night and by discussing with them by day."

The general term for spirits was *meginalew*, "people you cannot see," but in fact Mo-Bintang and his fellow shamans could see them: they were in no way mere wispy phantoms. Spirits were made of flesh and blood, in most respects just like humans. They came in many sizes, colors, and distinctive dress, and I knew I would never be able to sort them all out.

For all the forest Teduray I knew, the existence of spirits was never questioned. They knew that shamans saw them regularly, and so spirits were "observable realities." Shamans consistently saw, interacted with, and talked about them and their doings, and those who were not shamans accepted their reports at face value. Spirits were not "supernatural"; they were "things of this world," like trees and rocks. The whole cosmos was a huge natural community (I was later to find out just how huge!), which formed the ground and context for all creatures' lives both before and after death, and in which humans were merely one part.

Shamans had two principal tasks. Their most frequent work was to restore harmony with the spirit world when some human had inadvertently antagonized a spirit. The general rule for spirits, at least the great majority of them, was that they were just like humans; they treated you respectfully and kindly if you treated them that way. But it was easy to harm them inadvertently because they couldn't be seen, and the spirits retaliated by making you ill. This was the main cause, as Teduray understood it, of sickness.

When people were sick, shamans would go in their sleep to find the offended spirits. Shamans negotiated, the way sages did in legal sessions, a fine or some reparation to restore the person to health. The system worked reciprocally: if the spirit was at fault, it had to make some reparation to the ill person as well. The various tribes of spirits had their own legal sages to adjudicate disputes among their own kind, and they had spirit shamans to hold sessions with humans. By virtue of their gift to see and speak with spirits, shamans were the principal Teduray healers.

Most shamans were also *muwà*, or "physicians"—specialists who healed through medicines and other techniques. Physicians had intimate knowledge of the great variety of herbs, barks, and other medicinal remedies found in the forest, and were skilled in such physical therapies as massage, setting bones, and applying heat. By their medicines, their healing hands, and even their placebos, physicians brought a great deal of comfort and relief to injured people. Some physicians were not shamans because they could not see spirits, and their ministrations were occasionally ineffective; shamans, however—for reasons I will return to in the next chapter—"always succeeded."

The second specialized task of shamans was to lead the community in the four sacred meals called *kanduli* that were observed each year, meals that punctuated important occasions in swidden cultivation. Everyone was clear that without the cooperation of the spirits the fields would yield no harvest, and so the spirits were honored and thanked in every ritual feast.

Three months after I arrived at Figel, I experienced my first *kanduli*.

"Mo-Lini, come take a picture!" For the third time that afternoon, Mo-Emét was calling me to bring my Polaroid camera for a snapshot of a family arriving from one of the other Figel settlements to celebrate the ritual. When I got to the big house with my camera, the family readied themselves for the picture as they imagined they should, by posing with stiff posture and an expressionless face—their "legal session face." They did not want to compromise their dignity by smiling. My snapshots of Figel people usually showed them looking uncharacteristically stiff, even grim. But their demeanor immediately changed to glee when the image appeared from the camera and I offered them a copy.

By evening, Figel was fairly bursting with anticipation of the ritual feast that would take place the next day. Since I had been in Figel for such a short time, and since this was my first *kandulì*, the meaning of much that I was to see was beyond my understanding; nevertheless, it was impossible not to get caught up in it. The ritual wouldn't actually begin until the morning, but there was much singing and a high feeling of expectation.

I was out with my camera and notepads at dawn, not wanting to miss anything. Mo-Bintang and the other Figel shamans were already up, giving directions to all the people who had come, so that when the ritual began around nine everything would be in order. Most of the folks from the outlying settlements had arrived the previous day and slept in the big house or, if they had one, in their own house.

Finally, amid much gong playing and posing for my camera, a great basket was brought by two young men and placed in the center of the yard. When the basket was in place, members of each family (we three researchers were considered part of Ideng- and Mo-Emét's family) lined up holding a small basket with rice saved from its ritual plot and mixed with special aromatic spices. Mo-Sew, the other principal Figel shaman, stood beside the basket, and as the rice was poured into it he mixed it thoroughly to blend the rice from each family. During this process, which took about twenty minutes, Mo-Bintang made a short speech, welcoming the spirits to participate.

"The world is for all of us, and we all help each other. Come join our celebration," he said, facing east. Then he turned to the north, west, and south with similar invitations, including all the cosmic community. When Mo-Bintang finished addressing the spirits, and the last family's rice was added, the two shamans and their wives refilled each family's small basket with some of the blended rice and covered the receptacles with banana leaves.

This first mixing done, the gong music started up again and everyone assembled for a noisy, somewhat ragged procession to the river. The baskets of rice were left there to soak until late afternoon. None of this—or anything else to come in the ritual—was done in a noticeably "reverent" way. People were playful and the day was more like a party than a typical Western religious event. The only time people grew solemn was when they noticed me taking a picture.

In the early afternoon, several men prepared a cooking rack—a long pole, held up by supports at each end, over a bed of firewood—while the rest of the men played an hour or so of *sifà*. Several women strummed melodies on their bamboo zithers, and Mo-Tong treated us all to a concert of the haunting music of the homemade flute, one of his specialties. Each family cooked a chicken and hard-boiled several eggs, which would be eaten as part of the next stage of the ritual. During the afternoon, some of the younger folks danced in the big yard to the sound of gongs. Adult men occasionally took women's parts in the dances, and women, men's parts.

By about five the fire under the rack had burned down to hot embers, and the gongs struck up a particular melody that told everyone it was time to march to the riverside and bring back the rice.

When we arrived at the river, Mo-Sew thanked the caretaker spirits for keeping the rice safe. As soon as we got back to the settlement, each family took its well-soaked rice from the basket and put it into two bamboo tubes, each about two and a half feet in length. Next they sealed the ends so the soaked rice wouldn't spill out. Then, as the gongs played a loud staccato refrain, families exchanged their tubes of rice, passing them back and forth, so that they ended up with different tubes than they had started out with. This whole procedure brought on great whoops of laughter and glee. Finally, the tubes were taken to the cooking rack and left to simmer for the next several hours.

By about nine the rice was cooked and the tubes had cooled down enough to be handled. Mo-Bintang, standing at the center of the group, took a little rice from one of his tubes and placed it on a six-inch square of banana leaf with a slice of egg and a small piece of chicken. Then, to the din of many gongs, he laid it in the splayed-out top of a bamboo pole, where it remained as an offering for the spirits—their share in the day's food.

"We are grateful," he said, facing east. "We could not have plenty in life without your assistance. You help us in our gardens and you share with us as food the plants and animals you care for. We are in this life to cooperate with each other. It is just-right for you to be with us now, and we honor you." Then, facing north: "The Great Spirit has created us to care for the forest, and the forest to give us all we need. Join us in our festival." Toward the west he said: "We have grown this food by working together. We welcome you as our companions in the world." Finally, facing south: "You are our brothers and sisters. With great respect, we give you some of our harvest to eat and some chicken and egg."

Everyone seemed to know that the spirits would not actually eat the little offering. The point was the presenting of it, not as a sacrifice but as the sharing of hospitality and the giving of formal thanks.

The tubes of cooked rice were passed among the families once again, before being cut into individual-sized segments of about eight inches each and placed in the houses. Until well past midnight, people continued singing, dancing, and playing their musical instruments while they snacked on fruit and other foods that weren't part of the ritual; some who had been to the market in the past few days shared little cakes and cookies.

At two in the morning the gongs were taken up one last time, and a special melody, reserved for this moment in the festival, announced its climax. Every family—some in their own houses, some staying in the big house—ate the specially cooked and often-exchanged rice, the chicken, and some egg.

Exhausted from my long day of watching, questioning, and note-taking, I went to bed. As I drifted off, I heard the sound of singing in the big house.

The *kandulì* was clearly not just a meal; it was a ritual performance, a periodically offered communal feast shot through with spiritual significance. Although there was no notion that the rice became, even symbolically, anything other than just rice, the *kandulì* nevertheless struck me as having much in common with the Mass, the ritual focus of my own religious tradition. Concerned with more than the tangible world of here and now, both observances proclaimed and grounded everyday lives in a larger context of meaning. Both focused on the community and not the individual, and were dramatic presentations of how the community understood reality, in its fundamental structure and in its most central values. Both involved offerings to, and a sense of participation in, the full cosmic and mythical reaches of that reality. As rituals, they celebrated what *should be* in the midst of what *is*.

But if in these regards the *kandulì* and the Mass were alike, the actual content and feel of the two rituals stood in striking contrast to one another because, of course, the cultural matrix of each was very different.

The *kandulì*, like a legal discussion or a game of *sifà*, took place in an atmosphere of radical equality, infused with the interdependence of all things and all beings. The Christian liturgy, like the Church itself, is saturated with divine and ecclesiastical hierarchies and differences in power. The *kandulì* reminded forest

Teduray of a very different universe of thought, of action, and of strategies for day-to-day living.

None of these characteristics was explicitly grasped by the Teduray. If I had asked people why they did this ritual four times each year in every neighborhood, I have no doubt they would have simply said something like "It's what we do. We work together, we play together, we do *kanduli* together. It is our way to live." And in a way, such a simple, unpretentious answer would be quite accurate. Earlier, I described the way neighbors worked on each other's gardens, how they could not have done most of the stages of the swidden cultivation cycle without the whole neighborhood pitching in. In the ritual exchanging of rice this interdependence was dramatically enacted. Every family knew they were eating some of the rice from every neighbor's garden on which they had worked, in company with the spirits who had also made their indispensable contribution. A *kanduli* ceremonially stated and modeled the Teduray's most basic social truth. It said—in music, word, and action—that all persons were partners in the achievement of an abundant life and that they were utterly dependent on one another.

Another *kanduli*-like ritual, done on a much smaller scale and often presided over by lay physicians as well as shamans, involved food offerings to a particular spirit as a means of paying "fines" for past offenses. These offerings, determined in legal sessions, made *fiyo* the offended spirit's gall bladder and brought about the patient's healing. And there were many other situational rituals, such as the little one of cutting the "first fruits" of rice or corn prior to the general harvesting of the crop. But what was true about *kanduli* was true about them all: they expressed, and helped shape, the fundamental Teduray understanding of the character of the world. The people of Figel knew that they would experience "the good life" only if they lived out, in all aspects of their existence, the sort of gracious cooperation epitomized by the way they together planted, cultivated, and harvested that rice.

I found myself sitting in my Figel house for hours on end thinking about the world as these people knew it and pondering—often with a heavy heart—what I had always taken as "normal." I walked silently along the forest trails, especially during the long hours trudging to and from Lebak on the coast, my mind darting in and out of my culture and Teduray culture.

At a fundamental place within me I felt the Teduray were right. No competition, no hierarchy, no coercive force, no violence—the core of Teduray wisdom, as I came to understand it in Figel—were becoming principles I desperately wanted to live myself. I didn't see myself spending the rest of my days in the forest or becoming someone other than who I was; but my spiritual convictions about how life should be lived—at home, in my own native setting—were unmistakably changing.

I have called the Teduray view of reality their "spirituality" many times. The term "spirituality" means several different things in our ordinary way of talking. For me, our spirituality is whatever path we choose to journey toward wholeness and meaningfulness. I also like to think of spirituality as our vision of what will make us whole and well. All people are on a spiritual quest, whether aware of it or not; to seek meaning in our lives is a part of being human. Anthropologists and linguists have often discovered that in traditional, relatively isolated societies there is no word for "spiritual" or "sacred"—all of life is inherently spiritual and all things sacred.

All of life was certainly spiritual for traditional Teduray. Their sense of the good and meaningful life was one lived out in radically egalitarian cooperation through maximally gracious interaction. This sense was so basic to all of their social life and thinking, and so deeply rooted in each of their personalities, that it required no term of its own. If I probed for a word like "cooperation," they would just give me back words like "work" or "live." If I asked for a way to say "religious" or "spiritual," they just looked at me in puzzlement. Or they gave me a Muslim word borrowed from the Maguindanaon people or a Christian word that had arrived with the missionaries. There was no native Teduray word with that meaning. They had a word for "spirit"—the world, after all, was full of spirits—and there were names for the different sorts of spirits. They knew a great deal about where spirits lived, how the various ones behaved, what they looked like, and whether they could be trusted. But all of that was so intimately a part of the entire texture of Teduray daily life that no separate word for the whole thing was required.

In fact, it is because all of Teduray life was "spiritual" that they had no ideas or activities that I feel could properly be called "religious." The term "religion," in my view, is best applied to traditions and institutions that have developed to protect and promote some particular historic version of spiritual understanding. Buddhism and Islam and Christianity are "religions" in this sense.

I suppose I could say that, by my characterization of religion, all of traditional Teduray life was a religion. But that would be a strange way to talk, because the religions of the world have generally emerged as separate social institutions, with their own terminology and systems of thought, their own particular and ordained leaders, their own rituals, and even their own distinctive buildings. They form—as we Westerners see things—the arena of the "sacred" in contrast to the rest of life, which is "profane" or "secular." Teduray who found themselves forced into peasant life soon realized that there were major differences outside the forest between what was considered "secular" and what was thought to be "sacred." But for the Teduray of Figel nothing was compartmentalized. Everything was saturated with spiritual significance: the forest and all that live in it, the plants in their swiddens, the fish in the river and the river itself, the mountains, their own bodies, and all of their physical and emotional being.

14 🌿 Mirab Interlude V

Our American medical institutions are not always as congenial as the Teduray ones. And rural Philippine hospitals—at least the two I knew in Cotabato City in those days, the government Provincial Hospital and Dominican Hospital, administered by Roman Catholic sisters—could be even less so.

This was certainly my sense when I had to take Aliman to Cotabato in an emergency during the second week of June. My team had been planning to go back to Mirab for a "home leave" in about ten days, but when Aliman's old wound from the logging truck accident began to seep rather badly and appeared infected, we left right away. Aliman was uncomfortable but able to walk the long trail to Lebak, where we engaged a fishing boat to run us up to Cotabato nonstop. We moored at the city dock at about four in the morning, rousted a jeep driver, and went directly to Dominican Hospital. By that time, Aliman was dead tired and in considerable pain.

The hospital had no emergency room, but a woman on duty at the desk assured us that a doctor would evaluate Aliman in the morning, and she sent us up to a ward in the charge of an orderly. We were both quite dirty, dressed in our grubby, travel-worn work clothes, and we must have looked every bit as exhausted as we felt. The orderly led Aliman to a narrow bunk in the largely empty ward, unrolled the thin uncovered mattress, and wished him well. Although it was a warm and humid night, I thought she might at least have offered him a sheet!

She then turned to me and said I should put my sleeping mat on the floor beside the bed. There was nothing unusual in that. Since rural Philippine hospitals at that time had no food service, a family member would just sleep on the floor beside the sick person's bunk and bring food purchased from a nearby café or cooked over communal fire pits behind the building. Still, the thought of ending that long, worried trip with a couple of hours on another hard floor seemed grim indeed.

Suddenly I had a bright, if desperate, idea and did something out of character. I set my pack down beside Aliman's bed—he was already stretched out—and said in a firm, commanding voice: "I am *Father* Stuart Schlegel, and I would like a bed!" As the startled orderly literally raced to the door, I added: "And a pillow!"

In what could not have been more than a few minutes, a sleepy nun burst through the door, followed by two equally sleepy but nervous-looking aides with sheets, a pillow, and even a thin blanket for each of us. The avowal "We are so sorry, Father; we didn't know!" echoed throughout the ward several times as a bunk was hastily made up. The nun and her helpers all curtsied and disappeared. I figured the fact that I was an Episcopal priest and not a Roman Catholic could wait until morning! Aliman and I had a good chuckle, and I slept soundly and with an untroubled conscience.

The following morning, after contacting a relative of Aliman who agreed to come and stay with him, I took the bus to Mirab. Aliman did indeed turn out to have an infection, but antibiotics had him well within a week, and he made his way back to Figel a couple of days ahead of me.

On arriving home, Audrey told me that Will had also been taken to Dominican Hospital three weeks before. Audrey and Armenia were at the Upi market one Saturday, she said, and he had stayed at the mission to play. While sucking on a piece of split bamboo, he had fallen off a large sack of rice, and the bamboo stick was rammed into the back of his throat, puncturing the soft tissue. At the clinic, Anne Dumo, the mission nurse, calmed him down and cleaned the wound, but she thought Will should have a tetanus booster. When Audrey arrived, she objected to Will's having the tetanus antitoxin vaccine that Anne routinely gave; it was made with horse serum and, as Anne Dumo well knew, had caused a violent allergic reaction in me several years earlier at the mission. I had broken out in a terrible rash and experienced mild anaphylactic shock before Anne, Audrey, and one of the convent sisters who was a nurse could get me through the emergency. Knowing that I had nearly died from the antitoxin, and that our boys might well have inherited my allergy, Audrey and I kept in our refrigerator several vials of tetanus toxoid, the newer kind of tetanus vaccine, which did not use horse serum. The problem was that Anne was not familiar with it and was afraid to go with something unknown to her. She finally sent Audrey and Will down to Cotabato in Hammy's truck.

At Dominican Hospital, the doctor on duty was also unfamiliar with our toxoid vaccine and refused to administer it, as did several other doctors then in the hospital. Finally, when Audrey was about to explode with impatience and worry, someone suggested a young *doctora* who was newly back from training in the United States. Audrey tracked her down at her town clinic and found that she had learned all about the toxoid variety and knew it was being used as the vaccine of choice for tetanus by the American forces in Vietnam. She gave Will the shot, and mother and son dragged back to Mirab, exhausted by stress and tension. Audrey and I were relieved but also disturbed at how backward our own system of medicine seemed, at least in the Philippine hinterland, when a crisis hit.

When I told Hammy and Mrs. Edwards about my chutzpah at Dominican when taking Aliman in and we ruefully recalled Audrey's experience there with Will, Hammy looked at us and said, "Well, that's the same hospital where I had my appendix taken out a couple of years ago, when you were in Chicago." His married sister Cora had taken him down and was in the waiting lounge when a nurse came and asked her to come into the surgery and give Hammy a cigarette. It seems that halfway through the appendectomy they had run out of anesthesia and thought perhaps a smoke might soothe the patient while they finished the operation!

During that week in Mirab I suggested to Audrey that she and the boys—and Hammy too, if he wished—might like to hike back to Figel with me this time. I had been there for well over a year and the community was used to me; I figured that by then a couple of towheaded boys and my wife would not be too disruptive, especially if they stayed only three or four days. Besides, I had spoken of them so often that many people in Figel neighborhood were as curious to see Ideng-Lini, Lini, and Wil as my family was to see them and their much-described place. We talked it over. I said that I could send Aliman ahead and he could come back with some men to help carry their bags and the boys when they got too tired. Audrey thought it was a great idea, and Len and Will shouted "Hooray!" at the decision to make the trip.

The Schlegel family visit to Figel went without a hitch. Hammy took us all down to Cotabato on his truck early in the morning. (Two of the Edwardses' farmworkers had gone the day before to hold places for us so we didn't have to sleep on the launch.) The launch trip bored the boys, but they fished off the side of the boat part of the way and slept much of the rest of the time. Priscilla and Carlos gave us a great welcome, and, as arranged, Aliman and four Figel men met us at the first river crossing the next morning. These men carried the backpacks—including mine this time, a lovely change—and although the hike took a bit longer, and Len and Will had to be carried much of the way as well as across the river each time, we arrived at Figel before it was fully dark.

Everyone met us and there was singing and dancing in the big house that night. For three days, the boys played and bathed in the river with the other children from Figel, and Audrey met all the adults from all the settlements of the neighborhood as they streamed in to see what Ideng-Lini and the little white children were like. The time passed quickly, and on the fourth day after their arrival my family bade Figel good-bye and started the journey home. This time Mer, who had missed the previous Mirab trip, was to accompany them, while I planned to stay and resume work. But in the end I couldn't let them go alone. I was having much too much fun, glad that both my worlds had met and for a short time the stark lines between them had blurred. So I went back to Mirab too.

Having reached Mirab, I made ready after just one night's rest to head back to Figel, and Len asked if he could go with me. I thought about it and decided it should work. Audrey agreed. She had found Figel gorgeous and the people friendly and helpful; she said she could well understand why Len was drawn to return.

So Len and I went back into the forest together.

The plan was for Aliman to escort him home in a week or two. But Len's stay in Figel was shorter than expected. It was at that time that he got so sick and had to be carried out along the raging, flooded Dakel Teran.

15 🌿 The People You Cannot See

One and a half years into my two-year stay in Figel I had learned a great deal about forest Teduray spirituality, and what I had learned had affected my own spirituality in profound ways. But an incongruity in my research had become increasingly clear to me. Teduray spirituality was situated in a world that was shot through with spirits, and I had learned almost nothing about them.

That small irony, however, was about to change.

One day, when the rainy season was fully upon us, I was sitting in my house working on field notes. One of the Figel shamans, Mo-Sew, came by and we chatted for a few moments about this and that. At one point, he said to me, "Mo-Lini, you never seem interested in the *felindagen*"—meaning "cosmos," "the universe," "everything that is"—"and you never speak to us about the spirits."

"Yes, uncle," I said, rather lamely. "I guess we are just busy with other things."

"Would you like me to teach you about them?"

For a split second I hesitated. Then a huge smile spread across my face, and I replied with the Teduray equivalent of "Wow, would I ever! When can we start?"

"How about right now?"

Mo-Sew and I went to his house, accompanied by Mer and Aliman, and for the next two weeks we gathered there for a major portion of each day. He first explained that the world is flat and goes on far beyond where the sky touches the ground. He described the sky as being like a bowl. Artfully placing corn kernels on his spread-out sleeping mat, Mo-Sew drew diagrams of the cosmos and patiently, systematically, introduced us to its many different paths and places (figure 1). Fortunately for me, Mo-Sew was a person whose mind was both reflective and orderly. I wonder how many other Teduray—shamans included—would have been able to draw such a clear map.

It wasn't long before several other people heard us talking and joined what was becoming a seminar on the nature of the cosmos. Sometimes they asked questions, sometimes they debated a spirit's name or some other fine point, sometimes they told stories from their own experience. As the days passed, I often felt that even these Teduray people, who knew that world intimately, were receiving new and deeper insights from Mo-Sew. The lessons I was learning were in a sense "the world according to Mo-Sew," because not everyone interpreted the details in the same way. These points of difference, however, didn't seem to bother anyone.

In the dim light of Mo-Sew's house, while I was receiving the second round of theological education in my lifetime, I sat leaning against the woven bamboo wall and watched with fascination as the shaman took a handful of corn kernels and traced the universe to the east from the "Realm of Humans" to the "Region of the Great Spirit." He eventually would set out the cosmos to the west, north, and south as well, but he began with the easterly realms because through them ran the age-old path that shamans took when they wanted to speak with the Great Spirit.

In Mo-Sew's kernel diagram (figure 2) were nine *bangel*, or "cosmic realms." Going from realm to realm was, to forest Teduray thinking, a matter of going from one kind of spirit to another, not from one world or level to another. In any given cosmic realm all the people had in common a certain amount of what the Teduray called *barakat*. This term has its origin in an Arabic word borrowed long ago from the neighboring Maguindanaon Muslims outside the forest. Its literal meaning in Arabic is "blessings" or "numinous properties," which are attached to certain sacred things and beings. The Teduray sense of the word *barakat* is difficult to translate into English; the closest I can come is "charisma" or even "spiritual wonderfulness." The Great Spirit, the creator, had the most, and every class of spirits in between the Great Spirit and humans had its own particular amount. For Figel Teduray, the notion of *barakat* did not include the idea of rank or power, though that was the way the word was used by Maguindanaon and by many acculturated peasant Teduray.

The circle to the far left in Mo-Sew's diagram represented the *inged keilawan*, or "Realm of Humans." It consisted of all the ordinary, mundane areas where the Teduray and other human beings lived their lives. When you were in Figel, or in the surrounding forest, or in Lebak along the coast, you were in the Realm of Humans.

Many of the spirits who inhabited this realm along with the humans were *segoyong* (caretakers) of various aspects of nature. Here lived the Caretakers of Fire, the Caretakers of Bamboo, the Caretakers of Rattan, the esteemed Spirit of Rice, and other spirits who guarded the welfare of various forest and domestic plants and animals. Another interesting group of spirits who lived in the Realm of Humans were the Little Green Women. Teduray could generally tell you the stature of a certain spirit, the

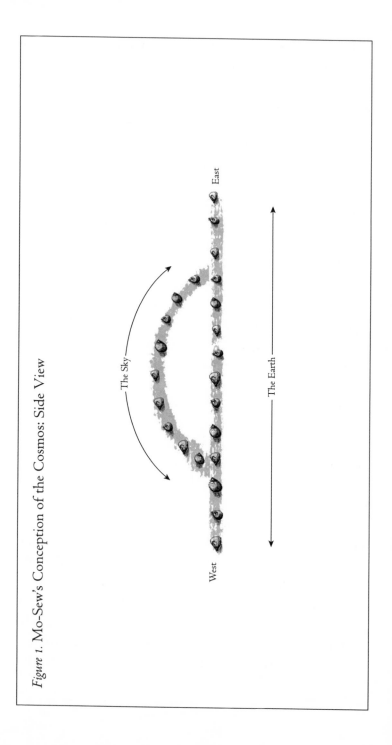

Figure 1. Mo-Sew's Conception of the Cosmos: Side View

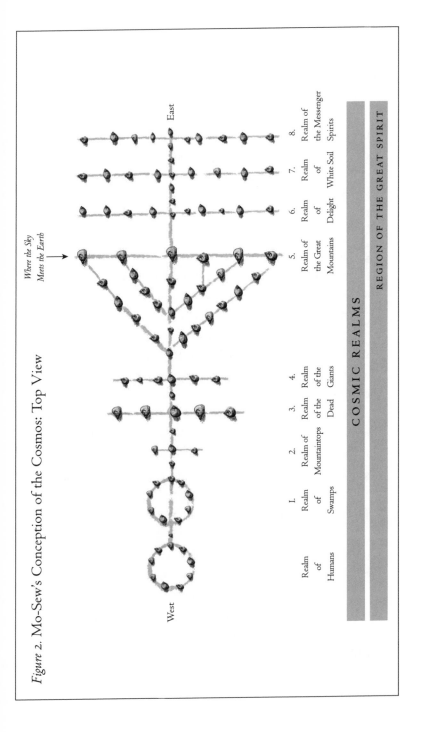

Figure 2. Mo-Sew's Conception of the Cosmos: Top View

color of its skin and clothing, and whether its hair was straight or curly. Little Green Women were short (pygmy-sized) green spirits who dressed entirely in green and had curly green hair. They lived around strangler-fig trees and had a great love and kindness for babies. I often heard in Figel one woman warn another woman not to delay giving her baby her breast if the infant began to cry, because a compassionate Little Green Woman might steal it away to give it better care, leaving her own little green baby in its place.

The *inged rasak*, or "Realm of Swamps," was by Teduray reckoning "the first cosmic realm to the east" (that is, to the east of the Realm of Humans). This has to be understood as the *cosmic* east, not the *literal* east, because anywhere you came across a swampy place, no matter in which direction it was from your home place, by cosmic reference you were in "the first cosmic realm to the east." All the spirits who lived in the Realm of Swamps (humans, of course, didn't live in swamps) had somewhat more *barakat* than the spirits who lived in the Realm of Humans.

A number of different spirit groups lived there. The Swamp Spirits, for example, were normal (human) sized, black in skin and hair color, and always wore black clothing; they were caretakers of the swamps and also of wild pigs. There were also elderly water spirit couples, one of which lived at every spring and kept the flowers around it fresh and beautiful.

On the path that Mo-Sew had sketched on his sleeping mat, the Realm of Mountaintops—*esudon*—was the next cosmic realm to the east. It was, simply, any mountaintop. As with the previous Realm of Swamps, whenever you were on any mountaintop you were in the Realm of Mountaintops, regardless of the earthly direction you took to arrive there. It was the home of a tribe of spirits—with, again, a somewhat higher amount of *barakat*—who were called Mountain Dwellers. They were short, their skin color was "shiny" or "glistening," and they dressed in fine, elegant clothes of various colors.

The Realm of Mountaintops had an interesting part to play along the path to the cosmic east. The trail eventually came to the place where the inverted bowl of the sky met the flat plane of the earth, and then, passing on through the sky, entered the "Region of the Great Spirit." So this path was the one used by human shamans when they wanted to visit the Great Spirit, perhaps to ask the Great Spirit for some sort of advice. While the shaman was asleep at home, her (or his) soul traveled east, finding in each successive realm a particular spirit acquaintance— perhaps a Springs Caretaker in the Realm of Swamps, then one of the Mountain Dwellers in the Realm of Mountaintops. The spirit who recognized her as a proper shaman endorsed her entry to the next cosmic realm, until, finally, she reached the Region of the Great Spirit, beyond the sky.

Sometimes, though, it was the Great Spirit who wished to converse with a shaman. In that case, the Great Spirit would request a Messenger Spirit, one of the spirits who lived beyond the sky in the eighth and last cosmic realm to the east and who had vast amounts of *barakat*, to go down the path and invite the shaman. The Messenger Spirits traveled west only as far as the Realm of Mountaintops, however, and there handed messages over to a Mountain Dweller to deliver to the shaman in the Realm of Humans. Therefore several shamans I knew said that it was important to have a good friend among the Mountain Dwellers.

"Why do the Messenger Spirits do that?" I asked Mo-Sew. "Why don't they just go on and find the shaman themselves?"

He said, "I don't know; they just do." Thinking about my

query for a moment, he suggested that it might be because Messenger Spirits have too much *barakat* and would dazzle humans if they went themselves. He actually said that they would "make humans sick," and I got the impression of something like radiation poison.

So I asked him, "Then, how do shamans handle the even greater *barakat* of the Great Spirit?"

Mo-Sew pondered this for a moment, unruffled by any inconsistency. Finally he said, "They just don't have a problem."

I chuckled, and we went on. That little "footnote" exchange was typical of something I had become used to in Figel. Traditional Teduray didn't have every last detail of their scheme of things worked out with the rationality of a Greek philosopher like Aristotle or a systematic theologian like Thomas Aquinas. When two scraps of information seemed illogical to me and I would ask about them, I would again and again hear both reaffirmed. And if I asked how both could be true, I would get some variation on "Well, I don't know. I wonder why." In time I just relaxed with this reply and figured that it was their version of my German grandmother finding no conflict between "Look before you leap" and "He who hesitates is lost."

Going on toward the horizon from the Realm of Mountaintops, you came to the third cosmic realm to the east, known as *tembas*, or "Realm of the Dead." This realm consisted of a number of settlements in the cosmic forest where there were many houses. This was the place of Bay Bonggò and her four sisters—all of whom Mo-Sew told us had once been humans, cousins of the great hero of Teduray myth, Lagey Lengkuwos. The five sisters cared for the Realm of the Dead and saw to it that all was just-right there. All the souls of humans who died nonviolent deaths went there, where they lived lives of great joy. Those who died from violent causes, such as a fight over honor, went somewhere else, where—as I will soon relate—they had an equally pleasant existence.

The Teduray knew two important things about people. The first was that every person, whether human or spirit, had three parts. There was the *lowoh*, or "flesh," "body," what you felt when you pinched a person's arm or rubbed somebody's back. Similarly, the woody trunk and limbs of a tree were called its *lowoh*. Then there was the *remogor*, the "soul" (as distinct from a *meginalew*, which I translate as a "spirit"). The soul gave living persons their life, the vital movement that animated their bodies and distinguished them from corpses. And finally there was the *ferenawa*, the person's "breath," which was visualized as a kind of string. When a person died, the breath-string was cut: the soul left the body and, after seven days of farewell with its kindred, went to its appropriate cosmic destination; and the body, now just a corpse without breath or soul, was buried and soon decayed—that is, was devoured by Corpse Eaters.

The second important piece of Teduray knowledge about people is that every birth was understood as the birth of twins. When what we call twins—two actual babies—were born (a relatively rare event), they were understood as being two sets of twins. Each set consisted of the baby itself and its umbilical cord. Both the baby-twin and the cord-twin had bodies and souls, but only the baby had a breath-string, so, unable to breathe, the umbilical-cord-twin could not survive after birth. However, as they were being born, the umbilical-cord-twin always asked the baby when and how it would like to die. The baby-twin might answer, "I would like to die of old age, when the rice is harvested for the first time after my last grandchild is born." The cord-twin then died and its soul went to the appropriate place of the dead (in this example, the Realm of the Dead). There it awaited the time its baby-twin had chosen, and prepared a house for her or him to live in. When the appointed moment came, the umbilical-cord-twin returned to the settlement of its sibling, waited for the days of mourning to end and its twin's soul to be ready to depart, greeted it, and tenderly escorted it to its new home. They crossed together a cosmic bridge that separated the Realm of the Dead from the Realm of Mountaintops, and neither soul ever went back across the bridge; they lived happily forever in the Realm of the Dead. No one had to do any work; they subsisted on the finest betel quid only; the men spent their days playing *sifà;* and the women had nothing to distract them from visiting with each other or strumming their bamboo zithers. No one was even tempted to cause anyone else a bad gall bladder.

Teduray had no fear of the dead returning to haunt or cause trouble to the living, such as is found in many other Philippine traditional cultures. Nor was there fear of dying, and this held true for whichever place of the dead people had chosen. I was often told this by Teduray women and men, and from my observation it was completely true. There was simply nothing to fear. Families and communities grieved the loss of loved ones, especially children, but they didn't worry about them; they died when they had chosen to die, in the manner they had also chosen, and they went to a place of great delight and ease.

Being a product of Western rationalism, I of course had questions about this understanding of death. "Do you mean," I asked Mo-Sew, "that a man who dies very young, or dies from falling off a cliff, has actually *chosen* that time and way of death? That a woman who dies in childbirth really *chooses* to do so?"

"Yes, Mo-Lini, that is how it always is."

"But, uncle, why would a person make such a choice, if they could select any death at any time they wished?"

"Hmm. Good question, nephew," he said to me. "I wonder

why they do that." There were a few seconds of silence. "I don't know *why* they make such choices," Mo-Sew continued thoughtfully. "But they certainly do make them—because people often die in unpleasant ways and at strange times. Some things are just puzzling, aren't they?"

Traveling on from the Realm of the Dead, a shaman's soul journeying toward the eastern skyline would come next to the *inged alagasi,* or "Realm of the Giants." This fourth cosmic realm to the east was where large white-skinned spirits, called Giants, lived. They were not caretakers of anything, but were the husbands of the Little Green Women who lived back in the Realm of Humans.

"Why do little green spirits want to marry giant white spirits?"

"I don't know; they just do."

"Why do they live in different cosmic realms?"

"Because they have such different amounts of *barakat.*"

"Why is that?"

"I don't know; they just do."

"Just-right," I said. "Let's continue." I should have figured.

At one point I asked another question that seemed to take Mo-Sew by surprise, because, I suppose, he felt it was such a silly question. "Uncle," I asked, "how do you know about all these places?"

"I've been there," he replied very simply.

Of course! I could only nod my head.

These huge spirits were completely good, but there were other Giants who were not. It seems that "long ago" some foolish humans infuriated some Giants who were too angry to settle it in the proper way through their legal specialists. They left the Realm of Giants and went to one of the realms to the west, where they lived lives of great cruelty and self-will. They are called Cruel Giants, and they hunted humans with dogs and then ate their souls. Whenever people found a body lying in the woods, perhaps partly eaten by a Corpse Eater (the spirit understood as the reason for organic decay), they assumed it had fallen prey to a Cruel Giant.

But mainly the good Giants in the east just played *sifà* all day long, and guarded the trail against travelers who weren't supposed to be there. They had a huge house where they all lived (I was never sure just how many Giants there were in this realm, but I gathered there were many), and while they played they stored their breath-strings in the cool shade within their house. That way they never got too hot or winded playing *sifà* under the tropical sun. I never thought to ask, but I suppose the Giants must have sometimes taken holidays to visit their wives down in the Realm of Humans; after all, the Little Green Women did have little green babies which they exchanged for neglected human infants.

If you had been a Figel Teduray, you would have looked up at the sky and seen a large, blue, inverted bowl that was resting on a flat earth. The earth's surface extended, you would know, well beyond the sky in all directions, and the portion underneath the sky was what you would have called the *duniya*. The stars all moved about on the surface of the bowl-like sky, and the sun and moon traveled across it in their different ways.

Right where the sun started its daily trip westward across the sky there was —along the path we have been looking at and at the easternmost reach of the *duniya*—a range of six cosmic mountains known as the *kawayan*, or "Realm of the Great Mountains." They formed the fifth cosmic realm to the east and were the residence of five spirit siblings and a Giant, all of whom, predictably, had a bit more *barakat* than the spirits of the previous Realm of the Giants. Each sibling—four men and a woman—lived on one of the mountains, and an especially glorious Giant, Malang Batunan, dwelt on the peak where the path met and passed through the sky. The other mountains were reached by separate paths that broke off from the main trail.

On the most southerly mountain of the Realm of the Great Mountains lived one of two Caretaker Spirits. The name of this spirit is difficult to translate but meant something like "Caretaker of Those Who Die Taking Blood Revenge in a Dispute"; I will just call him the Caretaker of Avengers. He dressed all in red, the color of blood, and he wore a kris decorated with a bright red bandanna. Bright red flowers bloomed all along the path up to his peak, which was separated from the next mountain by a crimson-colored river. This was the place where souls of males who died in acts of revenge dwelt. The next mountain to the north was exactly the same, except that it was cared for by a female Caretaker of Avengers and it was where the souls of women who died taking vengeance went.

By the tenets of Teduray moral thinking, these people should never have resorted to violence, however angry they were over matters of respect, and so they did not end up in the company of the souls of the more restrained and peaceful, the souls of those who had entrusted their provoked gall bladders to legal specialists for vindication. Nevertheless, these two mountains were emphatically not places of punishment and were not an exception to the general Teduray notion that everyone should be treated gracefully. The men and women with the Caretakers of Avengers had the same idyllic existence that people in the Realm of the Dead enjoyed. If some hotheaded soul were to cause a companion a bad gall bladder, the Caretakers of Avengers, skillful legal sages all, would settle the matter nicely. The only downside was that these souls missed their relatives who were in the Realm of the Dead. Their self-indulgent violence had not only endangered their community, but had brought about lasting consequences.

The Caretaker of Suicides lived on the next mountain, between that of the female Caretaker of Avengers and that of Malang Batunan. Teduray rarely committed suicide, but when they did it was almost always by taking poison. In the two years that Mer, Aliman, and I were in Figel we never heard of any suicides, but people said that on rare occasions young lovers who had been suddenly married to someone else would kill themselves. The Caretaker of Suicides dressed entirely in green. The path to his peak branched off from the path to the adjacent mountain of the Caretaker of Avengers and was densely planted with poisonous plants. A deep green river flowed between the two mountains.

The northernmost two mountains in the Realm of the Great Mountains were the places of two closely related spirits, the Caretaker of Drowned Mockers and the Caretaker of Struck Mockers. Here went the souls of persons who had committed the grave Teduray offense of what I can only think to call "mockery"—specifically, not respecting the dignity of animals other than humans—the punishment for which was death by drowning or lightning strike. Remember that the universal egalitarianism of these people included species equality; humans were not thought to be better or more valuable than any other forms of life. The classic examples of mockery in Teduray storytelling had several variations, but usually involved a man who specialized in hunting with dogs and who either spoke words of human language to a dog or "danced" with it (that is, walked holding the dog up by its front legs). This was thought to be not respecting the dignity of the dog, because it was not a dog's nature to talk or dance. Someone who did such a thing, or any other act that violated the gall bladder of an animal, would be immediately struck down, and the offender's foolish soul had to find its way to the Realm of the Great Mountains alone.

There was only one way to avoid these harsh consequences if you should mock an animal. Someone had to pick up the animal and pass it through a big wok, as if to cook it. The wok didn't have to be hot; it was a purely symbolic gesture. Perhaps the thinking was that if the animal were dead and ready for cooking it could not be offended.

I thought of Len and Will and the fits they had given Hammy's grandmother in Mirab. No wonder she was greatly concerned, I realized as Mo-Sew explained mockery. She and her wok had been all that stood between my sons and certain death!

"Why does that protect against the consequences of mockery?" I asked

"It just does," Mo-Sew replied.

"But *why* does it?"

His face slipped into a slight smile, an expression that I knew indicated mild frustration in a Teduray. I backed off and said, "Okay, uncle. Just-right." Then I added, "But isn't it a rather violent punishment?"

The shaman seemed amused. "Mo-Lini, no spirits who live to the east want to hurt anybody; besides, they don't have the power to do so. Don't you see?" I thought his voice carried just a hint of exasperation. "They're not like Maguindanaon datus. It is just nature. When you don't respect an animal's gall bladder, you will be killed. It is the same as your drowning for certain if you are foolish enough to jump in the Dakel Teran River at the height of the rainy season." Again the furtive little smile. "Is that so difficult to understand, Mo-Lini?"

It is the anthropologist's lot to ask many foolish questions.

Finally, with regard to the Realm of the Great Mountains, Mo-Sew told us about the mountain right on the main path, where Malang Batunan lived. He was a large spirit, actually a Giant, and like his fellow spirits in the previous cosmic realm, Malang Batunan had a house that was as huge as he was, so that he could stretch out his legs when he slept. He had no companions to play *sifà* with, so his work was just to rest and keep the souls of any false shamans from passing through to the Region of the Great Spirit. If one were to reach Malang Batunan, he would be gobbled up right away.

The *inged Tulus*, or "Region of the Great Spirit," was not a particular cosmic realm itself but was the whole large area beyond the sky to the east, and included several realms. The Great Spirit, whose specialty was to be creator of all things, had no fixed place but went around all over the region beyond the sky, visiting with those who lived in its various communities. The Great Spirit was the source of all things, all life, and all nurture—a kind of ultimate embodiment of the regenerative abundance and graciousness that permeated the universe—and had the greatest amount of *barakat* of any person. The Great Spirit was also regarded as the supreme model of how a human should live.

Unlike all other spirits, the Great Spirit was totally nongendered. Similarly, the Great Spirit was neither young nor old, but ageless, and therefore never referred to by any kinship term.

The Great Spirit created everything that existed, but certainly was not, in any way, "almighty." A specialist who was held in the highest esteem in traditional Teduray cosmology, the Great Spirit had no greater rank than any species, any human, or any other spirit. In the Teduray cosmos, everyone and everything was equal in standing; only people like the Maguindanaon—who "didn't know how to live"—thought otherwise. The Great

Spirit was not a "divine Father" (or "Mother," for that matter) and was neither omnipresent, omniscient, nor omnipotent. The Great Spirit was a helper, a friend, and an advisor—the perfect model for Teduray life.

I will never forget Mo-Sew's description of this region "beyond the sky" where the Great Spirit was at home. I feel certain that I wasn't fluent enough in the Teduray language to get the full beauty of his description, but he was clearly speaking in rapturous terms.

"The sun always shines in the Region of the Great Spirit," he began, "but it is never hot. It never rains. There is no forest"—this was a bit of a surprise, considering how much the Teduray loved their rainforest—"but rather there is only short, soft, yellow grass." What the Teduray generally knew as "grass" was the straw-colored tropical savanna grass that grew near Figel. Coarse, tough, and sharp, it rose to several feet in height and was a cultivator's nightmare—great for thatching a roof but good for little else, and hardly pleasant to walk on. Thus the grass Mo-Sew described in the Region of the Great Spirit was strangely luxurious and otherworldly. "It is like soft ferns," he said, "always covered with a light dew and blown by a gentle cooling breeze that makes the dewdrops ring like little bells." The other Teduray in the group nodded in agreement. They, too, seemed captivated by Mo-Sew's description.

"Beautiful, harmless lightning continually strikes the houses, to give the spirits who live in them great joy, but there is never any thunder to jar the peace. From roof to roof of every house rainbows always glisten, and everywhere you look you can see all kinds of lovely, shiny flowers."

I listened to Mo-Sew go on about the beauties that one finds beyond the eastern sky, and I thought to myself, "He is telling us about a place that he knows to be truly just-right."

Once one crossed the eastern horizon, passing beyond the sky and entering the Region of the Great Spirit, the next two realms were named the Realm of Delight (*lefinon*) and the Realm of White Soil (*futê fantad*). The Realm of Delight, the sixth to the east, was a settlement where a large group of Teduray souls lived who had been led beyond the sky by the legendary shaman Lagey Sebotan. The Realm of White Soil, the seventh to the east, was the home of the other group of Teduray who were led beyond the sky by Lagey Lengkuwos, the most famous of all Teduray mythical heroes and shamans, thus forcing the Great Spirit to re-create humanity (see chapter 5).

The journey of those people to the Region of the Great Spirit was told in the long, epic chant called the *Berinarew*, the Teduray foundational myth, their Genesis. The *Berinarew* described, in one part or another, the whole cosmos. Mo-Sew told me, as I mentioned, that he knew all about the cosmos because he had traveled it on his many nocturnal journeys—he had been there—and I do not for a moment question his experience. But I suppose that a Western dream analyst—one of our versions of shaman—might say that years of hearing the *Berinarew* with its evocative and colorful stories probably inspired the imagery of what the analyst would take to be Mo-Sew's dreams.

There was one last cosmic realm to the east, and that was the *inged telaki*, or "Realm of the Messenger Spirits." They were the spirits whose work it was to help the Great Spirit communicate with spirits or human shamans "under the sky."

It must have taken Mo-Sew about a week to describe to his rapt listeners the cosmos to the east. The next week or so of his teaching took us through the cosmic paths that led to the west, north, and south. There again we heard of strange and fascinating spirits, all having distinctive descriptions and characters, all living in different cosmic realms with different amounts of *barakat,* and all engaging in a great variety of activities.

Very briefly, to the cosmic west there lived many types of spirits known collectively as Cruel Spirits. They were aggressive and nasty, and they would do you harm if you let them. Teduray believed that spirits had the same range of character as humans did; most would not do anyone harm unless they were offended, but some were malicious. Among the Cruel Spirits were the nasty giants who liked to hunt humans in the forest with dogs and eat their souls.

Occasionally, and with evil intent, a Cruel Giant or another malign spirit would claim to be from the east and would give a human the gift of seeing and hearing spirits. This was how there came to be "false shamans." Such poor people's souls would wander about the cosmos, usually in its dangerous western regions, thinking that they were on the path to the east. Malang Batunan destroyed such misled unfortunates if they wandered into the east. Several Figel neighbors told me that they had themselves experienced what might have been a shaman's gift when they were children, but they had refused it and had never tried to be shamans. They were simply too afraid that the gift might have come from the dark cosmic west.

To the south was the Realm of the Flying Souls. These were human men and women, seemingly quite normal by day, whose souls left their bodies at night and flew through the air. They were tutored in their flights by other Flying Souls, and early in their training would be presented by their mentors with what appeared to be two pieces of chicken. Actually, only one was chicken; the other was a piece of human liver, which the mentor had stolen from a sleeping sick person. If the neophyte selected and ate the real chicken, she (or he) became a "good, just-right" Flying Soul; but if she selected the liver, she became a "bad, not-right" one who would always afterward crave human flesh. The bad Flying Souls loved to steal the livers of the sick and take them to their leader, who transformed them to look like the meat of a chicken or wild pig.

Interestingly, before he did this the leader always asked those present whether any were related to the victim. If a good Flying Soul could say, "Yes, he is my cousin," the liver was not transformed, and the good Flying Soul could take it and restore it to his kinsperson—who in the meantime, without his liver, had been lingering in illness, neither improving nor getting worse. When the liver was restored, the healing process could commence. As one of my Figel neighbors once told me, "We all need to have at least one good Flying Soul in our kindred." Everybody knew about Flying Souls, of course, and had considerable fear of them. Charms and amulets were widely used to protect against a Flying Soul getting at your liver if you were ill.

I occasionally heard speculation that this person or that might be a Flying Soul, generally a good one. (Of course, accusing someone of being a bad Flying Soul would have been a great insult.) But I never met anyone who claimed to know one personally or be one, not even the helpful kind.

The same was true of sorcery. Teduray believed that some people could make others sick by the use of a special charm, and most people had another charm, which protected against the first. But I never met a single person who knew anyone who had the malign charm, or who could even tell me how it was made or obtained. People might have been simply lying to me, of course, but I don't think that was the case.

My hunch is that although Teduray reality included sorcery and Flying Soul cannibalism, no flesh-and-blood practitioners of those dark arts actually existed. Even if my guess is wrong, the point is not that such things did or didn't exist but that, like revenge killing, they were never valued positively or encouraged. Teduray were quite realistic. They knew full well that there were always going to be people who could not live up to the moral standards of the society and who, for personal advantage or in the throes of anger, would resort to violence. But in the general Teduray mind (or gall bladder), such behavior was never just-right.

The final cosmic direction was to the north. That was where the spirits associated with certain fearful diseases lived, such as measles, malaria, cholera, and tropical boils. Each of these spirit tribes had the same name as the illness it caused. Although they did not intend to cause illness, if they left their home and came to the Realm of Humans—something they seldom did—there was a certain quality about them that gave the malady to all who came in contact with them. These diseases, not being intentionally inflicted, were therefore different from the sicknesses caused by angered spirits. Whenever one showed up, it caused terrible fear as well as suffering, because this was a sickness that no shaman could help.

Let me return to a question of healing that I mentioned in passing in the last chapter. Teduray believed that, when it came to curing sickness, shamans were *always* successful. ("Except," as one of my anthropology colleagues liked to say, "when they weren't!")

I think the reason people had such confidence in the ability of their shamans to cure illness was that *all eventualities were covered.* If a person was sick, basically three things could happen: the person could get better, in which case the shaman had been successful in the session with the offended spirit's shaman; the person could linger on and on with no change, which meant a bad Flying Soul had stolen her liver, and that was hardly the shaman's fault; or the person could die, which was because of the pact she had made with her umbilical-cord-twin. So the shamans were always successful—except when they weren't.

When we were not in the shaman's house, Mer, Aliman, and I mulled over what we were learning. All three of us were greatly moved.

What I heard when I listened to Mo-Sew tell all those stories, as well as when I spoke about the universe to others, was an image of reality as a great cosmic community, where the traits of true community—cooperation, unconditional care, gentle graciousness, nurture, and honesty—came first, and where those traits were understood as fitting with all that was and was meant to be. Even in death you were not alone: you had a twin waiting for you to love you, to escort you to a waiting and prepared community, and to be with you forever. People did not have to wrestle ethics out of a universe that was fundamentally unfriendly toward generosity and mutual assistance. Instead the universe provided a cosmic, oceanic oneness for all who lived in concert with its rhythms.

As I am writing this chapter at my desk in Santa Cruz, the comet Hale-Bopp is visible in the night sky over California. I pulled myself out of bed a few nights ago in the wee hours of the morning, when the full moon had descended in the sky, and I drove to the loneliest, darkest spot I could find nearby. I saw Hale-Bopp in all its wonder—the first comet I had ever actually seen. Its head was a dim, fuzzy ball, about the same size as a large planet but without that brightness or sharp definition, and its tail was a diaphanous smear that trailed along behind for several degrees of arc. I stood and just gazed at that celestial display for what must have been half an hour or more, until my neck and eyes felt strained. I was mesmerized with wonder at what I was seeing. It was spectacular.

Several comets have come into sight in my lifetime, but I had never been able to make any of them out. I suppose none were very bright or they were obscured by the luminance from the lights of whatever city I was living in at the time. We do not usually get in urban America, or in Philippine cities for that matter, those crystal-clear starscapes against a jet black sky that I so enjoyed in Figel, lying in the clearing in front of my house while old Mo-Baug taught me the Teduray constellations. I thought of this as I drove home that morning, and I wondered what Mo-Baug would have made of Hale-Bopp. Perhaps he would have heard about comets on some radio in a coastal market, just as he had heard about satellites, and would have simply said, "Mo-Lini, that is a comet." Or perhaps he would have given it some creative mythical location in his cosmos. I can't say.

But this much is sure: he would never have thought of it as a piece of ice hurtling through cold and lifeless space. He would never have located it as an event in the sort of vast, impersonal, and value-free universe that is described by Western science. His familiar universe, the ground of all he and his people knew and did, was shot through with life and connection and moral significance. It was a deeply personal world, saturated with meaning and brimming with relationships that bore directly on Mo-Baug's daily life. The shamans actually *saw*, with the eyes of their night-traveling souls, the totality of their world. And the rest of the people *knew* the world the shaman *saw*, and absorbed its wisdom into the very fabric of their life and thought.

My "seminar" with Mo-Sew occurred in July, just a few months before my time in Figel was to come to an end. Hearing him was a remarkable experience, and when I was through with my "lessons" I had hundreds of note cards full of information and a pretty fair working knowledge of the Teduray cosmos. From then on I felt at ease regarding the spirit world and the myriad aspects of that crucial sector of Teduray reality. Mo-Sew had given me the final thread that allowed the tightly woven web of Teduray spirituality to come together for me as a whole.

I knew that I was learning from my Teduray friends on two levels. I was sorting out, *as an ethnographer*, the particulars of their social and cultural ways as best I could, and arriving at the most coherent description I could put together of their formulation of the world, the good society, and the good life. But I was also struggling *as a human being* to listen to their wisdom, to hear how I, as someone who would spend my life outside that forest, might learn a better way to live.

Mo-Sew in those two weeks—and all his Teduray sisters and brothers over the preceding year and a half—had given me a powerful gift. Their vision was so elegant and so attractive, and their spirituality such a profound contrast with the cosmic and moral views of my own people and my own upbringing, that I was increasingly in awe at its brilliance. But I was also confused and anxious. Their vision was not some exotic dream that only they could dream. I knew, deep in my heart, the frightening truth that the principles the forest Teduray presented me as "the way to live" should apply far beyond Figel and the rainforest. These principles had begun to pester my consciousness. Their truth and beauty were transforming my own wellsprings of meaning, and I was starting to sense that I had reached a moment of decision, and that there could be no going back—if I wanted to live the rest of my life with integrity.

16 ❀ Mirab Interlude VI

With each passing week after I first settled in Figel, I grew more accustomed to my surroundings—the place, the people, the language, the thought world. By the time I had been there almost two years, Figel had a "homelike" feel to it that was quite remarkable. I had, it seemed, arrived at a stage where I had two homes.

In September of my second year, just a few weeks after Mo-Sew taught me the Teduray cosmos, I once again made my way to Mirab for a few days' visit with my family. The stay was, as usual, relaxing and renewing, and otherwise uneventful. It was almost as though, through familiarity with each scene, I had finally gotten past culture shock. The tension between the two ways of life seemed to have vanished, and the implications of the Figel community for me and my family barely entered my mind. I should have realized it was a "fool's paradise."

Returning to the forest, I threw myself back into my research, spending long days talking to people, taking notes, pondering the systematic logic of Teduray life and thought, and trying to act in ways that honored and respected my companions. As always, I strained every nerve to be sensitive, open, and receptive.

I tried to give appropriate signals, not only with my words but with my body language as well, and I attempted to pick up on all the subtleties of what I was seeing and what was being said to me through word and gesture. It was intense and consuming, this work, but I thought it had become familiar, routine.

And then I had a startling experience.

One day, a moment came when suddenly I felt strangely dislocated from myself. I felt tiny explosions popping off all over my body. I suddenly wondered if this was what dying was like. I felt cold and dizzy, and my knees began to tremble. The sun appeared unusually bright to me, the forest unnaturally still. It seemed for a few scary moments as though I had never lived anywhere else, spoken any other language, known any other etiquette. This was not just in my head; it was more a rush of feeling. Anxiety threatened to overcome me. It was all very strange.

I knew I had to break off what I was doing right then, which was talking with a legal specialist about a recent settlement. I asked his pardon and started for home. I made my way back to my house and sent word to Ideng-Emét and the others that I would not be eating that evening. When I lay down on my floor, I felt confused and disoriented. I picked up a novel I had brought with me from Mirab; it was *Ruben, Ruben,* by the dark and funny novelist Peter de Vries, whose humor and keen eye for American society I usually enjoyed. I turned to the opening words and read this:

> Given a little money, education and social standing, plus of course the necessary leisure, any man with any style at all can make a mess of his love life. And given these, plus a little of the right to self-realization that goes with modern

life, a little of the old self-analysis, any woman with any gumption at all can make a shambles of her marriage.

I found myself staring at these words, my mind a whirl, and then my consciousness seemed to implode. Panic grabbed me and twisted my thoughts. My mind darted from my little house in Figel, to my family in Mirab, to events from my early life. Scenes of combat in Korea crashed against thoughts of High Mass at the mission. My marriage had been experiencing some strains, to be sure; was it "a shambles"? Had I made a mess of my love life? Of my entire life?

Where was I? Who was I? Who were my people? I cried out involuntarily, and then recoiled; I had cried out in Teduray! What was my language? What was my culture? What were colugos—flying mammals or furry birds? What were the right ways of getting on with people? Of seeming pleasant? Of acting sensibly? Of being intelligent? Sweat ran off my body. I began to hug my chest with both arms, as though I were hugging a little child. I don't remember much of the rest of the night, but the next morning I got up, gaunt and shaken, and left immediately for Mirab. I felt that in some primal, instinctive way I needed to be back with my family, to plant my feet solidly on the ground of my own culture, language, and people.

Once back in Mirab with Audrey, Len, and Will, I held my wife and talked for hours and hours with her, and I seemed to want to hug my sons whenever they came anywhere close to me. I felt, in many ways, like a frightened little boy. The three of them sensed clearly that I was extraordinarily needy, and we huddled close together for a week and a day. No one suggested drives to Cotabato for a movie, or play time with Hammy; I needed my own people.

It worked. I calmed down, and whatever it was that passed for normal, in me and my head, seemed to return.

I read these words today and I know that I have managed to capture only a tiny part of that remarkable experience. It is easier by far to describe what one has seen than what one is thinking or feeling, and my thoughts and feelings had gone wild; I had been crazy with confusion. I think of that episode now affectionately as my "mad scene." For a few hours I had been totally, wildly detached from any solid sense of reality. I hurried back to Mirab because I needed to embrace my own world, to be among long-familiar people and ways, and it was healing to do that. Nothing else could have helped: of that I feel certain.

What I had encountered, I think, was not just a burst of recognition of the unfamiliar outside myself, but of something unfamiliar stirring deep within my being.

Somewhere in my consciousness, the truth had finally taken full hold of me that the trusty everyday patterns of our daily lives—what we believe, how we do things, whom we trust—really are no more than shared understandings in the society where we were raised. I had read and thought about this in graduate school; but that afternoon in Figel, in a flash of panic, I had felt it in my bones. I had found myself at the edge of a cognitive abyss, and I had cut and run back to the familiar.

In moments like that the most compelling question is surely not "What happened?"; it is, rather, "Who am I?" I must have realized, deep down, that I would never again be the same naive American that I had been before Figel. The questions that were welling up, inchoate but frightening, were fundamental ones. What was my world—America, middle class, Anglo? Was any of that really real? Or was it Figel, forest Teduray, academic sojourner—and was any of *that* real? Is there any "real" world for us human beings, or are there just the various "worlds" we have been socially and culturally given, worlds whose values, meanings, and order are not fixed and certain but depend on the precarious consensus of those who inhabit them, those who take a particular world to be "reality" and assure each other that it is true. And if that were so—as I knew inside it surely was—then what was *my* reality? Having struggled long and earnestly to understand another reality, what was I, now, to believe of my own? And how was I, now, to live?

For a brief span I was neither in my own known world nor in that of the Teduray, but in some unfamiliar terra incognita where there were no firm handholds. The old familiar stars still pierced the night sky and the sun still rose in the morning; people around me seemed at ease and at home—and they were. But I had been wrenched loose of both ease and home. I had felt the last vestiges of my original innocent hold on life vanish. For a few fleeting moments of emotional and intellectual vertigo, I had no idea who I was.

I now believe I had come to an awareness that was too tough for me to process in the fright of that moment, an awareness that I was not and could never be a Teduray but that I was an unhappy resident in my own world. In that brief spell of terrible disorientation, the lessons I was learning from these gentle, egalitarian, nonviolent people began to take coherent shape. I was learning who, what, and how I did not want to be anymore. I was learning how I did not want to continue to live, what I did not want any longer to accept as normal and necessary.

I had crossed a great divide. "People are not always of the country in which they were born," wrote Théophile Gautier, "and when you are prey to such a condition, you search everywhere for your true country." By my efforts to understand the people of Figel, I had been opened to a lifelong quest to live by new spiritual bearings, new ways of seeking meaning in my homeland of America.

In that brief moment of madness, I believe, my Figel period came to an end, and I began in earnest a long journey of putting together in my mind and heart a new understanding of what it means to be whole, to be alive, to be human, and to be able to love in a healthy and abiding way.

17 ⚹ Catastrophe at Figel

In late November my little research team packed up, bade farewell to the many people we now knew so well, and hiked out of Figel for the last time. Soon afterward my family was back in the United States and I wrote the dissertation on the moral and legal aspects of Figel Teduray life that completed my doctoral work at the University of Chicago. In the fall of 1968 I began teaching at the University of California, Santa Cruz.

I was sad to leave Figel, knowing full well that I would not find in America the overflowing graciousness of community I had so cherished in the forest. Still, I believed that I would return often, that I would live out my life in periodic interaction with those people and their generous vision of reality and life.

But that was not to be.

In the early 1970s, another bloody chapter in the centuries-long struggle between the Crescent and the Cross erupted in the southern Philippines when the Muslim peoples launched an armed revolt against the Philippine national government. Since World War II, the Muslims' old sense of connection with the greater Islamic world had grown increasingly deeper. Many new mosques and Muslim schools had been built, and religious teachers had come in large numbers from Egypt and other Muslim lands, while thousands of Filipino Muslims made the pilgrimage to Mecca and hundreds went abroad to study in Islamic universities. With this strengthening of ties, the Muslims' hatred of the Christian-dominated secular government and legal system, and their yearning for an Islamic state based on principles of the Koran, had only grown. Add to this their justified anger at politicians in Manila for handing their lands over to Christian homesteaders throughout the twentieth century, and their feeling that the schools set up by the Americans and perpetuated by the Filipinos were but thinly disguised outposts of Christian culture, and the time was ripe for trouble.

By the late 1960s there were some two million Muslim people on the island of Mindanao, and an equal number of Christian homesteaders. Tensions between them were reaching the breaking point. When a Muslim provincial governor began gathering popular support among the Islamic societies for independence, the general lawlessness that had always characterized the "southern frontier" started to take on a distinctly ethnic, religious, and political character. Civilian terrorism and military atrocities became common on both sides. Disorganized, almost random, skirmishes began in 1970 between Maguindanaon Muslim farmers along the Upi road and both Christian Teduray and lowland loggers. Soon a number of Muslim datus and Christian homesteader mayors emerged as what can only be called territorial warlords, their troops often virtually indistinguishable from the many outlaw bands and teenage gangs that had long threatened peace and order. By 1972 Cotabato and the other heavily Islamic provinces, and even some of their larger towns, were effectively divided into Christian and Muslim zones. The rebel forces coalesced into a bold though poorly disciplined army under the banner of the "Moro National Liberation Front," and President Marcos—for complex reasons that went far beyond troubles in the south—declared martial law. He promised to send an entire

Philippine Army division down to "annihilate the outlaws"; from then on, most of the fighting was between government and Muslim troops.

Within a few years the fighting had left many dead on both sides, countless families homeless, whole villages and even parts of cities laid waste. The Philippine government called the Muslims "savages," "pirates," "insurrectionists," and even "communists," but the Islamic fighters saw themselves as patriots and holy warriors, defending home and faith against infidel oppression. The war—largely ignored by the U.S. media—has gone through many hotter and colder stages, but continues to bubble to the surface to this day. I am told that, after all those years of bloody but fruitless struggle, most of the rebel units have actually become what the government has always called them: bands of brigands and outlaws, largely using the revolution as an excuse for murder, kidnapping for ransom, and looting.

Against this backdrop, tragedy came to my friends in Figel.

Santa Cruz, California; February 17, 1972; 11:10 P.M.

I was just about to turn out my bedside light when the phone rang. My good friend Hammy Edwards was calling from Cotabato City in the southern Philippines. There was no mistaking the anguish in his voice. As he spoke, I experienced one of the darkest moments of my life.

A band of Maguindanaon guerrillas from the lowlands had run into the forest to hide from Philippine Army troops. They made their way to Figel and there tried to force the people to feed them and provide them with women to use sexually. The larger Figel neighborhood community was gathered in the main settlement (presumably for a wedding or a ritual), and when they offered the guerrillas food but adamantly refused to let them have any of their women, the Muslim soldiers opened fire. The Teduray defended themselves with their bows and arrows, blowguns, and a few homemade shotguns, but these were no match against the intruders' automatic assault weapons. The rebels, Hammy said, had fallen into a killing frenzy and did not stop firing until they had murdered every man, woman, and child whom I had known in Figel.

Perhaps my old friend, overcome by emotion, was only assuming the worst and a few Figel individuals had actually survived. There was no way I could know. I just know that I was crushed by the news. I could not sleep that night, so finally, in the small hours of the morning, I got up. I brought out my notebooks and photographs and sat in my office weeping. At the university the next morning, as you know, I met my large lecture class and told them about the massacre. We stood together in shocked and reverent silence.

A year after receiving that terrible call, I went to do some work for the Ford Foundation in Indonesia, and from then on I made Indonesia my anthropological focus instead of the Philippines.

I often speak these days about the forest Teduray people and their way of life. I show slides that I made from those old black-and-white Polaroid photographs. I play tapes of the music. And, above all, I share the beauty of their spiritual vision. The women and men of Figel live on for me in those talks, in my field notes, in my lectures and writing. I feel commissioned to tell their story and pray that something of their way of life, which I have been so honored and privileged to know, comes through in this book.

A quarter of a century has passed since Hammy's phone call. I stayed in touch with him and his family until his death from cancer in 1990, but I never returned to the Upi Valley, and I never went back into the rainforest. Anthropologists typically return every so often to visit their primary research community, to report on the changes that have occurred over ten, twenty, or thirty years. Going back is one of the great joys of the field, but I simply could not make myself do it.

18 🍁 Visions We Live By

Only with the passing of many years did I fully realize how deeply the shape of Teduray spirituality had permeated my soul. The French philosopher Albert Camus once said that our lives are a long journey to find the images that opened our being. Looking back, I can see that since childhood I have been drawn in the direction of nonviolence and egalitarian cooperation, but it was my time in Figel that turned those concerns into major themes of my life. My years in the rainforest turned out to be much more than just a research project for me, a hoop to be jumped through on the way to a Ph.D. Figel deepened me. It helped me do what adults in every society must do—make sense of myself and my world and determine where meaning lies for me. Unlike the many Spaniards and Americans who sought fame and fortune in those islands, I had not gone to the Philippines to fatten my wallet. But I *had* come away with a priceless treasure, a treasure that the tragic end of the people of Figel has not erased.

The Teduray taught me how to live. Since Figel, the importance of respecting people's gall bladders has never ceased to whisper within me, and it has helped me know what it is to receive and give genuine love. It led me to take a stance toward the world that has not come easily, but that has greatly enriched my life: to honor myself and those whose lives I touch; to work at not making my love for people, including myself, so conditional; and to be more compassionate and less judgmental regarding personal shortcomings. By their words and their example, Figel people taught me to scan for the good in others and not for their faults, to try to help others out and not put obstacles in their way. I have found all those commitments to be a challenge and a daily struggle, but I believe that when I succeed I feel happier and more alive. When I get it right, I am a better husband, father, and friend. I now understand the urgency of my vote in local, state, and national elections, and although I often feel I am forced to make what a political columnist recently called "a choice between two weevils," I go faithfully to the polls and vote as part of my work toward a better world. I see the environment and the rights and needs of Mother Earth with different eyes than I did before hearing the stories of Mo-Baug; I feel compelled to give money, time, and a great deal of personal effort to peace and justice advocacy groups, because the violence and power hierarchies all around now stand out, as starkly to me as they would have to Ideng-Amig or Balaud, as "no way to live."

After finishing my doctorate, it was clear to me that I would not return to Episcopal Church work. Instead, with the Teduray in my heart, I taught for twenty years on the beautiful redwood-forested campus of the University of California at Santa Cruz, overlooking Monterey Bay on California's central coast.

UCSC was tremendously appealing to me in the early years, when it made a brave attempt to be something new and better in undergraduate education. The campus was founded in 1965, with a structure aimed at building a small-school atmosphere—an engaged, intimate community of faculty and students—supported by the resources of a great research university. The principal instrument of what we called the "Santa Cruz Dream" was to be the colleges, partly autonomous academic units in the manner of the English universities of Cambridge and Oxford. Students could take advantage of the whole range of campus course and independent study offerings but still be part of a small college. There they would get to know their fellow students and teachers well and they could benefit from uncrowded classes taught by senior professors, not teaching assistants. In short, UCSC was to have the good but not the bad sides of a mega-university like UC Berkeley, where a great faculty was relatively unavailable to undergraduates and students could easily get lost in the crowd.

I was immediately swept up in this vision of putting under-graduates first and encouraging close interdisciplinary relations among a diverse and caring faculty. On the opening day of Merrill College, where I was a founding fellow, the new college's faculty met the incoming students in the parking lot and helped carry their bags to their dorm rooms, something I fancy Mo-Sew and Balaud would have thought was "just-right." My office was between a sociologist specializing in Mexico and a political scientist who studied China; directly across from me were the offices of an African-American sculptor and a religious studies scholar who had been born in what is now Pakistan. It was a very different sort of academic environment, with many splendid Teduray-like nonhierarchical, noncompetitive characteristics, and I took to it with enthusiasm. This, I felt—with the Figel experience behind me—is what a teaching and learning community should be.

Increasingly ambivalent about Christianity, and thinking that I saw much more concern about the pain of the world among my university colleagues than among some of my fellow Episcopalians, I quietly dropped out of Church life. I didn't make any official break with the institution or with my priestly orders; I merely quit attending and I stopped making annual reports to my far-off diocesan office in the Philippines. I doubt the bishop there even noticed.

I did not stop my pastoral concerns or work; I just took the collar off—once and for all, I thought—and switched to living and stating my convictions in secular rather than theological language. It was an easy transition, actually. I had long since taken to expressing the same thing in both idioms. Teaching and counseling students provided a fitting context for many of my values and goals in life. In particular, I believed that teaching was not restricted to imparting information and theories to passive, receptive intellects, but was a learning experience for me as well as my students, a sharing in a quest for deeper understanding, not only of anthropology but of life. From the start, therefore, I didn't want to teach just concepts and data—what kinship systems are and how they work, what anthropological theory was like in the nineteenth century; instead I wanted to explore together with my students what other people in other cultures could teach us about the meaning and beauty of life, and in the process absorb some of the rich insights my students had to teach me about living well.

I walked with my students in picket lines to protest the senseless death and destruction in Vietnam. I did informal "pastoral work" in my office, where I spent hour upon hour listening to student problems of all sorts. And I took on some of the less attractive committee assignments—such as those having to do with academic cheating or dormitory squabbles—where I felt I could make a contribution to the quality of campus life. I also committed to publishing my research, to the extent possible, in the Philippines, where there was a fine professional anthropological community, and where, after all, I had gotten all my material. Many of my colleagues saw this as a strategic career blunder, but to me the issue was ethical and spiritual. At UCSC I believed that my vision of the good life, learned in a Philippine rainforest, could be made real in my life and in the lives of my students and colleagues.

By the late 1970s and early 1980s, however, UCSC had changed. There had always been strong traditionalists on the faculty, especially among the natural scientists, many of whom saw little or no good in the Santa Cruz Dream and regretted that our campus was unlike the "real" University of California. Although some of these were brilliant teachers, on the whole they seemed to regard time spent with students as a necessary but unfortunate distraction from their true work: research and publishing. Over the years, then, they quietly politicked to do away with what they thought of as irrelevant, Mickey Mouse innovations and to reorient the campus commitments to emphasize scholarly production. The campus, little by little, turned into an academic battlefield. Accusations flew between students and faculty holding contrasting points of view, as tenure and promotions granted and denied became the focus of bitter recriminations. Ill feelings flourished on all sides.

As California as a whole turned increasingly from appreciation to distrust of innovation, public favor for the UCSC campus declined, and with it enrollments. Students seemed to be less idealistic and more narrowly career oriented, increasingly more interested in getting into law or business school—and thus into the upper brackets of wealth—than in the problems of American life and the world. A general malaise and discontent, even disillusionment, emerged among the faculty, which I felt strongly.

In 1977, a new chancellor arrived who believed that the only solution was to "go mainline" and so began a radical restructuring of UCSC. He stripped the individual colleges, which had been central to the older, more intimate structure, of almost all their teaching role, and he grouped most professors in the now victorious academic departments. Graduate studies were emphasized as they had never been before, at least outside the sciences; interdisciplinary offerings were trimmed back severely; and negotiations were begun to create a large industrial park on campus for business-sponsored high-tech research. Although a bit of the old dream lived on in some of the faculty, it was clearly in retreat.

I was downhearted; the changes that were going on at UCSC were not just technical changes, but spiritual ones. What mattered wasn't better teaching techniques or newer equipment or more efficient administrative procedures; the key issue was what the university was for, what it was in its soul. In my view, UCSC had given up being a beacon of concern for students and cooperative education, and had been redefined as a little Berkeley on a redwood hill overlooking Monterey Bay. Some students and faculty regarded the transformation as a marvelous return to sanity, but I did not. As I saw things, undergraduates lost the most, but we were all diminished by the rise of faculty rank, power, and thinly disguised self-interest to their "proper" place.

In the mid-1970s, after I heard of the massacre in Figel, I went to Indonesia on an assignment with the Ford Foundation to help establish a social science research training center in a devoutly Muslim province of Sumatra. On a return visit in 1976 I again heard the call to prayer five times every day and, rather to my surprise, began to feel lonesome for my own religious tradition. No longer finding as much fulfillment in academic life, in spite of teaching several courses that I loved, I decided in 1979 to test the waters back in the Church, where there existed, at least in theory, a sense that it was good for people to be concerned about each other. For the first time in years I donned my clerical collar and began to assist without pay on weekends at St. Luke's Church in Los Gatos, a suburb of San Jose. The pastor was an old friend and a good man; he let me reenter at my own speed and, with great sensitivity, fed me increased responsibilities only when I felt ready to take them on.

When I "came out" on campus as a priest, many of my colleagues—a very secular lot—thought I had simply taken leave of my senses. They seemed unable to fathom why a fellow they knew as an intelligent scholar and popular teacher—and who had previously managed to shake himself free of all that foolishness—would return to such a life. I think their image of a Christian minister was drawn primarily from the ranting, money-grubbing ways of TV evangelists. My colleagues probably assumed I had not only abandoned social science but had taken up biblical literalism, self-righteousness, and the pious infliction of guilt as well.

In fact, I had done no such thing; I was simply shifting a part of my working and social life to a more congenial scene. Just as my commitment to a Teduray-like spirituality had once taken me out of the Church, and some fifteen years later had led to distress with a changing UCSC, that spirituality now drew me back to the Christian community, where concern for one another— what is there called love—was at least considered an important value. I returned a very different person and priest than I had once been. The Teduray experience had changed me, and now that I was back in the Church, the changes were evident. Instead of criticizing my co-parishioners for lack of zeal concerning racial equality and peace, I was now just glad they welcomed me as part of their journey to meaning and would be fellow travelers with me in mine. Instead of wishing to extend Christianity to far places, I now felt privileged and overwhelmingly grateful for what I had learned from a remote community of animists. I had come to see Christianity, at least in its more benign expressions, as a vast symbolic system of myth and ritual that encourages community and offers spiritual support for a journey of compassion and love. I could now understand the Church as a group of people who—when they get it right—hold in their concept of "the Kingdom of God" a vision of how to live the good life and work for the good society. That ideal, I realized, is very close, if not identical, to the Teduray's worldview.

This time around, I hardly noticed much of what had troubled me about Christianity before. Most crucially, perhaps, I had learned from anthropology that myths need not be taken as literally true to be the bearers of life-giving truths. More than that, when I looked at Episcopal parish life through Teduray eyes, I found myself much less concerned with whether people fully lived up to their ideals and values all the time—I know I didn't. Instead what mattered was what those ideals and values *were*. And I knew that, if I were to give my own values my best effort, I needed spiritual companions.

So I went back to Christianity, but with an altered and quite specific understanding of what it meant to me. I have no regrets about having left the Church—I needed to do that—nor any about returning to it. At the stage I had arrived at in my life story, I found it a challenging and nurturing place to be, far more so than academic life at Santa Cruz had come to be.

In 1984, when the pastor retired, I cut my university commitments back to part time and became the rector of St. Luke's.

In 1987, I retired from the University of California.

As the years have passed since leaving Figel, I have come to see my experience there as part of a larger picture. A key factor in my thinking is what Riane Eisler, in *The Chalice and the Blade,* calls the "partnership" and "dominator" models for society. These constructs gave me a framework for understanding what the Teduray taught me.

The forest Teduray were a "partnership society," in which men and women were viewed as partners in life. Therefore, family and social structure were egalitarian and social relations unranked and peaceful. Decision making was typically participatory. Softer, stereotypically "feminine" virtues were valued, and community well-being was the principal motivation for work and other activities. Nature and the human body were given great respect. The emphasis of technology was on enhancing and sustaining life.

The dominant American cultural tradition in which I came of age stands at the other end of the spectrum. In our "dominator society," hierarchy prevails throughout the social order, with males and the harder "masculine" virtues dominant. Work is to a large extent motivated by perceived scarcity and insecurity. Institutionalized social violence, like war and harsh criminal punishment, is commonplace. Technologies of destruction and control reign, and nature is something to conquer.

As human social groups evolved and diffused out from their primal locations to populate the earth, many no doubt began on the partnership path, just as many others were probably hierarchical and violent right from the start. But very few of the partnership societies survived. Some—like the Maguindanaon—developed private ownership of property, and with it came haves and have-nots; soon the whole scene of power as a tool of ranking and violence as a means of domination developed. Other partnership societies were overrun by dominator neighbors and either absorbed, like the Awang and peasantized Teduray; driven into a collapse following from apocalyptic hope, like the Alangkats; or simply destroyed, like my Figel friends. Today, only the

Teduray and a very few isolated peoples—the Semai of Malaysia, the BaMbuti people of the African Ituri forest, and the !Kung Bushmen of southern Africa, for example—can meaningfully be called partnership societies. Most of the world is dominator.

Must we sadly conclude that the partnership way cannot survive in a dominator world?

I emphatically do not think so.

The vision of a social order based on equality, cooperation, and peace must surely have continued among at least some individuals and groups who never lost their partnership bearings. Even in the most hierarchical and violent social regimes, this vision must have provided at least a *minority* hope for a better future.

I often wonder whether all the old-way Teduray communities in the forest have by now been either killed, quashed by disillusion, or drawn into the world of domination and violence. Or is it possible that some still survive in what is left of the forest, hidden away from loggers, missionaries, and killers? I hope so. Perhaps also, here and there in the hills and farms around Upi, some memory of a better way persists that might again be nourished into life and begin attracting people back.

In fact, even in the most heavily dominator societies of today, many partnership voices are heard, and numerous institutions, movements, and individuals draw meaning, life, and hope from that ethos. Eisler argues persuasively that in the last several hundred years there has been a discernible shift toward partnership, as evidenced by the enactment of the U.S. Constitution; the almost universal abolition of slavery; and the fight, led by the worldwide labor union movement, against terrible oppression of the work force in general and children in particular. In this century alone, political empire-building by European nations collapsed, and virtually every previous colony in the world became an independent and sovereign nation. Fiercely dominator political powers fell before nonviolent mass protests in the Philippines and in eastern Europe—protests led by courageous people who believed that there can be a better way. Women's struggles against sexism and patriarchal institutions have improved the lives of countless women. And liberation movements are growing everywhere to release people from the many other oppressions of our day, so that increasingly racism, classism, homophobia, and all the ways in which people hurt each other from positions of dominance are being seen for what they are—not a part of "normal" social interaction, built into "reality" itself by God or some earthly necessity, but profound abuses of the human spirit.

It is in this context that we can ask what Teduray spiritual wisdom offers us today. I believe what I have presented here is more than a romantic glimpse of a doomed and vanishing paradise. Teduray spirituality offers us all—as it offered me—a vision of what life can be at its very best; it is a kind of *utopian* vision, which cries out to us all to take it on, to plumb its depths, to align ourselves with its values, and to reshape the institutions of our societies.

People tend to regard a "utopia" as some impractical, escapist dream, but I am not using the word in that way. The notion began with Plato, who in his *Republic* set out to criticize Athenian social order by posing an alternative model to it, a model that would provide the best life for all. Plato didn't really expect his society to transform itself into his idea of perfection, but he felt that his portrayal of the ideal society held deep insights for how people could live richer, fuller, more satisfying lives. A utopian vision, in other words, is not some wistful but impractical dream, nor is it a blueprint for remaking the totality of society in some far-off day; rather, it inspires and points the way for living life *right now* in a social environment alien to the values it subscribes to. It summons its visionaries to personal relationships and social action of the finest and most humane kind.

The Teduray partnership way of life that I have been describing gives us just such a vision, and I have committed myself to it. I do not suppose for a moment that all of the world's dominators will eventually surrender their status and their resources; no doubt, there will always be those who cling to power and seek to exploit violence. But I believe the growing momentum of partnership thinking, as it comes to inform more and more of our social institutions, can have a telling outcome. It can soften the harsh edges of dominator control and draw people to its benign way of organizing and living life, until the center of gravity in our world shifts away from domination, violence, and inhumane ways of ordering social affairs and a new social consensus forms around peace, cooperation, and harmony.

We cannot just hope, however; we cannot just dream. The Buddha taught that if we would have the earth covered with leather we need first to put on our own sandals. If the world we seek is not to remain merely an optimistic fantasy, we must begin by reshaping and enriching the quality of our own lives. It is vital that we realize that visions of a better world—of utopia—do not exist only in the minds of philosophical writers. They exist in the gall bladders and hearts of people like the Teduray and like many of my closest friends who organize their lives around an alternate vision in what they perceive to be a destructive world. They exist in the will of people like you and me.

In his great sixteenth-century poem *Orlando Furioso*, Lodovico Ariosto contrasts a rather conventional earthly paradise, where we meet St. John and the Hebrew prophets, with a far lovelier one, the garden of Alaina. There, however, all is not what it seems to be, because Alaina's garden reflects upon all who enter it their own desires and illusions. The garden's power, Ariosto implies, *is not in what it does to you, but in what it leads you to do for yourself.* I am convinced that the Teduray vision of a better world gives us profound wisdom on how to transform ourselves and our immediate social surroundings, on how to live our lives right now, right here, in the thick of our present dominator society. The Teduray vision was borne by their particular myths and enshrined in their particular images, but it was not mere thinking; it was a script for living life. From time to time, they lost sight of their vision, but for the most part they did not; they lived out their values through their own particular way of meeting daily challenges and offering solutions. And those values captured my heart.

I have thought about the Teduray and about writing this book for years. I began working on it in mid-1995. I wanted to share the beauty of Teduray ideas of how to live and the influence they had on me. I wanted people to realize what that vision could mean to them. But from the beginning I had a significant fear: Would what I had to say about the Teduray seem too good to be true?

Ultimately the best test for the authenticity of the Teduray is the people themselves. I have tried to describe their spirituality—their understanding of the nature of the world and of how to live in such a world—with sufficient texture that their genuineness will be apparent.

They were not a "seamless robe"—no society is, not even one as relatively isolated and integrated as traditional forest Teduray society. Like all real people everywhere, they were not always consistent in their thinking or their acting. Sometimes the details of their systems of thought did not add up. In some instances, I may simply have missed or misunderstood a piece, but in others I am quite certain that the parts did not fit seamlessly together. I have no idea, for example, why they treated young brides and grooms in such an apparently abusive and inhumane way; it certainly didn't cohere with the rest of their attitudes concerning social interaction.

Likewise, Teduray did not always act as they knew they should. They occasionally turned to violence to settle their problems, even though their beliefs and institutions all said violence was never right. Much more than occasionally, they ran off with each other's spouses, even though doing so violated their most fundamental moral norm, and they knew it.

The Teduray didn't always live out every detail of their elegant and lovely vision of the good life, but it was not just a pious ideology. It shaped their existence at a very deep level. They were committed to it, and they embodied it again and again in what they said and did. They were certainly not goody-goody moral automatons in a never-never land of perfect harmony. But during the time I spent with them in the forest, I found the characteristic graciousness and kindness of these forest people to permeate the very air we breathed. And their ways have affected my life to its depths ever since.

I believe with all my heart that I have described in this book something that was not only very real but immensely valuable. If the extreme theoretical skeptics are right and ethnographic descriptions such as mine are merely dreams, little more than fables, then I can only say that the Teduray transported me into a wondrously enriching fable and that life among them was unquestionably the most beautiful dream I have ever had.

But I do not think they are right. I know I have been given something both true and infinitely precious, something I have tried as best I could to share with you in this book. I wrote it because I want the Teduray of Figel and their vision to remain alive.

Epilogue

I began this book with a story about my son, Leonard, and a gift given him by the Teduray. Let me close with another story about Len, and another gift.

By the late 1980s Len had become a computer scientist at SRI International, a Silicon Valley research institute. He had grown into a fine young man, big and strong with a goofy sense of humor and full of compassion and goodwill. He was doing some outstanding research, had many close friends, and loved to play softball and golf. He visited us in nearby Los Gatos often. One day in April 1988, Len told his mother and me that some lumps on his neck had turned out not to be sebaceous cysts, as his doctor had thought, but lymph glands swollen by melanoma cells. This was scary news, but neither Audrey nor I—nor Len, I think—recognized at first just how grim the diagnosis was and what lay ahead for him. I read later that, once melanoma has spread to the lymphatic system, the two-year survival rate is only 20 percent and the five-year survival rate is zero.

Within the week, a surgeon removed most of the muscles in Len's neck and shoulder on the left side, and found over fifty lymph nodes with melanoma cells. For six months, we all held our breath, but there was no sign of recurrence. Then in early December Len noticed swelling in his abdomen. Scans revealed melanoma tumors in his bones, his lungs, and especially in his liver. The doctor who broke the news to Len estimated that he had two to three weeks to live, and advised him that chemotherapy was of little use with this type of cancer. That evening, Audrey and I held our son and each other in our arms. We cried for hours, and we said, over and over, how much we loved each other. It was nightmarish, but our closeness transformed that evening into one of the most beautiful times of my life.

Two days later, Len flew to Hawaii, where Will lived with his family on the island of Kauai and worked for the large Westin resort hotel. Len and Will had become very close as adults, much more so than they had been as boys, and they wanted to say good-bye. Len was in such severe physical pain that he hardly got out of bed during the few days he was at Will's, but they, too, held each other and wept together.

Len asked his surgeon if he could at least *try* chemotherapy, and he was put in the care of an oncologist. He responded so spectacularly to the treatment that within half a year he was free of any sign of cancer in his lungs and bones, and the tumor in his liver had been reduced to the size of a marble. There things stood for about three and a half years, most of which was good time for Len. His institute put him on disability but urged him to come in and work on his research whenever he felt up to it. He played golf almost every day and even resumed playing softball, saying with characteristic good humor that since his weakened left shoulder no longer allowed him to hit for power, he would go for average. During those difficult times when the chemo would wear him down, Len came home to us.

Partly so I could have more time for Len and Audrey, and partly to relieve the stress that had come into my life with his illness, I retired from St. Luke's in May 1992, and we moved back to Santa Cruz. I did some anthropology writing and occasional teaching, and I led a few retreats, but mostly we concentrated on caring for Len. Every checkup with the oncologist was liable to bring devastating news, so Audrey and I always went with him to learn the results of his frequent tests and scans. Since things were holding steady and the liver tumor seemed dormant, the two of us decided to go ahead with a long trip in our camper-van around the country. After the first month, we were called home: Len's cancer had begun growing rapidly and spreading. He was given an experimental course of therapy with a drug called Interluken II, but there was no improvement. In December we three went to spend Christmas with Will and his family, now in Palm Springs. Len was sick and depressed during the visit and had to be taken home early; it was a difficult Christmas for us all.

By February, Len could no longer live independently under the care of his housemate, David, so we brought him home to Santa Cruz. He began receiving morphine from a bedside pump. This worked wonders for his pain, and during the last weeks of Len's life he had very little discomfort. Will came up for a week to have some time with his brother. Len's rapid decline devastated Will, who hated being so far away, and the weeks with Len in a hospital bed in our living room were extremely depressing for Audrey and me. We tried to fix him any food he wanted, and although he had many requests, he couldn't actually eat very much. He began to look like a concentration camp survivor, just a skeleton covered with skin. We rubbed his bed sores with bag balm, and we kept him as clean and comfortable as possible. Dopey from morphine, and well aware of how much ground he was losing each day, Len still tried to remain cheerful. We worked at that too, but it was tough.

Friends rallied to help us, especially people from St. Luke's and some of our old university friends. They phoned, sent flowers, brought food. One of my UCSC anthropology colleagues, a man from Benares, India, who had been a good friend since University of Chicago days, came one evening and just sat silently with Len in the Hindu manner. Jill and Lou, two of his dearest friends, drove from Menlo Park every evening, an hour-and-a-half haul through heavy traffic. They chatted with him and held his hand, not leaving for home until he had fallen asleep. Jill was an ex-girlfriend and still cared for him very much; Lou was the head of his research team. The two of them taught the three of us much about compassion and fidelity. Night after night they brought laughter and hope to the house: not hope that Len would be cured, but that he would not die alone. Hope that all of us would be able to buck up each other's hearts and make it through this horror.

But it was hard. Audrey was in utter torment, with a beloved child, her firstborn, dying before her eyes. Some days I would find her sitting alone outside our back door, smoking. I have no doubt that I will never fully comprehend what Audrey endured in those days. I know that I felt totally powerless myself, lost and empty. Sitting next to Len, I began to miss him even before he was actually gone, and my heart screamed in futility, confusion, and pain. Although Audrey and I had never been closer than we were in those weeks, I felt lonely. Irrational as it seems to me now, I even felt angry at Len for dying. Rage rose up from some black and melancholy place within me that hated fiercely what was happening to him.

There were up moments too. As his most prominent outer attributes drained away—his handsome face, his strong body, his intellectual and verbal subtlety—Len's gentle inner self shone through clearly. His brain didn't work very well anymore, but his heart was intact. A few evenings before he died, but while he was still fairly awake, I was holding his hand. I told him how much I loved him and how proud of him I had always been. And he said, "I know, Dad." The simplicity and the sweetness of his words meant more to me than I can describe.

On his last night, we knew the end was near. Len's morphine doses were by then so large that he was seldom conscious. He had not eaten for several days. Audrey and I took turns sleeping in the living room beside his bed, checking him every so often and putting moist swabs on his dry lips and tongue. This particular night was Audrey's shift, and I reluctantly fell exhausted into bed a little before midnight. I had been asleep only an hour or so when Audrey came in, gently woke me, and said, "He's gone." She had dozed off also, and had missed the exact moment when a change came in the rhythm of Len's breathing; each breath was a little weaker than the last, and finally there was just silence and peace.

We went to his bedside, and for a moment I just sat and looked at Len, conscious of the huge sense of mystery that is death. With part of my mind, I knew and accepted that he had died, yet it was hard to grasp with the rest of my mind. Words spoken by Mo-Sew came back to me: "Some things are just puzzling, aren't they?" We really know nothing about what happens after death; we only have our stories. But what pressed on my consciousness in that moment—less as a thought than as a feeling—were not stories about resurrection and heavenly banquets from the Christian tradition, but the Teduray story that Len had a twin, an umbilical-cord-twin, who had come to meet and welcome him and who was now taking him to a kindly, happy place in the cosmic forest, where all was well and where a house had been prepared for the two of them, where he would never be alone but would dwell in peace and joy.

Audrey and I stood together, our arms around each other's waists, saying nothing. We had to just let that dark moment happen, as countless families have throughout human history. We, too, were not alone. I felt—and I know Audrey did too—Will's anguish and his care from afar, and we drew strength from the support we had received from so many people. As I understand the Christian faith, it is through such things that we know the love of God. But in that moment of need, I also felt some of the profound peace, security, hope, and connection that the Teduray had taught me was the character of reality. And I clutched tightly in my heart all the deep truths they had given me—given all of us—about what really counts in this world as we make the human journey.

Works Cited

Along with the works cited in the text, given below, readers may wish to consult my earlier, more technical writings for greater detail on some of the features of Teduray life. The Teduray legal system is described fully in *Tiruray Justice: Traditional Tiruray Law and Morality* (Berkeley: University of California Press, 1970). The economic and subsistence practices associated with hunting, fishing, gathering, and marketing, both among the forest people and the peasant people, are set forth in *Tiruray Subsistence: From Shifting Cultivation to Plow Agriculture* (Quezon City: Ateneo de Manila University Press, 1979). Various aspects of Teduray life and thinking may be found in *Children of Tulus: Essays on the Tiruray People* (Quezon City: Giraffe Books, 1994). Finally, *Tiruray-English Lexicon* (Berkeley: University of California Press, 1971) is a dictionary of the language.

The works cited in the text are:

Ariosto, Lodovico. *Orlando Furioso*. London: Oxford University Press, 1974.

Bennasar, Guerrico, S.J. *Observaciones gramaticales sobre la lengua tiruray por un P. misionero*. Manila: M. Perez, hijo, 1892.

Borgman, Albert. *Crossing the Postmodern Divide*. Chicago: University of Chicago Press, 1992 (quotation in chapter 11).

de Vries, Peter. *Ruben, Ruben.* Boston: Little, Brown & Company, 1964.

Eisler, Riane. *The Chalice and the Blade: Our History, Our Future.* San Francisco: Harper & Row, 1987.

————. *Sacred Pleasure: Sex, Myth, and the Politics of the Body.* San Francisco: HarperSanFrancisco, 1995.

Eisler, Riane, and David Loye. *The Partnership Way.* San Francisco: HarperSanFrancisco, 1990.

Hudson, Christopher. *Spring Street Summer: The Search for a Lost Paradise.* New York: Alfred A. Knopf, 1993 (quotation by Théophile Gautier in chapter 18).

Malinowski, Bronislaw. *Crime and Custom in Savage Society.* London: Routledge & Kegan Paul, 1926.

————. *The Sexual Life of Savages in Northwestern Melanesia.* London: Routledge & Sons, 1929.

Post, Ursula. "The Phonology of Tiruray." *Philippine Journal of Science* 95 (1966): 563–575.

Radin, Paul. *Primitive Man as Philosopher.* New York: D. Appleton & Co., 1927.

Tenorio, José (Sigayan). *Costumbres de los indios Tirurayes, traducidas al español y anotades por un misionero de la Compañia de Jesus.* Manila: Amigo del País, 1892. (My translation into English of the Teduray text and my annotations on both the Teduray and the Spanish texts are in Schlegel, *Children of Tulus,* pp. 171–212.)

Tylor, Edward Burnett. *Primitive Culture.* London: J. Murray, 1871.

Acknowledgments

I am delighted to express my appreciation to the many individuals and institutions who helped me with this book's gestation and delivery. The way I wrote this book reflects its subject matter; it was a "partnership" book all the way, the most so of any of the books I have written.

I especially want to thank Riane Eisler, whose classic work, *The Chalice and the Blade: Our History, Our Future*, opened my eyes in a whole new way to how my Teduray experiences related to wide issues in cultural history and transformation. Riane's seminal volume thrilled, enlightened, and encouraged readers in thirteen languages and on every populated continent. Her research and her insights on the partnership way, now brilliantly continued with *Sacred Pleasure: Sex, Myth, and the Politics of the Body*, are a source of wisdom for many people ranging from scholars to general readers. Moreover, Riane is a warm and supportive personal friend. She and her husband, social psychologist David Loye, encouraged me in the writing of this book from its inception to its completion, and my gratitude to them both could not be more heartfelt.

Nor could I ever adequately thank my friends Frank Andrews, Melody Walsh, John Robbins, Paul Irwin, Bill Domhoff, and Roz Spafford. Melody and Frank, in particular, read and commented on each chapter at every stage of development, taught me how to write for general readers, and led me to weed out more unclear or overwrought prose than I like to admit. John, Paul, and Bill read full drafts and helped me—more than any of them probably realizes—keep my enthusiasm at a high peak through large doses of their own. Roz gave the text especially careful scrutiny and made suggestions that could only come from a writer with her exquisite sense of style and grace.

Several other persons read earlier versions of all or parts of the manuscript and weighed in most helpfully with their critical eye and red pencil. Among them were Gibson and Mickie Anderson, Rosemary Anderson, Dan Hood, Michael Kimmel, Nayan McNeill, Christine Meek, Ruth Royal, and Art Stevens. In particular, Belinda Breyer and Janaki Bakhle-Dirks gave me the benefit of their expertise as professional editors as well as friends; Chris Greenwood not only read and commented on the manuscript but, with José Araneta, also crafted the map; and Kathleen Mrachek drew the cosmos diagrams. Every one of these people helped tremendously to make this a better book. My thanks as well to Alfonso Montouri, Elliot Aronson, and David Szanton for their stalwart encouragement; they kept my gall bladder strong and hopeful. And so too, in many ways both demonstrative and subtle, did my clergy colleague group and my men's support group.

Several institutions have, over the past years, supported my research and invited me to speak on the issues discussed in this book. The American Council of Learned Societies and the Social Science Research Council generously funded my original Teduray research through the Foreign Area Fellowship Program, and both later honored me by asking me to be the first chair of their Joint Committee on Southeast Asia. The University of

Chicago anthropological faculty, especially Lloyd A. Fallers, Fred Eggan, and Clifford Geertz, inspired and shaped me as a field researcher and teacher. Frank Lynch, S.J., Mary Racelis, and Willie Arce of the Institute of Philippine Culture at the Ateneo de Manila University were good friends and a crucial help, as were the clergy, sisters, and staff of the Mission of St. Francis of Assisi in Upi. I thank my colleagues in Merrill College and in the Department of Anthropology at the University of California, Santa Cruz, whose friendship and intellectual stimulation never flagged over the two decades I taught there. And I was blessed with a huge number of outstanding students who, over the years, led me to far greater depths of understanding of my Teduray material than I could ever have achieved without them.

To Professors Triloki Pandey, Barry McLaughlin, and David Sweet—all of whom repeatedly allowed me to bring the Teduray story to their classes in anthropology, social psychology, and history—I owe sincere gratitude, as I do to the many groups that invited me to speak, probe, and discuss, especially the Resource Center for Nonviolence in Santa Cruz and the Benedictines of Los Osos, California. None of these individuals or gatherings ever allowed me to get away with easy answers to difficult questions.

Particular thanks go to Lynette Temple of the Primate Center at the University of California, Davis, and to Karen Killmar of the San Diego Zoo for their help with the identification of the kobol (chapter 3) as a colugo. And I am grateful to Arthur Stevens and Don Maruska for helping me see the significance of attitudes of abundance and scarcity, which I discuss in chapter 5. My appreciation goes also to Fred Jealous and Charles Kreiner for the understanding of an inherent healing process in human beings, set forth in chapter 11 as it pertains to Teduray law.

The following people all gave of themselves to me and my project in ways too diverse to list, but I value every one: John Beecher, my friends in the Breakthrough community of men, Terry Burke, Ruth Eller, Fred Jealous, Tom Johnston-O'Neill, Noel King, Timothy Krech, Charlie Kreiner, Kitty Lehman, Lance Lindsey, Bill Little, Virginia Mack, Don Maruska, M. Douglas Meeks, Annie Moon, Kathy Newman, Sherry Ortner, Forrest Robinson, Nick Royal, Richard Smith, and Mark Whitaker.

In the final stages of the project Jenny MacDonald, my agent, and Barbara Ras and Anne Canright, my editors at the University of Georgia Press, led me kindly but firmly to make this book the best it could be. Barbara, especially, believed in the project from the beginning and never flagged in her encouragement. I have been graced to work with such gifted women.

Many families worked wonders of hospitality, kindness, and warmth in the days I write about, but especially the Harrises in Upi, the Edwardses in Mirab, the Conchas in Lebak, and the Meades in Cebu. Not the least among my creditors are the Teduray people themselves, both as a group remembered with deep affection and as individuals recalled with a joy that is mixed with tears of grief.

Finally, my gratitude to my family is deep and abiding. For four decades my wife, Audrey, has given me unfailing personal support and critical advice. Loving me and others so magnificently, she helps me recognize love wherever I meet it, and so I see traces of her on every page of this book. She is the hidden, silent presence in everything I write.

Like Audrey, my son Will makes my life rich and full. I love him dearly and am proud of him beyond words. And I carry Len within me with a constant gladness. It gives me great pleasure to dedicate this book to Len and Will.

Every author knows how impossible it is to give adequate thanks to everyone who has made a writing possible. I reluctantly surrender to this impossibility and hope that all those persons, named and unnamed, who gave me a hand with this book will recognize themselves and their efforts in the preceding pages. I acknowledge them all happily and with profound gratitude.

Index

Stu Schlegel is professor emeritus of
anthropology at the University of California,
Santa Cruz, and an Episcopal priest.

For more about the Teduray and the author, and to
offer feedback, visit the web site for this book at
http://www.rainforestwisdom.com